Blessed with
Twice the Freedom

Blessed with
Twice the Freedom

❦

Domnitsa Uilean

Blessed with Twice the Freedom

Copyright © 2018 by Domnitsa Uilean All rights reserved.

This book is a work of fiction. Certain long-standing institutions, agencies, public offices are mentioned but the characters and the events are wholly imaginary. Any resemblance, to events and persons, is entirely coincidental.

In Memory of Mary McKee

Table of Contents

Introduction 1

Chapter 1: A Child Warms up a Chilly Train 3

Chapter 2: Hidden Lives Bound Within Two Covers 13

Chapter 3: Whispering to the Dolls 18

Chapter 4: Days and Worries 21

Chapter 5: A Duty to Endure 25

Chapter 6: Harsh Winter, Harsh News...40

Chapter 7: Two Blows at Once 50

Chapter 8: Looking for a Silver Lining 55

Chapter 9: Hardship, Harsh Winter 58

Chapter 10: The Tireless Going...66

Chapter 11: A Bruegel Comes to Life 69

Chapter 12: Candle's Tears 72

Chapter 13: Other Days Imprinted Deeply in Memory 74

Chapter 14: A Toast with a Banana..77

Chapter 15: An Overview..82

Chapter 16: A Transylvanian Echo 84

Chapter 17: Three Times the Nothing 94

Chapter 18: DDT, the Fragrance of the Time 97

Chapter 19: Endless Gifts... 103

Chapter 20: 1987- An Angel Hidden in the Inferno 108

Chapter 21: May I Be Happy Loudly? 116

Chapter 22: Sonia Follows the Sun 123

Chapter 23: Is There an Orphanage for Dolls?.................................... 128

Chapter 24: Family, Living Treasure... 136

Chapter 25: A Frontier Between the Old and the New.................. 146

Chapter 26: Falling Off the Cloud Nine 153

Chapter 27: Resilience! 171

Chapter 28: Is There Still a Great Moment?...................................... 179

Chapter 29: Terrible Means Terrific in Romanian 184

Chapter 30: Family Is More Than Blood Ties.................................... 199

Chapter 31: Thoughts Still Lingering in Memory............................. 203

Chapter 32: Every Life is a Song 212

Chapter 33: Virtue Triumphs Over Wickedness 222

Chapter 34: Open Doors to Opportunities 225

Chapter 35: Reverberations 228

Chapter 36: Wishes Sent Out Through a Window............................ 233

Chapter 37: Reborn from the Ashes 239

Chapter 38: Not Lonely 241

Chapter 39: Tragedy Hovering in the Sky 243

Chapter 40: Thinking Back to Transylvania....................................... 248

Chapter 41: Grandpa's Last Journey 252

Chapter 42: From the Heart of a Transylvanian Village 257

Chapter 43: Reflections on the Present and the Past 266

Chapter 44: True Love Never Dies 269

Chapter 45: Turning Back Pages.. 282

Chapter 46: An Old Scar of a Distant Spring 286

Chapter 47: Escape into Colors 292

Chapter 48: Just a Thought Between Us 296

Blessed with Twice the Freedom

Chapter 49: Lines Other Than Parallels 303

Chapter 50: Reviving the Past, Again.. 314

Chapter 51: A Resumed Path 317

Chapter 52: End of the Summer.. 330

Chapter 53: An Unbroken Connection 334

Chapter 54: 2011Moments of Grace and Remembrance............. 338

Chapter 55: The Priceless Years, Adolescence 342

Chapter 56: A World of Our Own... 352

About the Author... 366

Introduction

It's said, that no one cherishes Freedom as one who was deprived of it, and

"Blessed with twice, the Freedom" intends to be a meaningful testimony to this.

Such a truth, is illustrated through a long and tedious journey, of an immigrant woman of   Eastern-Europe, to the Promised Land of America.

Unfortunately, she is not only confronted with the injustices of a regime but also with an outdated idea, that a husband must be the leader and a woman, not more, than a follower.

At the end she wins it all, under the auspice of Freedom.

Along the way there are inserted aspects of two, totally, different social-political systems of East and West; one from behind the iron curtain, and the other one, with exit to Freedom.

The atrocities of the Communist Regime and benefits of Freedom, are not brought here up for antithetical reasons, only. They rather call for an awakening of the humans' consciousness to repel such a regime and never allowed to be revived, neither should any changes made to the quintessence of Freedom.

The magical power of Freedom, for those who don't take it for granted, it is revealed, and crosses as a red thread through the entire story.

Freedom generates hopes, and faith sustain them alive.

Freedom is as miraculous as is the *living water*, sprinkled over the wings, which were forced into forgetting how to fly.

As an immigrant woman, myself, who escaped from a Communist Country to a Freeland, I couldn't resist the thought of becoming the spokesperson for a crowd of women struck by the same fate; hardship, oppression, or abandonment. Despite to all of this, they reinvent themselves to rise up from being victimized to be triumphant.

For many women, from that part of the world, the benefits of Freedom are not only instrumental in their recovery, from a long social-political mutilation, but also in empowering them to stand up for themselves.

No road of recovery is easy and short.

Along the pages, hints and tools are offered, how a woman with a strong will, on a Land of Freedom, made almost the impossible, possible …

CHAPTER 1

A Child Warms up a Chilly Train

"The Express Train 371 for Cluj-Napoca, via Brasov, is leaving Bucharest North Station from track 3. Passengers please board!"

The raspy voice of the train operator, amplified by the megaphone, startled me.

My thoughts, which until then had been rushing in and out, were suddenly interrupted.

No wonder, I was sitting deep in thoughts. It was not a day like any, but one which turned the first page of a new year, and marking in a way or another, a new beginning for everyone and everything. It was 1985.

However, events from the year which just past, were still lingering in mind, while those of the anticipated future sneaked in. I let them shuttle back and forth and blend in on their own.

I would have liked, though, to foresee a bridge between them, or how they would connect, rearrange, and untangle by themselves, as the right path emerged.

As it is, though, such a balance between events is not so magical but rather complicated, especially when an outcome depends upon a chain of events with many broken links in it.

3

Nevertheless, reflections on yesterday's New Year's Eve many aspects of celebration were still vivid in my mind.

For us, New Year's Eve, or rebellion-as it is known in Romania, is the greatest celebration of the year. Revelers make plans in advance, targeting the best resorts, the biggest to-dos. The next day all the talk would be only about how the New Year's Eve was spent. There is also a recount of every happy moment of celebration, hoping that withholding on those moments, it would bring luck for the year to come; it was only source of hopes for us. At least for the day, we forget about our worries, renew our hopes, and burry any discontent.

As for myself, I would have liked to have spent it at a resort in the Alps, which for most Romanians now, would have been just a fantasy.

However, we had some shot at something like it, living as close as we did to the Carpathians. But at that time, my mom's house was the only imaginable destination for a holiday like New Year's. She was getting old and we didn't know how much time she had left to spend with us. The guilt of not being with her would have destroyed any joy we could have taken in a mountain resort.

My husband and I wished she had moved to Cluj with us, but there was no way to convince her. She had her own nest in Bucharest and it would have been hard for her to give it up. Eventually, we agreed with her; and so, we visited her in Bucharest whenever

In addition to the celebration, things related to my every day work, slipped also in my mind.

I was worried about the budget allocated to the medical office where I was working as a physician. The budget assigned to the needy was constantly being reduced. As a result, more and more people looking for the medical services were turned down and I felt superfluous professionally.

I was also wondering if the flu would strike again. Last winter, the flu took a devastating toll, especially on children and the elderly. Unfortunately, there are already predictions for another harsh winter and for cutbacks in energy resources, which would make the winter even worse. Both electricity and gas had already been rationed.

The other day at my mother's, I watched her struggle with the low gas pressure as she cooked. It took her more than two hours to boil a liter of milk.

But that's not all. Low gas pressure is not merely an inconvenience in the kitchen, it can be very dangerous, can precipitate explosions.

Politically, such events had to be kept secret, but of course it's hard to hide an explosion.

As a result, the Communist Regime started to fear another kind of pressure, the one coming from an uprising of the oppressed, whose patience was wearing thin. The government was aware that under such pressure, the country itself might burst, yet it continued to play its charades.

How – I ask you – can the explosion of a large apartment building in Aiud have been hidden from the people? How could they hide the very low temperatures in the birthing centers, where newborns entered the world shrouded in mist? It was that cold. No wonder some of them decided not to stay, but to turn back to the other world, a natural response to such a hostile welcome.

Nevertheless, we are told persistently, and constantly, that we are the luckiest people in the world, by living in a "Golden Era."

It is difficult and outrageous to agree with the propaganda, and yet, we have no choice. We must humbly accept it.

But on New Year's Day, at least for the day, people basked in the beauty and enjoyment of their New Year's Eve...

Soon after the dispatcher announcement, suddenly I could feel a bustling around and I knew that the departure time was up.

People wished each other, again and again, "Happy New Year!"

The pleasant noise of celebration was still alive in us all, pushing away, at least temporarily, all the gloomy thoughts which surely will rush to resume their place.

I did not go to the window to wave goodbye; there was nobody to see us off. It would have been too big of a sacrifice to have my mother out in the cold weather. Rather, I snuggled with my husband, Gil, and settled in for the 12-hour train ride. It was cold, so very cold on the train as there was not enough fuel to both run the train and heat it at the same time.

As the train got ready to leave, a stir of excitement filled again, the entire crowd. People down on the platform and those clustered at the windows hastily said their goodbyes. Despite the cold, there were crowds and crowds at the station. It was New Year's Day, and I guess, everyone liked to extend a little longer the other night togetherness and celebration. It is understanding. New Year's holiday is the only holiday on our calendar, where Romanians officially have two days off in a row.

People looked forward to it. It is, in fact, our only Winter Holiday.

We are not allowed to celebrate Christmas or even to have a Christmas tree in the house. The Christmas tree is called a "Winter tree" and is, officially, allowed only on New Year's Eve.

Santa Claus is not a name to be mentioned because Santa is a derivative of the word "saint." Any religious connotations are contrary to the Communists' atheism.

Santa is called "Gerila, the old", instead. The Romanian word for very cold weather is "ger," hence the name Gerila. Even the word Gerila makes me shiver!

As can be seen, the Communist Regime tries to control everything; but there is one place it couldn't reach; our souls. They could strip people of almost everything, but not of their faith.

There is a hope hidden deep in every oppressed heart that someday the Communist Regime would be nothing but a bitter past.

Luckily, thoughts are not audible. I was afraid, though, that my thoughts could be read in my open eyes. I personally could sometimes do that. It is not said in vain that the eyes are the window of the soul. So, I shut my eyes tightly. It was not only a way to hide my thoughts but also to relieve the tension created by a harsh reality, that was not safe to be spoken loud. However, I couldn't stay in such a captivity for too long and my trick to escape was to create room for positive thoughts.

My husband knew this habit of mine well and let me be until I opened my eyes.

He, tenderly put his arm around me, asking if I was cold.

"How could I feel cold next to you, my love?" I answered with the same tenderness.

Even though I was deep in my own world, I could still feel all around the rush of "Happy New Year "greetings from every direction again and over again, like nobody had any other words to say. Then the words let themselves be crushed under the train's rumbling wheels. Yet, through the open window "happy, happy, happy" still echoed vaguely. I turned, and reached for my husband's ear and whispered,

"Happy, happy, happy New Year."

"Many times, as much joy to you too, hon," Gil answered, looking lovingly into my eyes and hugging me tightly to him. It made all the cold dissipate.

Although it was just after mid-day, it was quite dark outside. The sky was heavy with clouds. Snow could come at any moment.

I had not yet examined the train compartment, as I used to do on long trips. I liked to study people's faces and make inferences about their features. It was not only out of curiosity but also to assess potential conversations I might have with them. It was an important test: we had to be very cautious with our words and avoid trouble.

Seated next to us it could have been a member of the Security Service. The trains were studded with them, everyplace was.

However, Gil brought my attention to the little girl who was seated across from me, next to the window. At the first sight, she resembled one of the paintings of Nicolae Tonitza, the unsurpassed Romanian portrait painter of children. The child was dressed beautifully and was looking intensely out the window. Right away, I noticed her black eyes and button nose. She was truly adorable. Next to her was her mother, I guessed. The mother was not sleeping, but she had her eyes closed and one of her hands around the girl's back. I assumed that, like us, they had no one to see them off.

"So Happy New Year to everybody!" said a young man who just came in from the window and took the seat next to the door. He was the icebreaker we all were waiting for.

"Happy New Year to you as well," could be heard from everyone in the compartment – except the child and the person next to her.

Soon after, the girl turned to that person and said,

"Mommy, do you have a napkin? The window is kind of cloudy and I cannot see the snowflakes through it."

The mother answered, smiling,

"Sweetheart, it is not cloudy, it is just fogged up."

The little girl's comment made us all smile, she lit us up like an electric light.

I examined their faces. They had many features in common. The mother's smile uncovered two rows of beautiful teeth. Because they were so perfect I wondered if they were truly natural.

I found the little girl to be unusually polite for her age, possibly, four or five. She turned towards her mother and in a very serious tone said,

"Thank you, Mommy, I am sorry for bothering you."

The mother replied,

"You're not bothering me at all, sweetheart," while petting the girl's head.

The mother's face resembled one I had known. I tried to remember who it could have been. Oh yes, she reminded me of the French actress Jeanne Moreau; they had the same smile.

I found myself caught in my usual game – guessing traits by reading a person's facial expressions and gestures. On her face, I saw inner peace even though she clearly had something important on her mind. I bet she was a Libra. Later, I would learn that I was right.

The snow had begun to fall. Its large flakes seemed heavy when they hit the windows. But, I thought to myself; that's a deception.

As soon they hit the glass, they flatten and turn into drops of water. Each drop then becomes a teeny tiny stream on the window, and strangely, tries to climb back up, against the grain.

I noticed that both the girl and I were watching the drop's struggle, and that's how we found ourselves smiling at each other. Caught in that complicity I dared, nonchalantly, to ask her,

"What is your name, beautiful girl?"

Right away she looked to her mother, blinking her eyes and waiting for her mother's approval. In a very calm voice, the mother encouraged her.

"Come on, tell her your name, it is not a secret."

"I am Corina, and my mother is Sonia," said the girl with confidence.

"I am Neli and he is Gil," I replied pointing to my husband.

That was how it started. Everyone in the compartment chimed in, but it was Corina who captivated all of us with her charm for the entire trip.

Soon I learned that Sonia and Corina were also traveling to Cluj, and strangely enough, that we lived on the same street, Lenin Boulevard. Lenin Boulevard stretched for miles through the city, so it was no wonder that we hadn't a chance to run into each other before.

We arrived in Cluj around midnight. A friend, who Corina called Uncle Justin, was waiting to pick them up at the train station.

It was very difficult to get a taxi at such a late hour, so we were lucky when Uncle Justin offered to take us home also. And we were also glad to travel in their pleasant company for a little longer.

That day was the beginning of a long-lasting friendship.

I learned that Corina and her mother had been in Bucharest for only a few days. Corina's father and her brother, Michael, had gone to the United States for medical reasons, Corina told us. The quiet girl from the train had become a true chatterbox. She proved the old saying that nobody can reveal a family's secrets like a child.

On the way home, she kept asking:

"Mommy, Dad and Michael will come back in three months, won't they?"

"Yes sweetheart, they will return in the spring."

"Which spring?"

"That would be the coming spring. Don't you know that always, after winter, only spring can follow? And with the spring, they will return."

Now, thinking back on Corina's question I feel the foreboding. Her father and brother never, in fact, did return.

The three months turned into three long years that neither Corina nor Sonia were prepared for, and little did they know then that their family would reunite in America.

After we met them, a day did not pass without having them in our minds. It was something I could never define; it was that feeling of having known each other forever. If asked, I would never be able to explain it. However, I can say that we met each other at the right time, for a reason. Corina, the bright and beautiful girl, filled my husband's and my heart with the happiness that only a child can bring. And Sonia, the deep and versatile thinker with her very generous heart, gave Gil and me many hours of enjoyment. Our feelings were reciprocated.

They say that time passes slowly, that the minutes drag when you're waiting. and three years have an awful lot of minutes. Gil and I talked about this.

Sonia, however, had found a way to look at things differently. It was easier for her to accept the long wait, because she did not count the minutes but the seasons. Sometimes, when looking at a peach tree in her garden, in the springtime, she would ask, "I wonder whether or not we'll still be here when the pink flowers of the peach tree turn to fruit?" Unfortunately, she would watch the peach tree grow leaves, flowers, and fruits, three times, until they could leave for the United States and have their family reunited.

Their departure was not easy for any of us. Yet, we tried to encourage them and look at it as a great opportunity and not easy to get.

We who were left behind had no future, Romania was suffering intensely under the Communist Regime. Even our economy collapsed, we were asked to tighten our belts even more. Everything was extreme. Be that as it may, no one could see that the "Golden Era" (that's how the Communists called it) was close to its end. If Sonia had known, if she even suspected, would she have left Romania? I really don't know.

The country she left behind was in a terrible turmoil. Romania was like a stabbed, hopeless animal, drained of all its strength. For so long the country waited, for help from the outside, to be saved from its harsh and powerful dictator, but no one would come to its rescue. Instead, it had to rescue itself.

It was almost impossible to predict that a revolutionary movement, and the fall of the Romanian Communist Regime was as close as it was.

When freedom did come, it came to a nation that had not known freedom for so long, that the people did not know what to do with it. Having escaped a political crisis, the country butted up against an economic one.

The regime itself was no longer in power, but these ex-communist-comrades, unfortunately, were still around, acting behind the scenes, continuing to create social and economic clutter.

I wonder if countries have a destiny like people do and whether heaven has anything to do with what happens on earth?

Sonia truly believed in an undefined entity, something that cannot be detected or measured by conventional means, only by faith.

She argued that "something, comes from above and from a dimension we are not allowed to know directly and visibly. Remember? Moses was not allowed to see the face of *whom* he spoke to."

I enjoyed talking with Sonia about unseen but existing things. She had always made me dig more deeply into the essence of such.

Faith meant a lot to her. Through faith she managed to eliminate the disabling negativity that sometimes takes over one's thoughts. Even resignation, for her, didn't mean quitting, but rather the point where surrender opens its possibilities. She was right, a storm cannot last forever; the sun will always come out no matter what, even though sometimes, we must wait a little more than we had wished. All of this challenged me, and I liked this kind of challenge.

Then there was also a special peculiarity in how she viewed events that might have seemed insignificant for others, but in which she saw the significance.

I see the truth of that now in how we met. It was not a simple coincidence. If I had caved into my mother's request to spend an extra day in Bucharest, I would never have met Sonia and Corina. How different our lives would have been! Yes, I like to believe that the heavens "set up" that trip for us from Bucharest to Cluj, on the first day of 1985. I shall never forget it.

CHAPTER 2

Hidden Lives Bound Within Two Covers

Many years have passed by. I have even stopped counting them, because no matter how long the time or the distance between us, Sonia and I have stayed connected. Modern communications technology has allowed us to stay in touch as if we were just around the corner, from each other. Chatting on the phone was our favorite.

But there was one phone call that was not like the others. Its ringing woke me up in the middle of the night. I jumped up, confused at first, thinking that I was on night shift at the hospital.

I did not expect it to be Corina because I had just spoken with her and her mother a few days before. Her voice was greatly changed, lifeless – I sensed that she was calling with bad news.

"Neli—I would like you to come to the States…My mom would have wanted you to see her off on her final journey."

After a moment of speechlessness, I assured Corina that I would be right there. Travelling to and from the United States was no longer an issue for Romanians.

Corina gave me the details. She explained that her mother and Adrian – Corina's stepfather -- had been in a car accident and both were dead. I suddenly remembered that Sonia had been in a car accident before, when she was still married to her first husband, Sabin. Sonia and her son Michael had almost lost their lives in that accident.

13

How strange! Michael's health issues, which possibly resulted from that first accident, had opened the path to America for her, and then another accident ended her life there and that of her second husband, as well.

I had been to America several times since Romania had become a free country, and I was familiar with the trip. I had no problems with the trip itself, but with the reason for the trip. Such a shock to lose Sonia! Such a sad day! Sonia, apparently, had been the first to go. Adrian lingered for a day in critical condition. He came out of his coma for a few hours, then sank back in, and never came back.

It was hard to believe that my dear friend had just "slipped away to the other side," as Sonia would have said, smiling her mysterious smile.

She and I often used to talk about "the other side," especially after my own husband passed away. We both believed that the spirit would live on. Now, I believe it more than ever.

Corina and Michael made all the funeral arrangements. They chose the most perfect music, Handel's Sarabande, to send them off. Sonia would have approved. I imagined her saying, "Well done, my children. This music stands in opposition to the war cannon's blasts, which could be heard when I was born." Sonia was a child of World War II. I imagined her stepping in time to that music's intense cadences all the way to the other realm…

At her children's invitation, I decided to spend a week with them, even though it was difficult for me to be in her house and not see her.

It was spring, the month of May. I found solace sitting on the deck where just a year ago we thought we couldn't be happier. May…I knew it was her favorite month. She thought it passed too quickly and she always longed for the next. Oddly, her destiny had its eye on May too. May once spared her life, gave her a shot at fulfillment, and then it betrayed her. That's the kind of spin she would have put on it.

Before I returned to Romania, Corina came out of her mother's office with a stack of books and handed them to me. At first, I didn't know what they were about, but suddenly I remembered how Sonia had often mentioned to me that she had kept confidences in her writings. The notebooks must have been those confessions.

"My mother put this package aside some time ago. She wanted it to be yours, if she were the first to go."

I looked at Corina in disbelief. In that very moment, it was as if I saw Sonia's eyes bore holes in me. But they were Corina's eyes.

That afternoon, I searched the journals and found her entry about our first encounter on the train. Clearly, Gil and I had meant as much to Sonia as she did to us.

I always knew that Sonia was a deep thinker and I could see it even more in her written work. She was always asking questions of life, questions that others couldn't or wouldn't. For instance, what guides and moves our lives? What is real happiness and how can we have it? What makes some people confront and conquer every obstacle, while others let themselves be conquered from the first?

In the first journals, the pages were dated chronologically. Later, the story followed its own course, freely, like a river which has its own song, until it vanished into the sea.

Sonia had enjoyed writing from the moment that she learned the alphabet. She not only enjoyed listening to new words, but she liked better to see them written down. She thought that in this way the words revealed their riches to a higher degree.

She craved writing. Her unspoken thoughts were like waters accumulating in front of a dam, building up a tension that had to be released. And she released it, peacefully, through writing. Thus, writing became her bedrock in earth shattering times. Writing was essential to Sonia's nature. If she read that, she would have asked, "But what determines one's nature? Are we born with it or do we acquire it?"

I am sure that through the pages of her journal, I will get to the answer. As a matter of fact, I'm just now remembering something pertinent. One day we came across a graphic map of the brain.

Instead of looking at it like we might have in a neurophysiology class, we compared it to a land of hills and valleys that sheltered mysterious treasures. We were awestruck that one's own universe of thoughts could be housed in such a little amount of matter, not more than three pounds. Even more amazing is how those "living wires" – the neurons – embedded comfortably in that small matter, created something as intangible and as intricate as a thought. Sonia said, "When you think that the same impulse to the brain can generate different thoughts, depending on different personalities, isn't it marvelous?" True again.

Sonia's sharp memory was clearly evidenced in her diary. She easily remembered names and faces, even places that I had become hazy about. Her secret was to be totally attentive to the subject in question until it had become concrete in her mind.

The diary also revealed her love for colors – not only in her paintings but to experience their benefits on emotions and relaxation. In that respect the green of nature, with its expression of vitality, was her favorite.

She also craved music and was endlessly thirsty intellectually. I, on the other hand – as a physician – I was left, sometimes, confused by the multiplicity of her pursuits. How could a person like so many things and not specialize totally in one of them?

Between the pages of the journal marked #1, I found a letter that was addressed to me but had no a date on it. Sonia may have meant to send it to me at one time but then she either changed her mind or forgot it in there. The letter is short, but it does reveal one thing, her intuition. She referred to it as a "whisper," and she listened to it often. She believed that ignoring the whisper had led her to her failed marriage with Sabin. Nevertheless, she was grateful for the two beautiful children, Corina and Michael, they had together, and eventually of the opportunity for a new life in America.

And that marriage I should say, was also responsible for our beautiful friendship, because without that trip to Bucharest to see her boys off, we would have never met each other.

Gil and I often wondered how she married Sabin. I am sure her diary will reveal the answer.

CHAPTER 3

Whispering to the Dolls

I could hardly wait to return home and go through all of Sonia's journals. Even though Sonia and I knew each other for a long time, I am sure that I would learn much more and much deeper about her life.

We had many things in common, including the medical profession, which we revered for its holy connection to the human health.

Gil was a physicist, and he was often captivated by our passionate talk making himself part of it. It was because all of science's pieces are related to one another, and he proudly would say that physics has its own approach to truth".

With his knowledge and our imagination, we travelled into the profundity of the universe and found its hidden beauty. Of course, we realized that there is also ugliness in the world, but we believed in our modest ability to bring some beauty to it.

We called our group the "Schopenhauer Club." We chose this name because Schopenhauer believed that human *will* and *desire* cause suffering and pain, but the contemplation of beauty or *aesthetics*, as he called it, is a way to escape distress.

We tried to keep politics out of our club. We knew that the walls could have ears. I was convinced that Sonia's walls and her phone were bugged, especially after her husband fled Communist Romania. So, we often talked in whispers, but Corina was too young to understand why.

"Sweetheart, those who love each other, talk in whispers. At our house and Neli's we should do that," Sonia said to Corina. Soon, Corina endorsed the new rule and started to talk in whispers to us and even to her dolls. She was more than adorable doing that. We couldn't keep ourselves from smiling when she came to our house and we heard her whispering:

"Hello Auntie Neli, where is Uncle Gil?"

For Corina, it was about love. For us it was about fear.

At that time whispering was a clever thing. We all heard stories about the security services spying on people's private lives, even in the least expected of places. These stories spread fear and anxiety; people could never know whether the next day one of them would be called on by police and even arrested without any explanation. It was that dreadful! Additionally, spies spied on each other as a performance enhancer, either in the hope of being promoted or simply not fired. They had to show loyalty to those they served.

Here's something that happened at a party. The host was a woman, and a director of a well-known company in the city. Without a doubt, she was a member of the Communist Party. Otherwise she couldn't have had such a position. It's also possible that she was an undercover security agent as well.

Anyway, it was around 7 PM. From 7 to 9 we had a TV program that consisted of a long series of shameless political propaganda pieces. Except, though it was a half hour of children show called Mihaela. Nevertheless, about 7 PM, one of the guests turned the TV on. The hostess said jokingly,

"Oh, please turn it off. I am sick of it."

The party continued smoothly and ended without incident. But the next day the hostess was called up to her company's Communist Party Committee. Nobody explained anything to her; they just locked her up alone in a room. Hours passed. At noon, the door opened, and a security agent came in bringing her a glass of water with a slice of lemon on it. With a quick look sneeringly said,

"Please drink this and so you won't be nauseated again."

For any outsiders it would have been difficult to understand what happened and why the agent was sneering, but she perfectly understood. Somebody at the party took notice of her remark and out of fear or loyalty to the party, couldn't stay quiet about it.

I have heard another one. Over summer one of my colleagues had some friends visiting from abroad. They talked and talked late into the night, when suddenly they could hear their own voices as if on a radio. The surveillance device planted in the wall had accidentally gone off. They looked at each other, perplexed. Visitors from the free world were dumbfounded by such a crass invasion of privacy. For the Romanians, though, it was nothing out of ordinary. No wonder we talked in whispers.

CHAPTER 4

Days and Worries

I find many days of worry in Sonia's journals, one of which dates from before Sabin's escape to America. Sabin had called from Italy, saying that he would not be home as expected but the following day instead. In any case, Sonia had rearranged her schedule to get to the kindergarten to retrieve her children before its closing, at 5 PM. Unfortunately, the bus she was counting on was late. Then, just to make things more stressful, the bus came to a sudden stop as it headed uphill. After some time, the driver found the cause of the problem. There was not enough gas in the tank for the engine to function in a slanted position. Here is how Sonia describes this event in detail…

"If you would like to get home, my dears, please get out of the bus and push it. That is the only way we can move it again. I have to pass over the slope and I cannot without your help."

We quietly did exactly what the driver said. We all got out of the bus and pushed it. Not a soul protested or complained. It was a true picture of Communism's approach to the gasoline crisis

While pushing, I thought through the road ahead, anticipating any other troubles.

"The most beloved son of this nation's Golden Era, Nicolae Ceaușescu!" I could not have been the only person to see the emptiness of that slogan; but nobody said a word, as we did not know whether the person next to us was a Security Agent or not. Saying one single word against the Communist Regime or President

Ceausescu meant jail time.

I looked at my watch. There were only twenty minutes to get to the kindergarten. As I, other passengers were worried of their being late, too.

However, the little ones can stay for "after-school" while they wait for their parents to pick them up. One – perhaps the only – good part of the regime is the educational system. You won't see children wandering on the street or parents not having a place to bring their children while they work.

But it is a catch to it. Since from the kindergarten the little ones, called the Hawkes of the Homeland, are indoctrinated with Communism Ideology, which at such an early age it is just a brainwash. For us those grownups it was a compromise in lack of any other options. However, we are glad that there are a lot of daycares called kindergartens, not luxurious places, but clean. And although there is not a lot of food, what there is had been prepared from scratch in their own kitchen. At least we can have peace of mind at work knowing our children are safe.

I was out of breath when I got to the school. Michael and Corina were only the remaining children to be picked up.

One of the workers on duty was supervising them. She had assured them that I hadn't forgotten them, that I might have been caught in traffic, which was very true. Everyone knows about the transportation problems.

If you are fortunate enough to have a personal car, you do not use it to go to and from work.

I have, in fact, a car, but my husband has made himself the owner of it. While he goes places mostly by car, the children and I either walk, for short distances, or take the bus, for longer trips. I learned not to make a big fuss of it not only because walking was my thing, but also because after losing my automatic shift car through the accident, I was not very passionate of driving a standard shift car. My husband was more than happy and never encouraged me to go

Blessed with Twice the Freedom

behind the weal.

Gas is rationed. Each car owner is supposed to get 40 liters per month. Even that little allotment is hard to be procured.

When the gasoline is delivered to the gas station, it is like a holiday for the car owners in the entire city. One could see cars lined up for miles and for days outside the stations. From above they probably look like huge colorful necklaces on gas-station streets. When gas finally becomes available, people must take time off from work to go get it. Otherwise they lose their place in line and/or the gasoline runs out. Many people push their cars to the gas station, either because their tanks are totally dry, or because they can save gas by not running the car.

Cars are a luxury. Those who could afford to buy one, must sign up, pay for it in full, and then wait years for the car to arrive. And we can only buy cars made in Romania.

Foreign cars can indeed be had with hard currency, and foreign money is not at everyone's fingertips.

Having hard currency, without a detailed, official explanation, is a crime punishable with jail time.

Nevertheless, there are many tourist places with stores called "Shops" for foreigners using hard currency; Romanians are not allowed to step into such stores. These stores can be found on the seashore or at other resort locations, waiting for foreigners to spend their money there.

Our children don't understand why all the treats they crave are only in those shops. They clamor at the window displays, insisting on a little piece of chocolate. Or they stick around the shop like ants sensing a grain of sugar, until the security agents chase them away.

Humiliating, yes, but we are used to living like this. Yet they indoctrinate our children at an early age with beautiful stories about Communism. Our children have nothing to compare it to and know nothing of the world outside of Romania.

One day coming from school Michael told me in a grave tone,

"Do you know, Mom, that comrades Nicolae and Elena Ceaușescu built all of the schools?" Without thinking I replied,

"Did you see them doing it?" The child was confused.

"Mom! How could you say that?" Immediately I realized how hastily I had spoken my mind. For fear that I had been overheard or that Michael would repeat it, I corrected myself,

"It's true, Michael, they built everything..."

Little Corina, who had just turned three and as usual didn't like to be left out said,

"Oh yes, Mommy, I think I saw them both, Comrade Elena and Comrade Nicolae Ceaușescu working."

It was funny to hear a three-year-old calling the president and his wife, comrade, but that was the way they were taught. I smiled at her and said, "Okay, sweetheart, I'm glad that you saw them."

We must be very careful about what we say in front of the children. In their innocence, they might repeat whatever they hear, word for word. They can make themselves part of a conversation even when they shouldn't. Little do they know what is safe and what is not safe to say. Nevertheless, both like to be taken seriously and any correction must be made with discretion. There is a fine line between what they are indoctrinated with and what they can hear from us. They are used to the rules at school and at home.

Corina often tries to find loopholes in the rules and even tries to break them, but adorably.

For example, Sabin is legendary for his rigid rules in the car. Eating, talking or touching the driver's seat when he is driving are all prohibited. She, of course, is too vivacious to stay still in the car. Often, I can feel her little hand pulling my sleeve as she asks,

"Mommy, may I sing?" Yes sweetie," I tell her, "singing is allowed." I say it just to notice the smirk on Sabin's face

CHAPTER 5

A Duty to Endure

"As soon as I opened the classroom door, both of my children jumped in front of me, ready for a hug saying,

"Mommy, Mommy we thought that you forgot us here."

"How could I do such a thing to such beautiful children? You are my priceless treasures; don't you know that?"

As a gratitude, they happily turned right away, their innocent gazes upon me.

The girl on duty at school that afternoon was "Comrade Mureşan ." That was the way little ones were instructed to call her. Outside of school, though, the children call her by her nickname, Muri. We all love Muri. This is not the first time they had to wait for me with Muri until after 5 PM.

Everyone knew that the public transportation is not at all dependable and often parents couldn't make it in time to pick their children up. However, I tried to apologize to her.

"I'm sorry for being late; the bus had problems," I said in a hurry. I knew that Muri should technically have been off-duty

"No worry at all, things happen," she said. "I'm just glad you got here safely. Be proud of these two. They were both very good and I rewarded them with an extra snack."

"I am glad to hear it," I said, with a smile of gratitude.

The children hugged Muri. Their faces lit up with happiness, as if I had been lost in a crowd and they had finally found me. I was happy to see them too; it had been such a long day.

"I have a surprise for you, my little birds," I said, while lovingly squeezing their little hands as we walked together.

"Mommy, mommy, what is it?" they cried.

"If I tell you now, it won't be a surprise when we get home."

Earlier that day, I had been lucky enough to find both oranges and a cake, which was their favorite.

As soon as we got home, supper was ready to be warmed up and served. Usually I cook dinner for the next day, after I tuck them into bed the night before. It is how I cope with our busy schedule.

Tonight, they were in a hurry to finish the food in front of them, while keeping their eyes on the surprise package. I gave them each an orange for dessert. Corina wanted the cake as well. And as a hint of her desire she asked:

"We cannot have the cake, Mommy, can we?"

"No, you cannot, sweetheart. You cannot sleep comfortably when your stomach is too full."

With an unspoken disappointment she accepted my reasoning.

However, she loves cakes. She is always first to finish hers, then she looks wistfully at Michael's. Michael is not in a hurry when it comes to his food. He is a slow and finicky eater. Corina tries to steal from him as soon as hers is gone.

"Hey, you magpie, you already had yours," Michael says. But he shares with her anyway. It's a trade. Michael, whose small motor skills are still clumsy, knows that he will need her help on other fronts. She can tie his shoelaces quickly, for example, or button up his uniform shirt when we need to hurry.

After supper, we have our own routine. First, they watch the only children's show on Romanian TV, "Mihaela." It's comes on for half an hour at 7:00.

They stop whatever they're doing and run from anywhere to watch. After Mihaela, is the reading time. They easily agree on the story. Corina is a good organizer. She lines up the books, and Michael agrees with her order.

When we kissed good night that night, I thought that Michael's forehead was slightly warm.

I had been told by Muri that a bug was running through the school, and I assumed there was a connection. I whispered to him that as soon as Corina was asleep, he could come sleep in my bedroom. I gave him some children's antifever medicine. I had no clue that would be the night that changed our lives forever: Michael had his first seizure.

We had both fallen asleep. A few hours after midnight, Michael woke up scared, asking to go in a hurry to the bathroom. I ran to bring the potty instead. As soon as I turned the light on, I couldn't believe my eyes. Michael was engulfed in a grand mal seizure. A dreadful fear drained all my strength away. I stood as if paralyzed, a helpless mother and nothing more. Any seizure is frightening, but this was of my very own child and I was aghast. My first impulse was to scream. Adrenaline clawed mercilessly at my heart, but I took a deep breath and composed myself. I dragged my phone into the bedroom and, keeping my eyes on him, I called the Ambulance Service. I also called one of my neighbors to take Corina to their house until the ambulance came. Corina woke up crying, not understanding all the commotion. Once my neighbor retrieved Corina, I held Michael in my arms and began to cry. I had to let out all the tension and fear, I had to suppress during the phone call. But my fear returned when Michael fell into a deep sleep, which looked more like death than sleep. I called his name desperately, but he was unresponsive.

The ambulance crew found me walking through the living room with him in my arms. The paramedic took him gently from my arms, brought him to the ambulance, and laid him down on the stretcher, he looked so tiny and lifeless on it.

Only in the ambulance did I realize that I still had my slippers on, but I couldn't have cared less.

We got to the Children's Hospital faster than I had thought we could. The doctor on duty was waiting in the emergency room for us.

It was a young pediatrician that I did not know.

My children's regular doctor is one of my friends, Dr. Cornea, whose nickname is Gabi. He and I graduated from the same college in the same year.

The on-call doctor, upon learning that I was one of Dr. Cornea's friends, invited me to go directly into the office.

The doctor there had a calm, but a solicitous demeanor in the same time. I watched him carefully and wished I could borrow something from his calm. I still felt the whip of my son's seizure lashing at me.

Nevertheless, I had to go through all the details again, answering all the questions. It has been a Deja-vu. I wished somebody else could have answered them for me instead. It was like trying to run away from a fire but being thrown back into it. But no matter how many burns I had from that fire, I had to keep responding by the best of my abilities. After all, it was for my son.

"How long do you think the seizure lasted?" the doctor asked, in his calm tone.

"I can't exactly say. For me, it felt like forever." I murmured, still heavily emotional. Then I continued:

"Without a doubt, this was a grand mal seizure. The very deep sleep, the unresponsiveness, the pale color made me wondered if he had died. This was even scarier than the car accident,"

The doctor remembered that Gabi had mentioned a car accident, one where a child belonging to one of his friends had been thrown out of the backseat and through the windshield.

"Yes," I said, "that was my Michael."

In the end, the doctor concluded that the high fever preceding Michael's seizure might have precipitated it, that this could be a one-time thing.

I opted to stay overnight with Michael, so he would not wake up scared and alone. I watched him all night. He slept normally, and eventually even his color returned, but he was still weak. And as I lay there, awake, I thought through possible causes for the seizure —was

Blessed with Twice the Freedom

it the car accident from two years ago, showing its rapacious claws only now? Was it the bug and the fever? Or was something else? I was inclined to believe that there was more than one cause.

I anxiously waited for Gabi to help me with my questions.

Since we were good friends, I called him early in the morning and he lost no time arriving. Michael's blood samples had already been sent to the lab, so Gabi was able to see some test results as soon as he arrived.

Gabi was, above all, a great diagnostician. When he got to Michael's room, my son greeted him with a smile. Gabi was no stranger to him. Gabi's kids were around my kids' age and they had been buddies forever. Moreover, Gabi – as Dr. Cornea – was well-known for his gracious tact with the little ones. At his very first encounter with a child, he secured the child's empathy.

Gabi acted as if he was not already in the know what Michael had been through. He gave me a conspiratorial look, pretending to be confused, as he asked Michael, "Hey, friend, are you paying me a visit at work today? What's the matter?"

"I don't really know how I got here, but my mom knows," Michael timidly replied.

"I will tell you how," Gabi said in a jovial tone, "Your mom brought you here because we haven't seen each other since summer. Remember when we all went fishing on the Someş River, and your friend Andy caught a big trout?"

Gabi talked about that trip and of our children in detail, convincing Michael that he was there just to pay a visit. Michael didn't realize that Uncle Gabi, which is what he called him, had already started the consultation.

While Michael ate his breakfast, we stepped out of the room. The on-call doctor who had admitted Michael exchanged notes with Gabi. When he left, Gabi invited me to talk to him. I didn't know exactly where to start, but somehow, I managed to find a way to put my thoughts into coherent words.

"Michael is four and a half now, and even though he did experience some high fevers as a baby, he has never had a seizure before. So, I am scared.

I keep wanting to blame the car accident from two years ago, even though all the tests at that time concluded that there was nothing to worry about. No lesion or scars were found on his brain. Could it be a late post-traumatic seizure?

It might be like a sliver hidden in the skin that goes unnoticed until it gets infected. It might be just like that; an insult to the brain that might have been deeper and more out of sight, that stayed dormant until another factor came to push it to the surface."

After pondering for a moment, Gabi expressed his doubts about my fingering the car accident.

"Sonia, I see you are a frightened mother today. I understand. It is truly torturous to watch a loved one, especially a child, going through a seizure. It is like an earthquake which once unleashed cannot be stopped until it runs its course.

We cannot deny, though, that most seizures are the result of brain injury, the more severe the injury, the higher the risk of seizure. Nevertheless, even a mild or moderate insult to the brain, could induce a seizure. It could happen right away after an injury or after days, months or years. In Michael's case, however, I doubt that the seizure is related to the car accident. He didn't lose consciousness, even for a minute, during the accident, and he has no scars on the brain. So, my dear, I think that his seizure was a one-time event due to high fever. Spiking high fevers are common in children. They are often related to a viral infection. You know that a high fever is the immune system's way to fight some viruses and bacteria which are sensitive to high temperature."

After his statement I objected,

"But all Michael's vaccinations are up-to-date. Just a few days ago the kindergarten nurse notified me that both Michael and Corina had gotten their mandatory DPT booster shot. And I should also say that my children have never had a reaction to vaccines. In addition, on the day of Michael's seizure, some kids, Michael included, had a stomach bug." As soon as I finished my sentence Gabi added,

"Sometimes, you know, even if rarely, some kids might develop a fever with a vaccination, and that bug might have amplified Michael's problem. It might be just a simple coincidence; Corina had nothing of this nature, right? So, the coincidence is plausible. Anyway, I will order an EEG and see what is going on with my little friend. We'll wait and see."

While we were talking, some more results had already come back from the lab. The doctor's eye spotted a low magnesium reading.

"Aha," he said, "the high fever overnight and the low level of magnesium could have triggered the seizure. You see, there could also be a metabolic factor involved."

"Oh yes," I agreed, "Magnesium is needed to turn glutamate into GABA, the inhibitory neurotransmitter, which keeps the brain's discharges normal and under control."

Gabi couldn't help himself. He said,

"Sonia, we would make a good team, wouldn't we?" I smiled. It was my first smile of the day. But Gabi didn't lose his train of thought. He added

"See, the fever has complicated the situation. We should find out where the fever came from, what triggered it. It too could have more than one cause."

I trusted Gabi with all my heart. His thoughtfulness would make him turn over every stone until he could get a correct diagnosis; yet, sometimes he needed more than his great knowledge. He needed great tools to work with and apply his knowledge. And I knew that the lab's EEG machine was so old it could be influenced even by street vibrations.

Nevertheless, Michael's EEG didn't show any serious abnormalities. Just like at the car accident, there were no indication of a scar or other injury which could have been the culprit for a seizure. We needed to investigate more deeply, but the tools to do so were not available in Romania.

At the time, we knew very little about MR. The technology was so new in Romania that really the most we got was newspaper references. I remember the first time I read about it. It was a kind of fantasy; through an electromagnetic field, an MRI could image the brain more precisely than an EEG, which does it by measuring the magnitude of electric impulses.

My biggest fear was that Michael would be diagnosed with epilepsy. I viewed it as a life sentence for my son. Gabi understood my fear and quickly told me that, even though it might look like epilepsy, it wasn't. With a sigh of relief, I asked,

"Then, what is it?"

"Given what we know so far, we have problems understanding seizures like Michael's. As you know, there are still barriers in the brain that we cannot yet pass. In other words, we are still confronted with areas in our knowledge that are grayer than the brain's gray matter itself."

He was right. In front of me I only saw barriers. And everything seemed to be even more difficult because in this battle of uncertainty, I was alone. My husband was always busy with other things and seemed not to be part of the team. Without saying it out loud, my hopes hung now on a trip to America, if Michael were ever to have another seizure.

At the car accident, I had had myself a head concussion, and an EEG done. The concussion did bring up some changed wave patterns on the EEG. For three months, I had to be on anti-seizure medication as a preventative, and that was enough to spare me from seizure.

Michael's EEG had not indicated a problem then, but had a seizure long after.

No matter how many times I was told that it might be only one-time thing, I had my hidden fears, though. Unfortunately, the hunch

I had was not just a false alarm. Michael had another seizure a few months later.

During his nap at kindergarten one beautiful, warm April day, Michael developed a high fever. Nobody thought that his flushed face was a reason to take his temperature. It is not unusual that children blush in their sleep.

I was told that when he woke up and tried to stand, he fell back down, and his body began to convulse.

It was just before 5, and as I had the day off, I was at home. A phone call from school, at that time of day, was not a good sign. From her first words, which I could hardly hear, his teacher's lifeless voice filled my heart with apprehension.

"Sonia, Michael is not well at all. Can you please come and take him home?"

"Yes, Stella, I will be there in no time."

I had no other words left, the bad news crushed them all.

It was hard to understand how pain of any kind, in the first moment, has an anesthetic effect on me. I feel numb. I feel like carved in stone.

But I couldn't let the shock overtake me; I had to move fast, my child needed me. I ran hastily to the school. When I arrived there, Michael was lying on his cot. When he noticed me, he tried to lift his head up and smile, but he was so weak that he dropped his head back down on the pillow. I bent over him and hugged his frail body tightly, pleading in my mind,

"Oh, God, if you let him be alive through that awful car accident, please make him healthy again. Please, God, please."

Corina was on another side of the building with her class, but at my request somebody brought her over. Both knew something had happened but neither understood what it was.

As soon as we got home I called Sabin at work, but I was told that he had stepped out. I left a message for him to call home immediately. He didn't call for a while and when he did he sounded grumpy. He didn't like to be called at work. Without criticizing the lagging of his call, I briefly explained what happened. I didn't have any time or patience for extra comments.

Again, we started a round of visits to Michael's doctors one by one. There was something wrong with Michael, but nobody couldn't say exactly what. It was something undetectable, but still it was there. Unfortunately, it was no longer a one-time event, as we had hoped for.

Another EEG was done and showed some nonspecific changes of the brain wave patterns, indicating a tendency to seizure.

I lived through a long stretch of uneasiness after that. Every time the phone rang, and Michael was not home, fear swept through me from head to toe. I became a fear-stricken overprotective mother.

Fortunately for him, Sabin was never there when Michael had a seizure. He never saw his child as if connected to an electric wire without a way of disconnecting as he stood watching, fearfully and hopelessly. Maybe a lived experience of this kind would have stirred up compassion and desire in his heart and be more attached to his family.

Now, both of Michael's doctors, the pediatrician and neurologist, decided to put him on a low dose of anti-seizure medication. They hoped that, as in my case, such a treatment wouldn't be necessary for his entire life.

Unfortunately, with Michael it didn't work that way. When the medication was stopped, the seizures came back.

Romania didn't have the necessary medical equipment to investigate further; we were at a dead end.

Gabi knew that Sabin had relatives in America. Located there was state of the art medical equipment, to which, Romanians did not have access.

One day, Gabi whispered to me,

"Sonia, Michael needs to have an MRI."

Soon after, without knowing Gabi's advice, the neurologist

confided in me. He had the very same opinion. An MRI would be our only hope of finding out what triggers Michael's seizures.

As soon as Sabin learned about his opportunity to take Michael to America, he suddenly became more affectionate. I have thought to myself, how pitiful.

I knew the game. He didn't know how to handle challenge, and always turned to me for help. Getting an approval for a trip to the United States, was a real challenge. He counted on my zeal to go to the end as I always did, when came to our children.

Even though it has been some transparency in all of this, I pretended of not seeing through it. I thought that I should deal with it later. Our child health was more of all. I couldn't afford to miss the only opportunity of my son having that EMR in which I had great hopes. Those hopes were with me day in and day out. It was not room in my mind for my husband double -dealing.

I haven't asked why he got more interested in keeping himself in good shape, than being next to me in the battle. I couldn't handle two battles in the same time, so I let him be.

He would leave the house early every morning for the city sport facilities. He found a plausible excuse to escape from home and his own things.

As for me, I wish there were more hours in the day to spend them home with the little ones.

So, Sabin had applied for a U.S. three-month tourist visa for almost three years in a row, but without success.

We couldn't mention the current reason for the trip, because that would have defamed Romanian healthcare.

However, the approval did come through this time, in part due to, we believed, another family's tragedy. The only child of a well-known family in the city, died from kidney disease just days before the child was approved to go to Germany for treatment. The entire city was outraged for, but the fear of persecution muffled the anger. Yet the fear of Communist Regime of being charged with non-compliance with Human Rights, it tacitly gave my son the chance which the other child unfortunately, missed.

However, as soon as Sabin had the Romanian passport in his hands, he stopped working conspicuously, on large projects around the house as he did before. It must have been just a cover up of any suspicion of hidden thoughts for "the comrades" who, for sure, had an eye on our house.

I had a hunch though that trip to America was more important for his own sake than for our son's.

Nevertheless, I was more than ecstatic. I saw in it my son's great opportunity to reach for the best in matter of diagnosis and treatment.

We the two people, in the same situation, reacted differently to the great news but it shouldn't be bugging my mind now. Yet, I can't chase easily away easily things which sometimes intrigue me.

Very often, people put the blame on heredity, as an excuse, when their life seems not to favor them. But heredity alone it not all.

About this, a parable from the Bible comes to my mind; the same grain of seed, thrown on arid ground or on fertile soil, won't grow up the same way.

In a sermon on this subject my father would say,

"It is not only the ground and the seed, but the care given to the offspring.

Imagine a little plant suffocated by overgrown weeds; if it doesn't die outright, it won't grow how was supposed to.

Many children in the world have the same fate; neither good ground nor weeding hands to help them grow into whatever they were meant to be.

I think of Conscience as a sculptor finalizing what the environment and heredity work put together. The result is unique; there are not two human sculptures exactly alike."

I have found a lot of truth in these words.

For sure, Sabin and I were two very different sculptures and over time we became more and more unlike, even up to a point of dislike.

Often, and unreasonably and out of blue, he would become grumpy and ready for an argument. Often the reason for it was totally laughable. His nonsense and endless disagreements made our children put their little hands over their ears imploring not to argue anymore.

That was the end of it on my part. I let him be grumpy, let him lose himself in his own blabbering. No matter what, he had to have the last word, and I let him have it. Unfortunately, he was not different with his children.

I never saw him playing with his children or lying down on the floor to giggle with them or tickle them. He was always too busy with his own world.

Outside of the house he wore the mask of an even-tempered, even meek man, but he took that off as soon he got home.

Without being totally aware, these kinds of thoughts crowded in, filling me with gloom. But it was not the right time to think about our marriage feuds, or why people act one way rather than another. Our son's health was the most important thing.

Finally, my husband's trip to America was granted by American Embassy also, issuing him a three months visa. The boys, as I used to call them, left for America on New Year's Day.

We saw them off at the airport. Suddenly the doors between us closed. Corina and I watched them until we could barely see them. Corina couldn't hide her tears but mine as always were kept behind my glasses. I told myself; it would be only three months, and Michael's health was worth the pain of separation. I rose on my tiptoes to be able to see them again. I could only see Michael's yellow hat, rolling like an orange further and further away. They left very early in the morning and we had all day long to be thinking about their trip. There was a seven-hour difference between time zones. We were seven hours ahead. While they were on their way to New York, we were on our way home to Cluj. Within one single day, we were already living in two different worlds. Corina and I said a little prayer that night before bed. We asked God to bring our boys home safely. But as always in my prayer, I added, "Your will to be done." We promised solemnly to accept His will no matter what the end would be. Then in the same day God's will has granted us an unexpected gift. We met Neli and Gil on the train taking us back home to Cluj."

God's will also grant Gil and me the reciprocal gift; our great friendship with Sonia and Corina began.

Now, I must feel honored that Sonia allowed me to go into her everyday existence, or into her "sanctuary" as she used to call it.

I was aware about a similarity between us. I can see it now even better going through her pages. We were like a fabric in which one couldn't foresee where one thread starts and the other ends.

Gil had good reason to call us Siamese sisters. He must have noticed how, very often, our thoughts, were conjoined as into a telepathic flux. It might have been in part because of our close professions and our passion for it, or just because we both were gifted with an extra sense. Sometimes we left Gil in dismay, and even ourselves with that.

In a country as corrupt a Communist Romania, where the truth could not be spoken out loud, crowds of words waited to be spoken, but were held back, choking us.

Then the communist demagoguery made us sick. And yet, we had to live our lives, use our minds let words flow out, without jeopardizing it all. Unless we haven't mention God, the science fields were often our refuge or other times sliding in long talks of fiction books, fashion and anything else but politics.

Sometimes, together, we contemplated the strands of DNA; and with our minds' eyes we admired its simply design and the marvelous work coming out of it.

We assumed that its two strands were created perfectly at the very beginning. That is how we saw them, perfectly coiled. But, as time passed by, little by little, with every generation, the initial perfection has undergone alters.

Where a repair to the DNA is not possible, but the DNA itself is still viable, nature makes necessary adjustments to deal with the imperfection, where we thought the personality traits have been born from. Eventually, as each generation passes along its adjustments DNA is found to be perfect. And neither are we.

And as we contemplated its myriad of possible imperfections, and its inner intelligence to overcome them, we left far behind any political distress.

We both strongly believed that such an intricate design couldn't have been possible without a Creator and His amazing artwork. It is amazing indeed.

CHAPTER 6

Harsh Winter, Harsh News

"We are used to harsh winters in Romania, but this one is hellacious.

Ceauşescu, Romania's beloved son, urges us to dress in layers — even in the house. Those of us who dress in layers bristle at the thought of his heated quarters.

I dress Corina like she is going on a North Pole expedition. I cannot afford to have her miss her kindergarten and I cannot miss work.

The windows of the buses running through the city are covered in frost. One day I heard some children fantasizing about it, pretending they were in a cosmic ship. All the adults sat smiling sadly to themselves. I wish there were a ship that could miraculously take us to a warmer land.

At home, Corina and I cuddle next to each other and cover ourselves in blankets on the sofa and try to read, to block out reality. We treasure the daylight because electricity is also rationed. Corina has a new favorite book. She got it as a birthday present from Neli and Gil. The title of her book is Fearless Nick. On the fly-leaf, Neli and Gil wrote: "To our fearless Corina," which totally won her over. While Corina keeps busy with her book, I read mine. It's a nonfiction about the drama of Romanian intellectuals and how sometimes their ethics conflict with the Communist System. Because I can find myself in its pages, it is hard to put down."

Reading about our gift of *Fearless Nick* to Corina so long ago gave me pause. Disgrace can befall a Romanian writer even after they've made it into the canon. As for the author of *Fearless Nick*, it came out that he had given some of his satirical verses about the regime to a dissident friend, at whose home they were later found. The dissident had once been a member of the Communist Party, but disappointed by the Party's deceiving stands, he chose to leave. He became a fiercely dissident and had been under surveillance by the Security Service. Once, during of one search of his house the police found $16.00 U.S., and with it they found as a reason to get him thrown into the most fearful jail, Jilava, where he was tortured to death. Owning the hard currency without legal evidence was considered a crime. Luckily, the author of *Fearless Nick* was outside the country at that time and thus he could ask for political asylum. He knew better than to come back. Now, I read on from Sonia's thoughts….

"I hear the wind whistling the same melody that I listened to as a child when I stayed at my grandparent's house in the country. A thermometer that hung on one of the porch poles, rocked back and forth, in a rhythmical cadence, adding its song to the wind's. That is the sound I am listening to tonight as I write this.

Tonight, for no special reason, Corina and I stood at the frosted living room window and admired the icy, beautiful design. We handed it over to our imaginations. The beauty of its flowers, castles, and clouds made the cold feel not so cold anymore. Our warm breath opened a gap and we could see the dusk outside quickly gathering into dark.

The gap grew bigger and bigger, until we could see the moon, which cast its metallic shine on the sky, as it does on freezing nights.

This week it was our street turn to stay in the dark as a contribution to solving the problem of the Romanian already collapsed economy.

Both of us were quiet for a while but suddenly I found myself saying, "I wonder what our boys are doing." Corina continued busily defrosting the window. "

At least they do not have to endure such cold," I thought to myself., a thought I could not communicate to Corina. It could have been of the potential for political trouble.

Little do children know what can say or not in a world where words must be carefully screened.

By the same token, I had to let my children be part of conversation, so I always was looking for inoffensive ones.

Not only I emphasized how important they were to me but also how grateful I was that they actively chose me as their mother. I let them believe that it was their own choice.

On their birthdays, I thanked them for it. They have always answered in their most serious way, "We didn't want anyone else to be our mother, but you" That sweet thought made me smile again.

I wish Michael were close enough now for me to thank him again for letting me be his mother.

The distance between us tonight is more painful to me than the cold and all shortcomings.

But today I have the reason to think of other kind of painful distance;

I am still in mourning for my friend, Aura. She died of leukemia not long time ago.

It pained me to hear that the blood transfusions she depended upon did not always arrive in a timely fashion to the Hematology Institute. In fact, because of the gasoline shortage, some deliveries were made by horse carriage.

Anyway, it broke my heart when visited her. Her hospital room always looked as desolate as her prognosis, it was difficult for me to talk hopes when weren't any. She however, remained uncannily beautiful. Weak and pale, she was still a beauty. I often called her Ali, because she resembled Ali MacGraw, whose character in "Love Story" also died from leukemia.

Aura left behind two little kids, too young to understand death.

Fortunately, their father is totally devoted to them.

I won't leave those children out when I bake cookies. I'll tell them that their mother sends the cookies, that she has not abandoned them, but that she has been called far away. It will comfort them.

Corina catches me out though. "Mommy," she asks, "you won't go, will you? Even if you are asked?"

Without hesitation I answer, "I will stay forever in your heart, little star." This she accepted though.

I want my children learn to always have a sense of appreciation and gratefulness for everything that has been done for them. Grateful hearts are tenfold honored. They should always remember that".

*****

"Winter vacation is over. Hundreds of students walk again to school, the blue of their uniforms taking over the streets, the pleasant sounds of their giggling delighting our ears.

Corina's kindergarten is right across the street from Michael's school. Before I dropped her off this morning, we both instinctively, were looking in the schoolyard to see Michael in the crowd. I said nothing about the trap an old habit caught me in. However, Corina asked, "Mommy, Michael will be in this school again, won't he?"

"Oh, yes my darling," I reassured her, "he will be back soon."

That night I realized what big fool I was by thinking and saying that.

It was late in the night when the phone rang. I jumped up, knowing that it had to be from overseas.

It was Sabin and using double meaning talk, he let me understand that they would never be coming back. Even hidden deep inside I had long suspected it, but I was not truly prepared to confront it. It came through that wire and hit me like a bolt of lightning.

A cold chill, which I couldn't distinguish as heartbreak or fear, ran through every fiber of my being until it stopped in my heart. My heart, confused, sent out strong beats as if it were in a panic attack.

That moment split my world in two. My eyes and my mind refused to see or to process things the way they used to, the way they always had.

Sabin let me talk to Michael. I felt the same fear in his voice that I knew was in mine. I swallowed all my tears, because I didn't want to cry in front of my child. Also, I couldn't forget that our phone was doubtless under the eyes and ears of the Security Service ever since Sabin had gone to America. I let Corina talk too. She was happy to do it, and then went back to sleep. She understood little. I am left alone now to ask myself questions I am unable to answer. On the phone, everything was vague - it had to be, although I am sure that despite our evasiveness, the Security Service still understood. I wanted to smash the phone to bits, so Sabin could feel my anger and my disappointment, yet I had to stay quiet and very calm. I was bursting with unsaid thoughts.

A friend from Germany was on his way to Romania to deliver an uncensored letter from Sabin – that would do the real talking. We had to rely on such subterfuges because all the official mail coming from outside of the Communist Bloc was censored.

I tried to end the conversation as if nothing was out of the ordinary, but not before telling him several times to take good care of Michael. He mumbled something back, but I was not listening anymore. I felt humiliated. I let my hand drop the phone down. I hated the phone for giving me such news. I too wanted to run away from this prison disguised as a country, but with a man I could trust.

I ran to take a shower. It was our week to have hot water, and luckily there was still some left. The shower was my refuge and there I had a bitter cry. I didn't want Corina to hear me; it would have been too difficult to explain to her. It came too fast and found me unprepared. I needed time to process all of this. I tiptoed into Michael's room and crawled into his bed. I pulled the comforter over my head and cried some more. I can hardly wait for the dark to vanish and for daylight to come. Everything seems worse at night, as my mom used to say.

I thought about calling my mother but didn't dare to. Before I could explain it to her, I would have to explain it to myself. Time was always a good adviser for me. Then I was afraid that if my mother called, I wouldn't be able to hide it from her. But she didn't call. The phone was ringing, yes, but I was relieved to find that it was Neli. Pure telepathy.

Neli said that she had woken up out of the blue and was compelled to call. She wanted to have us come over for dinner the coming Sunday. She and Gil are extraordinary people. Other friends of ours had distanced themselves from me after Sabin left for America. They were suspicious about Sabin's departure. Now I see that they were right to avoid us. They foresaw the outcome. It was not safe to be associated with a fugitive's family. This was not because they were not good friends but because we posed a risk for them. Many of them were high-level officials and of course had to be Communist Party members (which was a must for high ranking jobs). They easily could lose those jobs. It was that precarious.

Neli and Gil on the other hand, had no affiliation with the Communist Party. They had no aspirations to higher positions, not because they were mediocre, but because they were not impressed with the Communist Regime, how could anyone be? As soon as I had answered the phone, Neli sensed that something was wrong".

Sonia was right. I had sensed right away that something was wrong…I remember it perfectly. Sonia was not herself, but she said it was because she was tired, that she'd been having insomnia. I didn't question her further. We were excited to have them over on Sunday. We made the dinner table very festive. About two o'clock Gil took a quick glance through our living room window.

"Here they come," he said as he hurried to the door. I think it was Corina who rang the bell; and Gil opened it before the bell had even stopped ringing.

"Sonia, Corina, welcome, welcome, we are happy to see you!" we said in unison. We were so excited they didn't have a chance to say a word.

Corina held a nice bouquet of flowers in one hand and a coloring book and crayons in the other. I suspected that she liked to entertain herself when among adults. By the same token, I guess, Sonia wanted her busy when the adults had important talking to do.

Corina politely offered me the flowers.

"Hey, munchkin, how did you know that Neli likes the tuberoses?" Gill said warmly.

"Because, my mom likes them too," Corina answered.

"Corina, my dear, don't assume that what I like everybody else likes too."

"But you do like tuberoses, don't you?" Corina said as if she got it.

"Please make yourselves comfortable and feel at home," I said as I gestured to them to sit down.

I knew that we would have to do some talking without children's ears around, so I was prepared also. I had purchased some dolls and children's books for Corina, but she had her own travel set.

I assume Corina already knew the rules. The children had to keep busy in their own world and let the adults be comfortable in theirs. I mean if you weren't careful, children could repeat things they didn't understand and there would be trouble.

Sonia and Corina were our special guests and dinner should be special as well, although there were survival protocols around sumptuous dinners. For example, for the last few days, Gil and I had been busy getting everything we could from our "personal suppliers." You could share a sumptuous meal, but only between good friends, otherwise suspicions could be raised. So much for the Golden Era.

After dinner, Corina left us at the table and went into the living room to entertain herself. It was fun to listen to her, how she introduced herself to the new dolls and posed as their teacher. How precious is a child's innocence and imagination!

On the other hand, Sonia did not have a smile; I felt even more strongly that something was troubling her. Eventually, she shared her news.

Sabin, as we have already known, had gotten a three-month tourist visa to visit his relatives in the US. This tourist visa was just a pretext, the real reason for his visit was their seven-year-old son's health. After the child had the MRI, which was available only in the States, they should have returned home, but they weren't going to

In the Communist Romania, such a decision was considered betrayal and punished as such; and not only Sabin was made guilty of it, but Sonia, as well.

In the Communists 'eyes, he was traitor and so was Sonia. Nevertheless, he was in a safe zone and she was not. For her was just a beginning of more hardship. Her fate was in the Communists' hands, and it was a scary situation to be in. She was waiting for a letter from Sabin with more details to get through Germany to her. Gil and I were appalled.

As Gil often said, "character without intelligence can do a lot, while intelligence without character has no value."

And I, after reading all the things that Sonia had confessed to her journal, grew angry again at Sabin, angry with all his family. I feel something rotten in this whole story. Sabin's parents returned from the States from a visit with the other son, Sabin's twin brother, just before a visa was issued to Sabin. It is hard to understand.

Have they sent two elderly parents back home to be in Sonia's care, or what else? Gil and I couldn't make sense of it at all. Gil was first to say what I was also thinking; "wait and see, there must be a trap here not only for the Communists but for Sonia also" And. Gil couldn't have been more accurate. Throwing Sonia to the Communists was like throwing her to a pack of wolves..

In a week or so, their friend from Germany came with the letter.

Sabin wrote, "I know it will be very hard for us, but we owe our children a better future." It was the only phrase that made sense in the entire letter. We all spotted the blackmail in it right away. Sabin knew that Sonia would do anything for her children, even let him, Sabin, off the hook.

She had also relentlessly believed in the miracle of changing the father into a better man, and the man into a better father. And here it was his opportunity; he all alone taking care of Michael for three months. It is true that a miracle, very often, hasn't happen overnight but for a man as Sabin, even three-month wouldn't be enough time for change to happen, I guess.

Nevertheless, she would have done anything to keep a father in her children's lives. I don't think Sabin was ever worth the effort; all he wanted was to be free of family responsibilities.

But Gil had a saying for this, too: "No matter how late, the truth will surface just as oil does in water." Here's how the oil surfaced for Sonia. A nurse I work with, who had no clue that Sonia and I were close friends, told me how one of her friends was brokenhearted over her lover's departure to US. First, I thought that it was a simple coincidence with Sabin's trip. Unfortunately, it wasn't. That lover was none other than Sabin. How disgraceful!

Now, I got the answers to some of Sonia's complains about not having him home when most needed. It also explained his need to keep himself in good shape when his family had totally different priorities. What a sneak!

Gil and I refrained from talking about him. We also suggested to Sonia that she rip his letter into pieces, so the Security Service won't have a chance to read it. After a long debate, Gil and I decided not to say anything about Sabin's affair.

We were sure that the Security Agents were already mobilized by Sabin's case as soon as they intercepted his phone call home, and we were right. Only a few days later, Sonia was invited to the Passport Office which was a part of the Security Service network. It was also the office that had granted Sabin permission to leave Romania.

In the crowded waiting room, she was harshly scolded and called a traitor. They said they had no doubt she was his accomplice. On her way home, she stopped at our house in tears to tell of this. Corina was not with her, she was still in school, so we could talk freely.

She had to answer some difficult questions about her husband. If only they knew that she was more surprised by her husband's action than they were.

Sonia's day at the Passport Office was the beginning of a long hardship. It was hard to prove that she had nothing to do with her husband's decision to flee the country.

Even though Sabin's delivered the news to her which stirred the Security Service action, yet during those three -month of visa stay, he was equivocal with her about his decision, leaving her more than confused. Then there were his parents left in her care. She would have to provide them with those needed when shortage was on everything.

Gil and I, no matter how we tried, we didn't get to the end of puzzle. But Gill said again; wait and see…And he was right, within one year after, his parents applied to move out of Romania for good. The approval came easier for them, not only because it was any need for them in their late 70's, but because they both were born in US to parents who spent some time working in America.

It was a trick on Sonia very well-orchestrated!

CHAPTER 7

Two Blows at Once

If I could, I would have erased these pages not only from the journal but from Sonia's life entirely. But the past cannot be erased, only forgotten. Nevertheless, I should look at her resilience. If, as soon as you survive a major blow, and you are immediately hit with another, it can be the end. And yet, some can survive blow after blow. Sonia was one of those; I see it in the page to follow which personally I witnessed. And she goes:

"Corina and I had just gotten home and as usual I picked up the mail. I paled when I saw an official-looking envelope. I opened it and learned about an order that had already gone into effect: half of my house was to be seized. Corina could read on my face that I was upset.

"Mommy, what happened, what is wrong?"

"Honey, give me a moment, I cannot talk right now." Corina became worried and insisted, "Mommy, please, what is it?"

I had to find the right words not only so that she could understand but also to minimize the importance of the situation, so that Corina would not feel like sharing the news with anyone.

"We will be giving up half of our house," I said without any other explanation.

"It is not about my room, is it?" That is how a five-year old related to such news.

"No, it isn't; set your mind at rest about that. Remember, there are things we do not question, discuss with others, or refuse."

Blessed with Twice the Freedom

As the paper warned me, a comrade by the name of Carp, would come to knock on my door the very next day.

I had a strange feeling that the earth was slipping away under my feet and my house with it.

Just as the notice said, the next day comrade Carp came to my house. We didn't exchange more than a few words. They were regarding the only two options I had. I could keep the entire house by paying rent on one half which was seized, or let the State rent it out . I was shocked at first, but then I chose to pay rent on my own house. For sure, any tenants they chose would have been members of the Security Service who would have made a *spy- nest* in my house

After the comrade left, I could hardly wait to call Sabin, even though at that point there was not much to say. He had thrown these dice behind my back. I wanted to vent my frustration. I felt trapped and I was ready to talk to him loud and bluntly. Finally, the switchboard connected me to the U.S. but ironically, it was to a wrong number. It was a real test for me. It has been the first time to hear an American voice speaking English to my ears. It was like a smash in my face. I understood nothing. My fear grew by every breath. It was the language that soon had to be my everyday language. Nobody should blame me for that fear, I had been in my late 40's and, yet I had to pass the hurdle of age with no cry.

I wished I were a robot without feelings. Sabin's perfidy hit me more strongly than the seize of the half of my house. How dare he? Since I couldn't confront him, I could only panic to myself, not in front of Corina. I realized that I did not know Sabin at all. We had spent almost twenty years together, but I had created a vision of him that was everything I wanted to see and had pushed away everything I didn't like. How wrong I was! I had created a virtual man, but relentlessly thinking that love could transform flaw. I felt cornered and I started sobbing.

Then I remembered that my parents were on their way to my house, so we could take my ailing father for some medical testing.

51

They would be arriving at any moment. I had to dry my tears fast and hide my sorrow, which would finish off my father's heart more quickly than his existing problems. I could not tell my parents anything from what was lately going on, as they were both so fragile.

Neli was coming too, she was going to drive us, but there wasn't time to bring her up to speed on the situation with the house. I felt so alone and as well as being thrown out of my hose.

My father urgently needed to be admitted to the hospital. I called his cardiologist to let him know; Paul Corniş the best cardiologist around. But – as we had experienced with Michael – in medicine, great skill without great technology is not enough. Paul started all the preliminary medical tests.

It was a rainy day. Paul's office was dark and heavy drops of rain hit the window noisily. I was sensitive to the sound of them hitting. Their pummeling filled the pauses Paul made between words as he gave us the bad news. My father had suffered a heart attack and it seemed that another was on its way.

I had not recovered from the news about the house when the news about my father's health hit. These two blows were too close together. They felt like they were coming simultaneously. Both Neli and Paul noticed that lost look on my face and as if synchronized said, "Come on Sonia, cheer up, everything will be okay." I didn't answer. There was more than just one okay I was waiting for.

My father was moved right away to Intensive Care. Unfortunately, in Romania at that time, ICU was just a name and the care there did not resemble proper intensive care. There were two beds in the room, one for my father and one for a younger fellow who watched us with a sad smile on his face. His sadness was consonant with the situation, everything looked gloomy.

The bedding was clean, as was the room. However, I was more concerned with the condition of the two old monitors. I learned from Paul that they were a donation from the West a long time ago. They were not only outdated but too run-down to work non-stop.

We left the hospital late. My mother couldn't stay overnight with my father because she had a broken foot in a cast. Both Neli and I were ready to spend the night in the hospital, but Paul didn't want us to. The hospital was hot and humid and there was not enough room for us to be accommodated. Paul assured us that only he would be there all night and that it was only necessary for him to be there.

Very early the next morning, just as we were heading out the door with food and clean bedding for Papa, the phone rang. Neli looked at me with alarm. I picked up the phone.

"Good morning Paul," I managed to say with difficulty. The words were stuck in my throat. There was a pause on Paul's side, so I asked directly,

"Something is wrong with my father, right?"

"Yes, Sonia. Unfortunately. I have to say, yes. He passed away. Last night. In front of me. I was unable to help him."

We stood still in consternation. Corina was there, too, ready to go with us. She opened her eyes wide, not understanding what was going on. I had to hide the deep grief I was feeling. Corina would have time later in life to share this grief with me, but she was not ready for it now. The burden of losing my house perched on one of my shoulders and the weight of my father's death rested on the other. Before, I had wanted to unload on Sabin; now I did not want to talk to him at all.

***

"My father left the world without knowing about Sabin's falseness. It was best that way. And he left the world knowing that my mother was not alone. He knew that I was there for her. We buried my father next to my grandparents in the cemetery of the village where he was born.

Today I walked through the old cemetery to get to his grave. Only a few crosses with names on them were still standing.

I thought of the phrase, "for dust you are and to dust you shall return." It is an implacable truth which in a place like this becomes sonorous.

All along the path, bluebells were trying to push in among a crowd of daisies. They marked the path as if they knew that the people walking there would be looking down and that their humble beauty would be appreciated.

This cemetery is a page of the village's archives. As a child I wondered if those predestined to come into the world would at some point cross paths with those who had been called back. Only God knows the order…

Sometimes my children would ask me kind of similar questions. I have admired that kind of thinking in my own children. A child's thought is simple and direct."

CHAPTER 8

Looking for a Silver Lining

How I wish Sonia had dated her journal entries! Sometimes she seems to be writing at the time of the events she relates, and at other times, she seems to be writing from a place of perspective. I found these passages compelling:

"I better turn things around and look for better outcomes. I can't let them drag me down.

After my father died, I wanted to talk things over with my mother; her words of wisdom have always come to me as a lifeline. At this point, with Sabin's mixed messages, I don't even know exactly where I stand. So maybe I can't talk this over with my mother. I can't add to her worries.

After that first communication about the house, things unfolded quickly. I found a note from the official assessor in my mailbox. It was an order to assess and then confiscate half of my house. I surmised that Sabin's phone call was the trigger for this retribution.

The assessor seemed to be a good person, but he had his job to do, after all.

The order was not only to pay rent on a part of my house but if allowed to leave for good, to pay off my entire mortgage.

I was like a pawn in a game of chess, and the players were Sabin and the Communist Regime.

I finally told my mother what was going on.

"Are you saying that Sabin made this decision by himself?" she asked as soon as she heard the news.

55

"Yes."

"I always had the feeling that that man was trying to hide something. His face was perfect insincerity; but I never thought that he would go so far. You must think twice before following his lead."

"I know, Mother; you are right, but for my Michael's sake I think we should make peace with Sabin."

I said that to calm my mother down, but then I realized that I was quoting Sabin. It was hard to hide my feelings from her, though.

She sensed my struggle and said, "May God have knowledge of you, sweetheart," a line, which looks that she had borrowed from her mother-in-law, to use it in times of trouble.

"God sees farther into the future than we do, and let's ask him to direct our steps in the right way. Let us be at peace with His will."

I had heard her make this advice many times before, but it felt like good, new advice just the same.

Next day, I woke up with a little more zest for my future, and my mind was clearer.

My mother's words always had an extremely calming effect on me. She never used words in vain, or just for the sake of talking, her words were a bridge between her heart and her mind. I always tried to get a grasp on it.

She woke up every morning grateful for that given day. Her sense of Christian gratitude brought joy to her heart, and I could read that joy in her eyes. It was a humble joy that would spread light into every dark corner.

From her and from my father, I had learned that no matter how challenging an event is, it has within a seed for hope, for belief in something better. I nourished that seed of hope and deep down I believed in the light at the end of my tunnel of my troubles.

Such a belief sustained my fight, along with the faith that in this fight I was not alone. God was omnipresent. Some call that belief mystical. I would call it magical. Many things have happened to me where I could have considered myself lucky. Sometimes it was luck, sometimes it was magic; I grew up in an environment where magic was considered sacred.

I have been plagued with difficult questions, but answers have been revealed to me through my faith; my firm belief in something for which there is no a physical proof. Nobody sees or sense an electromagnetic field around us either, yet as soon as we push a button, electromagnetic waves connect with our senses. The waves existence proves by itself.

I was amazed to learn that when matter is divided far and deep into nothingness or into the subatomic realm, it behaves as in God's realm, where there is no future and no past, where time is condensed into specks of the everlasting present.

Even as a child, at a lower scale, I contemplated it. I was wondering how time comes and in the same moment disappears, letting me stay in a present which flow along with me. That was the time of innocent thinking.

I let my thoughts again wander for a while, to free my mind of the worries of an uncertain future.

Unfortunately, the reality around hasn't let me stay for too long faraway from daily uneasiness.

It has gotten cold again, both inside, and outside. We can't set our thermostats higher than 50°F. Sometimes we don't take off our coats and gloves and go to sleep dressed in layers.

God willing, it will be my last unbearable winter. In secret I have started to nourish the thought of leaving this hardship and go to America too. I realized that such a thought is already helping me. I complain less about the cold as warm thoughts emanate from my dream, America.

America is the most beautiful dream anybody could have here and now – and that dream is mine. No matter how hard the beginning might be there, it couldn't equal the hardship from here."

CHAPTER 9

Hardship, Harsh Winter

In these bits, Sonia sounds sadder and sadder. When we were together, I had become used to her jovial nature but there is always a straw that breaks the camel's back:

"Sabin, Sabin, Sabin. We haven't seen the sun under the same sky for a long time now. At the end of the day we pass it to you, so you can start a new day there. The next day when we look at it is rising, we know that in its tireless journey, it is coming from you. I wonder how you are at its arrival and departure. We are waiting here for spring's blessing. This winter has been not only harsh, but also long. Sometimes the wind feels like cuts from a hot knife, it is that cold. It is blowing from all directions drifting our ways and not just metaphorically. We feel trapped here.

At least you are protected there and are free from the shortcomings we have here. The other night Corina would have liked to have a slice of bread with butter and jam. I only had the jam. My mother had a lot of plums from her orchard and made it for us. But it was no butter. Corina didn't complain but accepted what was on the table.

The day after you left I made some new friends, Neli and Gil. They have been a Godsend. When you first meet them, you are overwhelmed by their kindness. They adore Corina tremendously. They do not have children of their own, so they spoil Corina rotten.

They were indignant about the *bitter* butter story, as we ended up calling it. Neli reprimanded me saying, "You know that I always have a little butter for my little friend. You know that, don't you?"

I do know that either of them would have come in a heartbeat with the bitter butter, but I didn't dare to call. It was already dark outside, and the roads were covered by heavy snow.

Since then, whenever I visit them, she has a little bag ready to go and slips it into my purse."

Oh, how well, I remember the *bitter* butter. Gil and I used that expression for butter even when the butter became *sweeter* and we didn't have to stand in line to get it.

I imagine Sonia sitting down at her kitchen table to have her steamy morning coffee and to write. Her coffee time was the only time she really had just for herself, early in the morning – before Corina got up and the real day started. I liked her kitchen. The warm orange color of the walls and all the tchotchkes she coordinated with them gave it warmth even when it was cold. But I will let her continue her story.

"Sabin you won't believe. The thermometer in the room shows 46 degrees Fahrenheit. I feel like spring is very far away. I'm all wrapped up in my blanket, so I can enjoy my coffee in peace and think of the both of you. I miss you dearly. I hope you make our son your priority. Your decision to stay in the States longer than your visa allows makes me wonder. What is there you're not telling me?

These days I am knitting a sweater for Michael. A friend is visiting her brother in the States and promises to bring it to him. I knitted my love into it. He might not need to wear it inside, like we do. I know that you have four seasons there also, but I am sure that in the winter the windows are not frozen like they are here. Talking about seasons, your little munchkin asked me one day with high curiosity, "Mommy, where do the seasons come from, and where are they going?"

I said, "It just happens. They come and go just the same as we do."

Right now, I am alone. Sometimes I need to be. I listen to people's problems all day long, at the pharmacy, no complaints about that; it is the nature of my work. Fortunately, I manage to just listen and help and not dwell on their problems when I'm at home.

During the day, I always set something aside for later, something to think about later that will cheer me up. Today that something is painting, colors. It has been a long time since I have had a brush and paints in my hands, since I have let the colors stretch as they will on the canvas. Unfortunately, it is too cold now, and such work cannot be done with gloves on. But I like thinking about it.

Now more than ever I am waiting for the spring. Spring is my favorite time and the time I am thirstiest for colors.

In the spring, the sun generously spreads its light and heat over us for free. It defrosts the windows, so it can come inside. Even though it comes at no cost, in my heart I feel that I owe it something for the gift of its light. My much-loved green of spring is nothing other than a reflection of the same frequency from the green of the sun's spectrum.

You might still remember my ritual; I like to be alone with just the light, the colors, and the music. I let them blend into each other and then I let their tide sweep me into their world. Spring will come.

While some old friends are too afraid of losing their jobs to associate with us, I still have some friends around. Your decision to not return home put us in a bad spot. I mostly refrain from talking about it out loud. I only talk freely about it in my journal or letters like these that I never send you.

I find myself humming a little song from my long distant childhood.

The garden flowers are blooming,

And the blue sky looks like a mirror,

Throughout the orchard flying,

The bees start their work

Ah! The warm thought that joins my morning coffee! It makes me smile. As a child, I liked to romp under the blossoming trees of the orchard singing that song. They say that it is good for the soul to slip down into childhood, that's how we drink from the fountain of youth.

A phone call, however, interrupts my peaceful morning. I am not jumping to answer it. It is too early in the morning for a regular call. Corina is safe home and you guys must be sleeping. it is not the ring pattern my mother and I have agreed upon. It must be somebody else and they can call again later.

And yet I am disturbed. I prefer to start my day conversing with my faithful friend, my journal.

I know that for you, with Michael, it is a little more difficult. But this is your chance as father to learn that at his age, he needs you now more than ever. Let this situation teach you that you should make him your priority and put yours aside for the time being.

The chores for the day ahead are already piling up. I have so little time left to talk to you today, dear journal-friend-husband.""

***

Mostly I try to keep the events in chronological order, but sometimes I find myself backfilling. It is only natural. I need to convey the true emotional load of the events I relate. The thoughts must come one by one and genuinely, the same way they were born in my mind. They can't come all at once and bump into each other like in a traffic jam; there is an order to be followed. If a day seems too crowded with events and cannot be sorted out easily, I let a night or even a day pass to give them time to unravel themselves. It helps to keep me calm.

It is, for sure, one of the many lessons I have had to learn: to stay calm, to be patient, and to look at things in my life considering all their aspects. I guess certain tasks come repeatedly in my life until they are learned so well, that they can be integrated into my nature.

Sabin, Sabin, Sabin. You were always quick to remind me that I am not perfect. You were quick to amplify even those little imperfections which were just sketched or feel victorious when you thought that found more.

I think a good physiologist would call it a mirror reflection on yours.

It must have been your nature, which was meticulously hidden from me when we met.

Now, I remember your saying, that you had no desire to go home, because of your parents' endless quarrels. You hated it, and oddly you, often, would be looking to stir senselessly, one. Like you did then, our children do it now; they cover their years imploring us to stop arguing. That was the point when I took a passive position in front of your many criticisms, while you took it like having the last word in the *debate*. It greatly satisfied your ego. You haven't stop there but took over the family affair pretending to be the only one decision maker. You see, this is virtual talk, which we should have had long before. But such a talk, face to face, would have been impossible.

Nevertheless, you played it so well as nobody could have ever thought otherwise.

It was a time when I have thought that I was so fortunate to find a true love for the second time. Unfortunately, often you let me feel that it was nothing but a deceiving thought. Our *honey moon time* has been way too short.

Even before we had become close friends, we were open about our past, and Adrian was not a name you never heard. You have learned how Adrian and I had to give up on each other. I have also learned about your experience in such matter; never being appreciated for who you were. I found it unjustly for you; there were too many qualities in you to be easily overlooked. Too good to be true…at least that you made me believe.

Now, I refrain from comparing you with Adrian, but I would like someday to understand the choices that I have made. How could I let myself mislead?

The difference between you and him is like between day and night.

Adrian was never caustically critical of me. When he did, it was lovingly, and just to tease me. He used to often call me Droplet, because of my precipitated feature when excited about something. He didn't see anything but charm in it, but you would always mock me for that.

I try to find such moments with you in my memory but there are only a few and far in between now...

For the longest time I tried to refrain from comparing you to him.

I told you all about him and the reason for our split a few years before meeting you.

I was not looking for another man to love, you just appeared as perfect as a man could be, at the moment I felt healed from an old scar.

You see, a forbidden relationship, when broken, heals differently from one full of guilt. If ours ever broke it would be out of guilt, you know that, don't you?

I hope you don't take offense that today Adrian fills my mind. I don't know why. Or it might be because you let the mistrust slipped between us.

My marriage to you didn't come to fill a gap because there were not any gaps at that point. It was love on my part, one which came from a heart that had been broken but was then healed.

Until we had our children, you even helped me remove any traces left behind that scar. You were that kind of husband any woman would have like to have.

However, after that, you took a turn, sometimes very difficult for me to understand. Were the children too much for you? I couldn't neglect them in favor of you, and if you feel that I did, it was because you left me be a single parent.

We both brought them in the world, didn't we?

Now this question is just for me. What if I had never gotten married?

As far as I know Adrian never got married but instead continued his education as an architect and received all the degrees and designations that he could. He is quite well-known architect.

I am proud of him and wonder if he would ever have a reason to be proud of me or if he had any regrets that I was married after the Communism failed.

We sacrificed our love in each other's names, and we were the martyrs for that forbidden love. It was forbidden because, as thought, of my family discrepancies with the Communist Regime. We were considered *political heretics* and could be easily *burned* at the stake, without anybody knowing, though. The regime had no tolerance for *heretics*. We were very aware of that.

My *burn,* I am sure, would have hurt him more than hurt me.

But I should stop right here and now and let past stay in the past. I better let myself being caught in the present.

Oh yes, look the sun is out, I find myself saying. It pushes, suddenly, the clouds away and the rolled in. What a gift light is, at least for us, who very often, have only that from the sky.

March 1st will be here in a few days. It is the day when we are looking forward to offering the gift of Spring, March's amulets, to our loved ones.

You remember the excitement, we had especially during of high school's years, don't you? It was a reason that encouraged us to step out nonchalantly, from a platonic love.

I noticed Corina was secretly working on them in her room. She was in a big hurry because it was already a little late for Michael's gift.

You told her though that they don't have such a tradition in America, which slowed her down.

Instead of a March amulet, Michael sent me some beautiful pictures with a little note, "Here are some signs of spring for my dearest Mommy." There were drawings that he had made for me.

He was right; on that day, my spring came; even the sun felt brighter in the sky. Good news can bring to the spirit what a few days of the shining sun can bring to nature.

I remember my grandma calling the sun the Holy Star when she looked for it in the sky. It does have indeed the merits of a saint. It has been chosen to give us our daily light; life would be impossible without it.

It doesn't ask for anything in return but to appreciate its generosity – no wonder Grandma called it holy.

It seems to me that those who are generous have something like the shining sun in their faces. They are happy. Such a state of mind cannot resonate with a greedy heart. Selfishness attracts greed like a magnet; it is that never-satisfied feeling.

I don't bring any intentionally hint here, I am just saying this".

CHAPTER 10

The Tireless Going

Gil and I called Sonia and Sabin the Grasshopper and the Ant. Well, mostly we called Sabin the Grasshopper. Every time he called Sonia from the States, he would have for her more and more, to add to the must-do list. For him was easy. He left, but all his financial obligations were left behind, and always he asked her, that they to be done first.

Before we learned what kind of man he was, we were thinking of how much appreciation he should have to his wife.

Corina attended many after-school programs: piano, swimming, modeling, ballet, voice lessons, and more. We often jumped to help Sonia with Corina wherever when her days were overloaded. We loved pitching in. It was our desire to help, and to get a taste of parenting. We were always invited to all of Corina's shows and recitals. Even her father was a fugitive, the multi- talent student was not push away from the programs.

Once, when Corina not was even five years old, she was chosen to open a show of the "Children's Little Town," which was part of the "Winter Season" show.

She wore a beautiful knitted outfit that her mother had made for her. There was a knitted bonnet-shaped hat that accented her rounded face and her dark playful eyes. The rest of her colorful apparel made her look like she'd been cut out of a fashion magazine. We couldn't take our eyes off, of Corina: she looked like a living doll. We could hear others around whispering, "Oh, she is adorable." She was indeed.

I remember Sonia knitting stylish things for her boys and sending them overseas. I told Sonia that one day I would like her to teach me how to knit. She, right away, replied, "Do you know that knitting has a therapeutic and an anti-stress effect?"

Looking at Corina's outfit I couldn't help from saying, "And, I should say, a creative effect."

We walked through the "Little Town" together. There was a little train that loaded and unloaded kids at short intervals, taking them from one place to another. There were little houses of different shapes – mushroom houses, ladybug houses, and flower-shaped houses.

True, they could only offer a poor assortment of children's goodies; we were still in the midst of our typical shortages. The important thing, however, was that the children were happy and proud of their performance.

Sonia, Corina, and I stopped at the bakery on the way home to buy a special cake, one of Corina's favorite treats.

Gil was unable to be at this performance due to a work commitment. He waited for us to return with the treats and the story of the day.

"Your little friend was the prima-donna of the show. She really was," both Sonia and I reported.

That afternoon Corina had another surprise for us. Until then she just played notes at random on the keyboard we had given her. Her mother told us, that she had practiced for days to play "Für Elise" impeccably for us. We were so excited to hear Corina's first concert.

The following spring, we were pleasantly surprised to see that she was a talented dancer as well. On the National Theatre's scene of the city, a group of little girls graciously presented a ballet show. This was an annual event and all the girls were always stunningly beautiful and received many ovations from the crowds. For us, of course, Corina stood out.

Gil and I looked in each other's eyes and read in them again our regret for not having a Corina of our own. In the next moment though, we returned to the realization of the joy we had found in Corina.

CHAPTER 11

A Bruegel Comes to Life

More from Sonia's journal:
"A beautiful winter panorama viewed through the window of a cold room, can eventually lose its appeal. Its immaculate white color speaks with more bravura than innocence.

For sure, my grandpa would have seen the snow as a shield over the wheat fields. They used to grow a variety of grains sown in the fall. The fields of the newly sprouted plants required a thick coat of snow.

I remember my grandpa's eyes full of joy watching the heavy snow that came as a blessing from above. With my grandpa's joy still in mind, it is my turn to find something more in the winter than its freezing cold face. I must look for its beauty, even if it is so physically cold and psychologically harsh. Like my grandpa's little plants, I must survive.

Pure, clean, white snow stretched across the ground everywhere we turned. For many weeks, we couldn't see even the smallest spot of ground. There was white, and only white. It was a winter wonderland.

People preferred not to wait for the bus but to walk instead. Corina and I would dress warmly and walk to all places within walking distance. With snow coming down every day the paths and roads were not slippery. I had never seen the city alive like that before. It was a beautiful display that reminded me of the Pieter Bruegel's winter landscapes.

Corina would hold my hand through my glove. I could tell when it was too cold for her, and that it was time to head home.

I would tenderly, squeeze her little hand and she understood the body language and squeezed my hand back. It was our sign when we both agreed with an unspoken feeling. Even, by her nature very talkative, on a weather like this, my little hiker refrained from talking. Without asking details about it, she knew that she might get sick easier from the cold air, and I couldn't skip work.

She knew how to dress herself in layers, asking me just to help with a scarf over her face. She was cute, like a little babushka to whom I could only see the black playful eyes. Our time together was precious. We adored each other.

It started to grow dark; it was time to get home. Good thing there wasn't much walking left.

Without the sun, it was not only dark but almost unbearably cold. So, we hurried our steps to get faster home.

In the front of the door we caught each other eyes and could read in them the same thought; we enjoyed it but happy that our strolling around was over.

"What story would you like to read to me tonight?" she asked me, before getting in. I could say smiling; I could read the smile in her eyes.

"As always, it will be whatever you would like."

My little girl, even from a very early age, was very neat and organized. The books were kept in order of her preferences. Sometimes, though she would make an exception and choose one randomly.

At this time, she was too exhausted, and fell asleep in the middle of the story.

Next day it was too cold, to walk and unfortunately, in the following days it got worse.

The wind added to the cold and helped to build great snowdrifts. The schools had to be closed, so I sent Corina to stay with mother for a week because I still had to go to work. The house was so empty without her. I realized how lucky I was to have her. One night that

Blessed with Twice the Freedom

week, surprisingly, the boys called.

"How are you, mommy?" I heard Michael's voice. His voice was a little raspy.

"I am fine, thank you sweetheart, but missing you a lot. How are you? Do you have a cold?" I asked my questions quickly, worried.

"Yes, I do have a little cold," he answered equivocally, and then to avoid the details he asked, "Where is Coco-Little?" That was what he called Corina, possibly to emphasize that he was the big brother. He probably noticed that she was not around, ready to grab the phone from my hand, to be the first to talk to him as she normally did.

"She is with Grandmother. You know, I must go to work and she couldn't stay home alone. The schools in the city are closed for a week."

I dared not to say why. If our phone conversations were being listened to, it could have sounded like a complaint and we were not allowed to complain. It could have been misunderstood.

I guess Sabin got hints from our conversation that I'd be home alone for a week and he got on the phone to somehow express his discontent with this. I assured him that there was nothing to be worried about.

"Come on, you must forget about it. It's cold and busy here, as I guess it is busy for you over there, right? No time for nonsense," I said, knowing him well.

He had probably taken advantage of my absence to find company. He got "lonely" easily. So, I wanted to remind him of busy-ness.

"Oh, no, I didn't mean to imply anything like that," he said weakly. And then, "Here is Michael again; he wants to talk to you some more."

"Mommy, I miss you and love you. Please tell Corina the same."

I managed to say, "You betcha." Then the phone's click threw us back into our two separate worlds.

71

CHAPTER 12

Candle's Tears

"What are you hiding in your hand, Corina?"

"I have something that I would like to keep."

"What might that something be?" I asked looking straight in her eyes. I could see that her tears were ready to burst. I knew her well; it must have been something sentimental and she didn't want to talk about it, but I still insisted,

"Please tell me, what is it?"

We had this conversation stepping down the church's stairs. We had stopped at the church where my father served towards the end of his career. We went to say a prayer and light a candle for his soul. It had not been long since he passed. Even though I tried to hide how much I still hurt, she still picked up on my distress. She would have liked, sometimes, to reverse the roles and take care of me. She had an innate sensitivity. It must have been that sensitivity that was speaking now.

When we got down to the end of the stairs, she pulled out her hand from mine and opened her fist, asking with a quivering voice;

"Have I done anything wrong picking the tears from the weeping candles? You lit them for Grandpa, didn't you?"

For a moment, I couldn't say a word, I was so moved. What a beautiful way to think about a candle melting down in tears.

"No, no sweetheart, you, beautiful thinker, you haven't done anything wrong. Grandpa is smiling fondly at your thoughtfulness from his place in heaven."

72

I took them from her hand and looked at them. The wax kept a round shape as it rolled, dripping down from the scorching flame. They took the form of petrified tears. Ever since then, when I watch a burning candle I also watch their tears respectfully. All of us are like burning candles, but our tears are different from those of candles. Our tears vanish. I recovered the candle's tears from Corina's hand. I still have them in a little jewelry box. They are indeed the jewels of that moment and remain a permanent reminder of that day.

It was a difficult time. I missed my father so much. But equally as hard as missing him, is now the realization that if I was to leave and go to America, then I would be leaving my mother alone. She will be without my father and without me. I stayed still in a front of a lit candle and for a moment I didn't know what I should pray for and what I should cry over.

The borders were tightly closed under the Iron Curtain. We would not have been surprised if, one day, even the birds of the air had their flights regulated. Romania seemed to be at the end of its rope, yet the Communist regime was still strong. It was hard to believe that Romania would ever break the heavy chains of its Communist Regime and head towards freedom.

Meanwhile I was on my way to break some of my own chains and. I was hoping that my mother could live with me after I arrived in America. Of course, I was not able to tell her about it, from fear that it might not happen.

CHAPTER 13

Other Days Imprinted Deeply in Memory

The sun penetrated the clouds only in the afternoon. For a few days in a row it has been overcast. Without the sun walking across the sky I sometimes feel disoriented.

My grandfather taught me to read time from the *clock* in the sky. Such a clock is never late or ahead, it fragments the day exactly.

At my grandparents' country house, I used to watch the shadows grow in the evening. When the shadows grew tall we knew there was not much left of the day and that it was time to return home from the fields.

Nature seemed to extend as its shade stretched further and further, first to embrace the dark, blend into the night, and then return, shorter the next day, just to grow taller again in the evening.

But sunlight does more than play with shade. No other season shows it better than spring, when all of nature returns to life.

Today is one of those spring days when you feel pushed out of the door to go outside. Corina and I enjoy walking; we can go for hours and hours without feeling tired. I try not to forget though that her little steps must do twice the work of mine.

Vivaldi's Spring was playing loudly from an open window. Corina turned to me and without saying a word let me know through her eyes that she recognized the piece of music. We have at home a cassette with all Vivaldi's' seasons. In the next moment, she was dancing.

Blessed with Twice the Freedom

"Come on Mom, let's dance together."

I assured her that I found pleasure in just watching her. If there were not so many people around I would have joined her without thinking twice.

She knew that at home I would let my steps catch the rhythm at every sound of music. She would do the same. We used music to dance away and shake off our problems from the turmoil we were in.

We did the same with our feelings of frustration on evenings without electricity. In the dim lighting, we pretended that our dinner was served at a fine restaurant by candlelight. Joy is a state of mind.

I remember exploring the power of imagination and make-believe many times in school. The best example is the Laws of Thermodynamics from my physics class. For some reason, it was not something I was naturally interested in. Yet I made myself believe that every word of those laws was there to communicate a great truth to me. I got it and then I loved it. I was amazed to learn that even uncertainty can be measured. Entropy is the unit of measurement for it.

Down the road, I followed that pattern for similar experiences. In front of any seemingly difficult obstacle I would put another one, even more difficult, first. Miraculously the first obstacle would be conquered and then the less challenging one would let itself be vanquished.

With Corina's jumping and my thinking all along the path we got to our friend Beata's house before we knew it. The plan was to visit the Botanical Garden that afternoon. Beata used her teaching skills on Corina as soon as we stepped in the garden.

"You know Corina, this garden is one of the most beautiful in Europe. You can see thousands and thousands of herb species from the entire world here.

You see, even in early spring there are many people visiting. Look ahead, there are the magnolia trees blooming. From a distance, they look like a tree covered in snow, don't they? And of course, they are

75

the garden's main attraction now.

"After a long winter, everybody is anxious to see a sign of spring, so they flock here.

There are also plants that do not resist low temperatures and those are kept in the greenhouses. We'll get there in a minute. Be prepared to see things that will stay with you for a long time."

Bea was right about such a visit. The living world left Corina speechless; she was all eyes and ears. Then we walked in a temperature-controlled greenhouse to see the tropical plants. Corina was ecstatic. She couldn't believe that the carnivorous plants such as Drosera and Drosophila even existed. She had fun gently touching the Mimosa plant which had drawn timidly inside right away. Corina was in disbelief. A new world had opened in front of her."

Many years ago, Corina had excitedly told me about the Botanical Garden in a great detail and now here I am reading it in Sonia's journal! Bea took some beautiful pictures of Sonia and Corina and made copies for me, which I still have. Gil and I had them framed and kept them in a place where we could see them every day.

CHAPTER 14

A Toast with a Banana

A year passed by. For some maybe it passed too slow and for others maybe too fast. In this respect Sonia and the two of us, Gil and I, are not in the same category. While Sonia would have like it shorter, Gil and I, without being selfish, would have like to last longer. It has been one year since we met. Now it seems difficult to be without them. But who could change the pace of time? Even though implacable in his passing, yet it may be playful with our imagination.

I find Sonia writing on this page about the New-Year Eve of 1986, seemingly in spurts, but it's hard to tell, because the handwriting is smooth and continuous.

"I decided to celebrate this New Year's Eve at home with Corina. As usual, Neli and Gil, spent it with her mother in Bucharest. It has been a year since we were given the opportunity to meet them in the train taking us home to Cluj.

It has also been one year since the boys left for America.

Tonight, the boys will be calling us, and waiting on that call has kept us home.

I am alone, nestled in the corner of my living room sofa, reviewing this past year of my much-tested life.

For the sake of an anticipated easier future, I must let the past and present find a common denominator – my children.

I hope that at least on this night our room's temperature will be a little higher than the rations allow. It is a hope for this evening only. Otherwise it will be painfully ridiculous to hold a crystal glass of sparkling champagne in a gloved hand.

Corina is playing with her chosen group of dolls, organizing them for a New Year's Eve celebration. She is dressing them up in the dazzling outfits she has seen on adults to welcome the celebration of the night. It is a pleasure to listen to her and watch her. She has taken words and mannerisms and applied them carefully to her dolls.

And she has a banana. She was more than happy to get it from her friend Victoria earlier this evening. Victoria received two fruits from another friend, and she shared with Corina. As they say in Romanian, "a gift from a gift is a piece of heaven." And so, it was. They both decided to save their bananas for the middle of the night and to call each other while taking bites. They are calling it the "banana toast."

I told her, "My dearest, I hope your sincere appreciation for one banana will soften heaven to bring us bunches and bunches in the new year to come."

"That means that I am going to be with my Daddy and Michael, doesn't it?"

"Yes, little chick, that is what I meant."

"I will send Victoria a bunch too, won't I?"

"Yes, my love. You are such a good, generous girl."

Since the boys left, Corina has chosen to sleep in my bedroom, and her room has become a playroom. She left her bed hosts her dolls. Looking to them, lovingly, she persuadable told me: " Mommy, I shouldn't let them sleep on the floor, should I? So, she has ended up in my bed.

From her room, she took only one little bear, Michael's first stuffed animal, "Mo-Mo." Corina considers the bear an orphan and thinks it is her duty to care for it until it can be reunited with her brother.

Indeed, she has never liked to sleep in her room. As soon as she learned how to jump out of her crib, she would take her blanket and sneak into our bedroom. Then patting my shoulder gently she'd ask me to make room for her. Now we are roommates again.

One day smiling, she told me, "We are three: you, me, and Mo-

Mo.

And I replied, "Yes! Ma-Ma, Mi-Mi, and Mo-Mo." It cracked her up.

I have often wondered how I would have made it through the year if Corina had not been with me. My mother was right when she said, "God sent His compassion to you through this child." I guess it was because only He knew how much I would need her.

My house is so pleasant tonight, due in part to the increased temperature and since I have decided I won't worry about my problems tonight. I am trying to empty my mind. But then I wish my mother was here. She was here for Christmas, but it was too cold for her to come out tonight. She might be nestled in a corner of her sofa like me, trying to process the events of her own life.

I have gone through a few cups of tea and even a cup of hot chocolate with sweet bread, an old family recipe. My entire kitchen has the aroma of chocolate and sweet bread. Just the scent of it is enough to bring me back to my Grandma's house. There was always a pleasant bustle in the kitchen around the holidays. The fire in the brick oven and the rising of the sweet bread dough had to be perfectly coordinated. My Grandma couldn't be taken away from that very important task, even for a minute. One simple fault in the coordination could ruin her entire work. So, she never wavered. Her loaves of sweet bread would come out of the oven with the tops a perfect golden brown. She would say to herself, "Well done." What a sweet memory!

When I think about moving to America, it is not like moving a piece of furniture. I'll have to move my entire world with me; otherwise the pieces left behind will hunt me down and leave me longing for them forever. I wish I could bury this year's pieces. For my country, the beautiful Romania, I have deep sorrow. I felt like a deserter running away from a loved one who has been dragged down and left behind to die.

I am now in my mid-forties; and could easily be fifty by the time

I get permission to leave Romania. Becoming successful again after starting over seems unlikely. My mother believes that I will root again, no matter where I go. She looked back over our stately family tree, which no storm can tear down, and she says I have the sap of that tree. I have inherited from my Romanian ancestors the stern desire to win, not for the simple sake of winning, but to fulfill that mission that has been given to me and to each of us in exchange for the gift of life. Nobody is skipped. With each gift, come special tools, and a *free will* how to use them, hence unlimited diversity. Even though it comes and goes, life is not given in vain.

"There is an everlasting Heavenly inheritance coming from God and going back to God who gave it originally. That's the Spirit," my father has often preached.

He ended every sermon with a quotation from the book of Ecclesiastics urging his auditors: "Fear God and keep His commandments. That is our duty."

My father enjoyed the dense wisdom in the Book of Ecclesiastes, which he called a pure distillation of thinking. I miss my father so much. I miss his deep thinking.

I have been alone all night on this special night and have spent it thinking and writing.

I have tried to focus on the people that I love and all that I have to be grateful for, tried to turn this night into a night of beauty.

Even though it is long past midnight I can still hear the noisy streets. There is exuberance in this night; you can feel it as soon as you look out the window. Like all things, the euphoria also is transitory.

It's getting on to 5:00 AM, the time the boys might call.

I cannot believe that at her age, Corina was able to stay up until midnight to have the banana toast with her friend Victoria! But because of the time difference, she won't be awake for a call at 5 :00 AM. As Gil once joked, "At least we are ahead of the Americans in something." For them it was only 10:00 PM. We have already passed into the New Year and they still have two hours to go.

Blessed with Twice the Freedom

They called! And the sound of the phone work Corina up. We had an usual chat, wishing each other luck and patience – until we see one another again.

Corina has just gone back to sleep. She insisted, of course, that I come too, but I want to get this down. I also want to let my thoughts wander a little more first. I still have the voice of my dearest boy in my mind. If I go to sleep now, I'll lose that. His voice was a little raspy, as it has been recently. I hope that he is not sick but rather that his voice is just changing. In one year, a child can change a lot. I also noticed a slight accent. I said to myself, "If only you knew how much I miss you, my Son-Sun."

Sabin – again – was not in a good mood. During our conversation, I felt the emptiness that words can't fill. Then there was an awkward silence. Then suddenly, without any context, he said, "Time is money."

I asked, "Are you ready to buy it or to sell it? What about your feelings? You are not in a New Year's state of mind, aren't you?"

But I got nothing from him. The call was over. The phone clicked.

CHAPTER 15

An Overview

Here's what I would say to Sonia if she were still around: "Oh, Sonia, Sonia, how many chances have you already given this man? Your trying to understand him is in vain; he has never appreciated what he had, but tried always to look for something new, instead'.

She didn't know the facts behind his moodiness on the phone, but Gil and I did. We said nothing at that time, because we believed (as she did), that there was a chance Sabin would tire of his affairs. And in the end, we were comfortable with our decision to keep the affair we knew about secret. It was not the right time to speak of it; too much sorrow at once can be devastating. Sonia needed to be strong for Michael...

Gil and I went around and round, though, analyzing Sabin and his actions. This was tough because we didn't have access to his emotional side. Here's where we ended up: Emotion was Sabin's secret room that only he had the key to. But he didn't want to shed any light in that room. To illuminate the room would have been an illumination of chaos; so instead, he spent energy trying to escape the room. And the excitement of cheating was how he escaped. Every betrayal required diligent planning, a successful cover up. The planning kept his mind busy. He no longer had time for his family, his profession, anything but his next adventure. The fear of being caught kept him alert. And that was another source of excitement for him.

"Is it incurable?" Gil asked.

Blessed with Twice the Freedom

"No, it is not. But to be cured of it, Sabin would have to admit he has a problem. Now, based on what I have learned about him, he is a classic narcissist; and by a definition a narcissist has no problems with himself. He is in love with himself. He is the best, everything he does is the best, and he never makes mistakes."

There is real struggle in Sonia's writings. She struggles to articulate a silver lining and yet at the same time she struggles to be honest about her bruised emotions. It was understandable. Generation by generation in her family it was not heard of a divorce, and a marriage considered inviolable. It is not wonder, that she had, relentlessly, tried to view things from many angles.

CHAPTER 16

A Transylvanian Echo

Here's what I mean about Sonia's ability to tell a story from multiple simultaneous angles:

"From afar, I heard the Town Hall clock tower use the cuckoo's song to mark yet another hour. Just as the bird's return heralds another spring in the Transylvanian Hills, the cuckoo clock in the tower reminds us, that time doesn't stand still. I heard six cu-cu's. It is six PM.

Instinctively I held Corina's hand tightly. Evening was approaching, and I was afraid to lose her in the bustle of the street.

The crowd flowed like a tide pulled not by the moon but by the changing of a traffic light. We flowed with the rest.

At that time of day most people are in a hurry to get home. Corina and I were heading home too. Once a week she takes a piano lesson and for that we must go across town to her teacher's house.

Her piano teacher, Virginia "Gina" Voicu, was at the top of everyone's list, so we didn't mind traveling across town. Gina is one of those people who use their own vocation to help others find theirs. Corina likes her very much.

Gina hums "Corrina, Corrina" at the beginning of the piano lesson. It's an old song that had recently become popular again. Corina feels special knowing she had a famous name.

We let ourselves move with the flow of the street. Nevertheless, my eyes captured the fast-changing panorama like stills from an instant camera, so many, so fast, that they give the impression of a live movie.

On the imaginary screen, the weary faces of Romanians, whether furrowed by time or by nagging thoughts, appear. There is no spark in their eyes. They let themselves be pushed ahead by the streets' flow. Some of them carry little bags filled with whatever was available after they had waited in line for hours.

Next, groups of young people – no longer sad and monotone – but joyous. They move with the elegance and confidence of youth. There are pairs of boys and girls holding hands. They look in each other's eyes as they talk. You cannot hear their words, but it is not necessary to hear them; you can easily guess they are talking of love.

"Feeling love, feeling happiness, it makes you beautiful," Gil would say. "Happiness is the best beauty expert."

I find myself smiling, as I think of the poem "Wonder." Corina won a contest reciting that poem when she was only four years old. She loved it, and for a while she would be ready to recite it any time the word "beauty" came up in conversation.

"Hey, Corina, do you remember the poem "Wonder"? The one you got the prize for reciting?"

"Of course, Mommy. Would you like to hear it?" she replied, with a joyful pirouette.

"No, sweetie, not now. We cannot stop now, in the middle of the road."

"But I can do it when we get home, can't I?" she asked, as enthusiastic as ever. She would hold a strand of her hair, closed her eyes ecstatically, and let her beauty engage with her joy. I am sure this was exactly how the poet Ana Blandiana, felt when she wrote it…

I remember that I had experienced a moment of happiness as beauty, on my own. It was the day, my son got the approval to go abroad for his health reason.

After three long years of many attempts, finally, a passport was issued to my husband to accompany our son to America.

Happiness burst from me, I felt it inflate my chest. This was a once-in-a-lifetime event, meant for sharing. First, I called my Mother, then I called my friend, Magdy, telling her that I was on my way, to visit her.

She was waiting for me with the door opened. I didn't have to say anything. She read the happiness of my heart in my face. She grabbed one of my hands. "What's going on?" she asked, "You are excessively beautiful today. Please go around the corner, there is a photographer. Have your picture taken and then come right back and explain your beauty to me." I did it. I got my picture taken right then and there, and I still have that picture today. I treasure it and the beautiful memory within.

I hurried back to Magdy's house to tell my story. She was anxious to hear it. She got the news, and to my surprise she was a bit reserved after she heard it. First, I didn't understand her concern, then I *read* between the lines. I was in the middle. On one side, I had my son, for whom this trip was vital and on the other side I had my husband who might have in mind something else than the real purpose of the trip.

She had never met Sabin. However, from what she had heard about him and from what she read in my heart sometimes, she didn't like him at all. She had her suspicion. He might snatch our son and used the boy's health to flee the country.

I didn't want to go into any more detail with Magdy. Blandiana's lines swirled around in my mind. This small touch of sadness, coming from my fears and my doubts about the future, was melting my beauty. I would have liked to keep that beauty born from happiness, but unfortunately it was as fleeting as the click of the camera.

Magdy was not only a famous designer, but a great person, a great problem-solver, almost a visionary. She had a piercing gaze and when she spotted a solution or an idea, she let you know.

When she issued her pronouncements, it was almost as if she were breaking a spell.

However, I was reticent with her on this:

They say that opposites attract. It must be true. Sabin and I are 180°

apart. Magdy doesn't totally agree with me about opposites, though. She has a more profound theory taken from her own experience.

"Two people, even opposites, who have attracted each other perfectly at least once, over time, lose their *magnetism*, a continue difference in *magnetic potential* is necessary to maintain the force of attraction". She also would often say:

"Two hands playing the same notes on the same keyboard may not make the exact same music." She was right, who could argue with that?

I pondered these things while walking through the crowd towards the bus stop. Corina left me alone to think without any interruptions. Even though she is still little, she recognizes the moments when I would like to be with myself. She becomes quiet too; she might be busy thinking also.

I noticed that in the meantime she had pulled her hand out from mine and held my arm instead. For her this was a step up. She would say that only little kids must be held by hand. She enjoyed hearing that she acted old for her age - which she often did. She was born with an old soul.

Corina was first to spot the bus coming. Glancing at the crowd I realized there was no hope of catching this bus, so I decided to wait for the next one. But, it was already dark outside, and I knew that the gap between two buses' arrivals might be longer than what we could tolerate at the end of the day. Everyone else had had the same long day we had had and was in a hurry to get home. There was no politeness or any respect for children, the sick, or the elderly. The survival instinct becomes obvious at a crowded bus stop, and I didn't want to see my child crushed against the door.

As I appraised the consequences of waiting versus jumping on the bus that was coming, a sad story surfaced in the back of my mind. Not too long ago a young man was killed while traveling on an overloaded bus. Even though the passengers were not actually permitted to ride in the bus stairwells, people in their eagerness to get home often ignored the regulations. In this case, when the bus took a sharp turn, the young man lost his balance and fell out, hitting his head on the pavement. He left behind two little kids who would know their father only through pictures and a young widow who for the longest time would see in every bus a killer. But the true killer was not the bus...

By the third bus, Corina and I could board without too much pressure. Finally, the children and elderly were let in first. It cost us time but at that point we were not in too big of a hurry. Nevertheless, I remember situations when I was running against the clock and was packed into the bus like a sardine.

As we waited for the bus Corina and I played some guessing games she had learned in school. They were fun and educational and made waiting not so annoying. Suddenly she asked, "Mommy do you know what we play at Kinga's house sometimes?"

"No, I don't, but if you tell me, I will. You've made me curious now, go ahead."

I listened to all the details of their game carefully and realized it was the same story my colleague Marga, Kinga's mother, told me about the other day. Marga and I were friends from the Pharmacy School. We both have husbands that are musicians, so we would spend certain holidays or vacations together and so did our children in their spare time.

There were many children of Corina's age in Kinga's neighborhood. Their place was not very far from ours, so when she was free, Corina could be there in a heartbeat.

Yes, it was the same story, only Corina's version was more enthusiastic. Corina got to play "Mariana", the girl from the grocery store, who favors some of us with a little more food than the rations allowed.

Marga and I laughed but felt pity at the same time. How easily the little ones imitated us. Because they knew it was a challenge to put food on the table, the kids wanted to participate in that challenge.

Marga jokingly said,

"Good, they will get great skills from it."

Corina, playing "Mariana" improvised a counter out of a board. There were pebbles representing eggs and all kind of weeds, as vegetables.

Marga's humorous comment was, "At least they weeded my flower beds. Luckily they knew the weeds from the flowers."

Even though there were a bunch of kids involved, everyone had a designated job in the "Store Game." Many of them were customers that would wait quietly in line, holding tickets. Some of them, however, were more favored than others. I didn't get what the criterion was.

"The favorites were the ones who most resembled us, Mariana's good customers," concluded Marga. Of course, this conversation was just between the two of us. No witnesses.

Then I remembered my own childhood games. I loved my dolls and took good care of them. Because of this, my grandma had foreseen in me a great mother. I smiled at that memory. She might have been right; my children are the light of my life.

Meanwhile my father had foreseen my eagerness to succeed and he encouraged me to do so.

"First you must have a plan that you don't abandon until you fulfill it. You break that plan down into steps that lead from the bottom to the top. No skipping steps. Your eyes should be on each step and on the final objective at the same time. It doesn't matter if the target is as far away and as high as Mount Everest or if it's as near and small as your front yard, the rules are the same."

I didn't have to ask my father to describe the people who have a hard time succeeding. I knew that these were the people who could only visualize projects in their entirety, from top to bottom, without breaking out any steps. This makes a project seem so complex that they feel powerless to accomplish it, and they give up without trying. And not only that, but the lack of accomplishment, creates a strong negativism which is fed by the envy they project onto others. On the other hand, people's enthusiasm frightens them, and they try to kill it, so no one gets ahead of them. I was lucky to have a father who could teach me these things.

Think about a toddler's first steps. We tell them,

"Come on, go ahead, don't be afraid," and they head toward us knowing that we are there, ready to catch them if they fall. The day they take their first steps on their own is quite a memorable day. If nobody is there to assist them, some toddlers give up after the first fall. They are afraid of other falls and, so they return to crawling, putting off the achievement, giving into fear. On the contrary, other toddlers pull themselves up after every fall, face their fear, push it away, and continue until they can walk."

Sonia is right again. Our own nature and the nature around us determines who we will become. Surely, those who are already frail will never grow strong if they hear about nothing but their weaknesses. Life is a challenge. And just like a cracked window that might not withstand the noise and rumblings of the streets, so it is with children's wounds. It is scientifically proven, that damage done in childhood takes a long time to heal, and sometimes it can never heal all the way. And some wounds that look healed can be reopened. Deeply repressed feelings can awaken and trigger unanticipated reactions. It is a big mistake not to take a child's feelings seriously.

There are so many dangers! Children's innocence can be altered if they are shuttled back and forth between parents. Manipulative parents can create manipulative children. Criticism and ridicule cut the wings of enthusiasm and self-esteem. Gifted and personable children can turn into submissive and reclusive adults in the face of excessive criticism. It is not easy for parents to find a balance between too much or too little attention.

Next, I came across a few pages where Sonia recorded her dialogs with her children before Michael left for America. It is delightful to "listen" to them. So, I would like to pass the "microphone" back to

Sonia and her children, live:

"As soon as the children could sit on their own at the table, we shared the four seats and each of us knew our place; I don't know how and when we even made such a decision. I guess it just happened. As Michael was more fastidious and finicky when came to eating, needed more help, so his place was across from me. Corina was across from her father or very often across from an empty chair. One-night sharp-eyed Corina asked,

"Why do I have to face the empty chair again? May I move next to Michael, so I can see you better?"

Before she could ask any more questions, I said,

"Daddy has a rehearsal tonight."

"Rehearsal? Why don't you ever have a rehearsal?"

"Well, I have chosen a profession that doesn't require rehearsals."

"Mommy, I want to be like you, no rehearsal."

"OK, darling. You will choose whatever profession you like best."

"You know, mommy, I like many things and I would like to be many things at once."

I could only smile; I thought the same at her age.

"Corina, my love, you won't have time for everything. You can be only one or two things."

Michael expressed his own choice,

"Mommy, I would like to be a pilot. I would like to fly. Do you know, Mommy, why the planes and birds fly?"

"Yes, I know, my love. But now, we are talking too much and there is still more than half left on our plates. Eat up; we must go to bed soon. You know what I always say."

"Yes, yes, we know," they said at once and then quoted the poem:
Sleepy little birds to drowse,
Toward their nests guide their flight,
Hide themselves amidst the boughs,
So, good night.

"And you are those little birds, remember?" I had taught them that rhyme as soon as they learned to talk. It was their sleeping pill. When I was their age, my mother had whispered it to me and I always went to sleep with that tranquil picture in mind – the birds, their nest, and their last chirp…

Later, on the couch, after we said the poem Corina would ask, "Mommy, would you like to be my twig?" That meant that I should take her in my arms and carry her to her bed. She was longing for the last cuddle of the day. Next, we would read a little. Some days they wanted more than one story and then they would beg me. "Please, please, Mommy, please!"

"Oh no, we must sleep so we'll be refreshed and joyful tomorrow."

Once, Michael said, "Daddy is less happy, because he goes to sleep late."

Corina couldn't help but add, "But he sleeps late, doesn't he, Mom?"

"Alright, that's enough for today; now think about the little birds in their nest. So, must you be."

Sabin never shared these beautiful moments. It is possible that he would not have enjoyed it anyway. He was living in a totally different world. As the children had noticed, he was late to bed and late to rise, but not very wise.

I never had a hard time waking the children up in the morning; they would rise without any need of an alarm clock. They knew the routine. Their uniforms and other garments were lined up and ready for them to jump into. That was my last chore each day, which saved us time in the morning. Once, Michael called to me, concerned that one of his socks was missing.

"It must be there, sweetheart; I put a pair in your shoes last night."

"But I still can't find it. Will you give me another pair, please?"

"Of course, my dear, but please speak softly, Daddy is sleeping."

"Wow, at this hour?" Corina said critically.

"Corina, please mind your business now. We don't have time for comments. You have to be on time for kindergarten and I for work."

Blessed with Twice the Freedom

"Mommy, mommy I found the missing sock!" Michael said happily.

"Where, where?" Corina and I asked earnestly.

"It's funny; I put both on the same foot."

"Oh, well, Michael your career choice is perfect; you will be good at flying. You already have your head in the clouds. I am sure you will be a good pilot."

We were amused but laughed softly so not to disturb Sabin. Corina was often under the impression that I gave Michael more attention than her. When she accused me of it, I would always say, "I love you both the same, but your brother needs me more."

It was a very honest statement. Nevertheless, she was very caring when it came to her brother. In school, she would check on him as if she were the older sister. She also liked to visit Michael's class because of his teacher, Stela. Corina liked Stela very much, and her love at first sight was reciprocated. In fact, all the parents hoped their children would be in Stela's class. One could easily read the kindheartedness in her eyes. She would choose a suitable approach and tactic for every child. She would say,

"Every child is different and therefore the quality of your attention for that child should be different as well. We, the educators, are not only called to lead them in the right direction but also to decipher the bud of talent within them."

CHAPTER 17

Three Times the Nothing

Here's another thoughtful entry from Sonia's journal, from just before she leaves Romania.

"There is not much time left before I leave for America; we are now counting down the days. I would like to spend as much time as I can with my mother. She has reconciled herself to the idea of me leaving. Her generous heart frees me from any guilt about leaving her behind. Without hesitation, she told me that my place was next to the other part of my family rather than with her. I will always keep her sacrifice in mind and will use it as a model for my own children. She said, "A parent should never be selfish."

However, because of my plans to go to America, I had long thought it would be a good idea for my mother to move closer to her other relatives. Growing old alone is not a pleasant option. My secret hope was that once I was settled and held American citizenship, I could reward all her sacrifices and bring her there to me. I said nothing about that to her because it was still too early. And knowing my mother, she might never agree to anything more than a visit, anyway.

So, about a year ago, my mother moved into my grandparents' house, which we had used as a summer home after they passed. My father was buried there, and she had been longing to return to that village for a while. It was a place of sweet memories, and with them she never felt alone.

I watched her try to take as much as she could from her flower garden. She knew every flower's place in the ground precisely. She packed all the bulbs up carefully and moved them with her. For years and years, they gave her great joy, with all their brilliant colors. They had become as much a part of the family as the humans. On hot summer days, she would understand the hardships they went through and would speak gently to them, as if she were speaking to young children.

She looked nostalgically at the linden and walnut trees. They had to be left behind. As with very old people, it would have been too hard to uproot them. Memories of the linden's fragrant blossoms and the thick shade of the old walnut tree would return to her mind every spring and summer, as they returned to my mind also.

Visiting her in the spring, I was glad to see her waiting for a chick to hatch. She confessed that every spring she longs to hear a hen cluck with love for its chicks. I smiled, I loved it too. There was something endearing in the clucking hen and her struggle to scratch out food from the ground. When she found a few crumbs, she would call her brood. She herself would have nothing until the little ones were satisfied. Or I would watch the hen before a storm or at bedtime stretching her wings protectively to cover her chicks. They spoke their own language. I wish I could decode it. I suspect that the mother hen spoke to her chicks in the same way that I spoke to my own. However, all of these encouraged me to contemplate further…

There must be a balance in everything but sometimes we lose the balance between giving and receiving. Supposedly one shouldn't get more than one gives. Unfortunately, too much receiving is conducive to selfishness and an insatiable craving for more. Selfishness is a bottomless hole, whereas altruism is a mountain overflowing with generosity.

We come into the world with nothing and leave the world with nothing. In between these two extremes, opportunities unfold, calling for the perpetuation of life and always for a next step. But without the instinct of love between those two extremes, life is empty. It becomes one more nothing. Three times nothing – a life in vain.

I spent as much time as I could with my mother. I no longer used the phone to empty my heavy heart to her, I visited her a lot. There was no privacy on the phone and we had much private talk to do. I needed her so. I needed my mother's words of wisdom and encouragement. No matter how bad I felt, she would always give me a seed of hope.

My parents taught me to find joy in every little thing and consider every day a gift. Waking up to an acknowledgement of that gift allows a feeling of gratitude to glow from the inside out, leaving behind an inner peace. I owe it to my parents; they taught me these simple things.

Nevertheless, nobody is spared unhappiness, and when I become unhappy, I call up the joyful moments of the past and bring them into the present. Very often they are small joys, but they as colorful as the wildflower fields of my Transylvanian Hills. They never fail me.

True happiness ignites inside and burns like a sacred fire. It engulfs the mind and heart at once but does not scorch. Nobody can buy happiness. Those who think they can, are selling themselves for the false promises of addiction. Addiction feeds an insatiable fire too, but it is a destructive fire that burns the addict to the ground.

Searching for happiness is not always rewarded with happy experience.

Happiness is strange! You can give it away even when you don't have it, but like a boomerang, it comes back to you. In this respect, it is as simple and as true as a rechargeable battery. The magic key to the secret box of happiness is this: give and you shall receive. This is the only true and constant rule of happiness. Everything else is a counterfeit.

CHAPTER 18

DDT, the Fragrance of the Time

Gil was right. Sonia and I could start with a word and end up with a story. For instance, one day when Gil suggested that we have scalloped potatoes, a dish which we hadn't had for a long time, I thought it was a good idea because outside it was a raw day of early spring and we were craving a warm meal. Sonia swung by as soon as the dish came out of oven.

"Wow, I got here at the right time, didn't I? In weather like this, it feels good to have a steaming dish on the table." Then she added, "I know both Sabin and Michael would appreciate something like this too."

While Gil was helping her to hang the coat on the hallstand he said, "Don't you worry about them. They must have many other goodies over there to choose from."

Instead of an answer she sighed…

Browned potatoes look appetizing, but unfortunately a specific odor came to spoil the aroma of the dish. It was DDT. We looked at each other just waiting for the other to start, but Gil did.

"You know that there is a ban on it".

Even though he didn't say what "it" was, we both understood. IL continued his train of thought:

"You know, that even the decision was implemented at the beginning of this year of '85 in this country. Nevertheless, what we have on the market are potatoes of '84 which are still loaded with the disgraceful odor."

To Gil remark, Sonia pitch in, in a hurry:

"But you know that even banned, pesticides like DDT won't be out of the soil or our potatoes for years, right? DDT is a chemical label for an odorless and tasteless substance. Yet we know the taste. Who knows, it might have been misused or overused."

Sonia delivered all of this in a flash when she felt her turn to talk had arrived. I was sure we would continue exploring this subject after eating, and indeed we did.

Gil excused himself and withdrew to his office to finish a project with a looming deadline. Sonia and I dug in. True, we had another reason to dig into DDT. We were faced every day with new issues in public health, which a decade or two ago were unheard of. Then Sonia brought this issue closer to her home:

"Sometimes, I wondered whether Michael's seizure was somehow, caused by an environmental factor like DDT. It could have been possible; it accumulates in the body in the fat tissue when the liver failed to eliminate it. It might be released slowly, passing again through the liver and overtaxing it.

It is hard to take away from the table a mashed potatoes dish, my kids, love it. Even though I don't serve it too often home, I have no control on it at the school, where they might have it every day. It is an affordable one. Don't you see? No matter where you turned, the smell of DTT is present. All public spaces and many of our crops are loaded with DDT. We can smell it. It is the fragrance of the time."

Sonia was right with everything she said, Nevertheless, nobody could complain about it, or inquire and explanation for such a strong odor on the crops, when this insecticide is promoted as odorless.

DDT odor, for sure, is not felt, in the food of high ranked communists.

We are kept in a bubble, separate from reality, but the bubble must ready to pop. It is behind our tolerance. Yet, we are not sure what

Blessed with Twice the Freedom

would happen after that. It is difficult to tell or speculate, on that. We have a wish, though, and that, it is just between us. God forbid, if it slips outside, our future would be over.

However, when the negative energy of suppression built up, we would turn, almost unwittingly, to other subjects, which without jeopardizing our future, somehow, let us vent out our discontentment.

To calm our attitude towards many difficulties, our topics were often philosophical, like this one for instance; we agreed that greed and ignorance were the root of the many things that were going wrong, and that the Evil of all Evils was greed.

Of course, talking about all Evils, we couldn't avoid talking about *Pandora's Box* which very well fit our subject.

As the legend goes, Pandora couldn't resist her curiosity and open the gift- box with the instruction on, *never to be open*. But how can someone refrain from opening a gift? And, thus, all the Evils have escaped, only the Hope was left behind, but in the end Hope freed also.

Sonia contemplated for a moment over the myth rendering, then said:

"To us, though, the opposite is true. We, first, make out of that Hope a shield, and leave all Evils behind, don't we?"

"Yes, Sonia you are right, but once out of the *box* and spread in the world, Evils could never be returned and locked, again, up. They are lurking around, instead."

I knew that Sonia would have an argument to it, and she did, indeed

"See, Neli, there is Hope around us also, as a source of unceasing desire to fight Evils and claim victory. Hope stirs up the wisdom to create antidotes to every Evil; they are the Virtues. Ever since, every Evil is challenged by its contra part Virtue. Nothing kills Greed as Generosity does.

Unfortunately, there are more vices than virtues, in our world. The vices have grown as a plague repressing the virtues".

And we have gone on and on with this…

At one point, kiddingly, Sonia compare our passion, for knowing more and more, and never satisfied, with an *addiction*. We had a good laugh on it, even Gil came to see what was going on. He added, jokingly also:

"No laugh ladies, sometimes, oddly, success can be a form of intoxication, coming from a form of addiction. We see people who, after achieving success, don't know what to do with it. They fall prey to unfulfillable desire, they are frustrated by that desire, and they fall like shooting starts".

"That's right Gil, they disregard the gift of life by voluntarily cutting it short". Sonia came to complete Gil's thought.

Success, career satisfaction, and happiness were, also, very often a frequent topic.

Like her I also believed, that tiny joyful moments, were the building blocks of the beautiful edifice of happiness. True happiness, keeps one anchored, to the earth.

But there is not true happiness without the foundation of first and foremost complement to it; an appreciation for the given, precious, gift of life. The happiness within, it was the reality. Always keeps one anchored to earth.

Self-destruction is nothing but a rebellion against that gift.

We went over such a ground many times, because around us

Our endless talking about just everything made time pass fast, but realized that we had to stop right there, it was time for Sonia to take Corina out of school.

After she left, I contemplated over their leaving to America…

Gil and I will miss Sonia and Corina terribly. I don't think we'll meet such a great and exciting friend again, and a sweet girl as Corina, with a voice like a pure sound of a crystal bell.

Soon an immense stretch of land and sea might be between us and we no longer will live on the same street, in the same city. I bet this is in their mind also, even though for now, they hardly wait to see their family as whole. Sometimes, thinking of leaving Cluj, which she was so found of, become kind of melancholic.

Besides all the visible shortcomings of the Communist Regime, our city still, keeps alive its charm. Sonia, often, highlighted those charms.

One day she confessed to me that she would miss the little things, so dear to her. "No matter the season, Cluj has its own, and specific beauty" she would say.

Out of all of seasons, she cherished spring.

Walking together downtown she would bring to my attention the colorfully dressed gypsies, selling the first signs of spring. They have been seen at every corner of the main streets.

She was touched about how they kept the snowdrops and crocuses nestled in their little baskets, covered with thick fabric and bundled up to keep the flowers warm. She went saying;

"You see Neli, such flowers, have more meaning than those from the florist-shops. Even, humble, and gentle, they are coming out of the harshness of winter. They carry within the victory of survival. No wonder why the lovers cannot pass by without buying a bouquet of them for their sweetheart. I remember how they have been handled to me many times. There was no a greater feeling…"

I felt myself smiling at this; against of all vicissitudes she was confronted with, she had remained an incurable romantic.

Then she would mention the flowers of the peach tree and the lilac bushes from her garden. Even though so ephemeral, their color of early spring, stayed long in her mind. They would serve as a source of inspiration for her paintings when the nature was deprived of colors.

She made me make a promise, that I would take pictures of them and send to her every spring. She would say:

"Each spring, the photo shots, even they will reflect current flowers, in time, in time it would be hard to tell one year from another, it would be just a flow of colors. I would say that the same happens with the events in our life. Even they might be very significant for a moment, but over time, when memory recalls them, they don't have a well-defined place, but all merged into flow of the past".

I was listening to her, not saying a word, but contemplated about it; she was so right. The events lose their contour in time.

"And I would like you, also, record the song of the rustic swallow in the spring." She said. "I know, I will be longing to hear them, if swallows don't populate that land".

With all these, wishes, I could see her struggle to break away from her Motherland.

Gil just happened to step in the room and caught our conversation about swallows. Seemingly, he got a hunch on the subject, because he entered directly in conversation.

"Don't you worry Sonia, hummingbirds might visit, instead, your backyard. You might find them very interesting birds. I just read recently an article about migratory birds and I learned every imaginable detail about these exotic, miniature birds. They truly are unbelievable!

This little bird challenges the physical laws, as we know them. It is hard to explain how a bird that weighs less than one ounce and measures no more than five inches at most, can fly up to 500 miles without stopping. Even a car would need to stop for fuel in that distance ". I guess Sonia, felt like adding:

"I guess it is not about the size but the design". And Gil resumed:

"Everything, is unbelievably condensed in such a creature, as is their memory which is also extraordinary. They can remember the flowers they've taken nectar from and how long it will take for that flower to recharge. Also, just as our swallows do, they know the way back to their temporary home. They, also, remember all the flowers that continuously feed from". At the end I also had a say in this:

"I still wonder, how do such birds find their way back. All of this is just amazing, isn't it?.."

CHAPTER 19

Endless Gifts

I know why Sonia loved music and used it a lot during her time of hardship. It was more affordable than food and it was necessary for her survival. It was food for her soul. One must feed the soul.

So, I was excited when I heard that Corina would like to make a career in music. I knew from the beginning that the piano would be her faithful friend. She took piano lessons at an early age and she spent a lot of time on the keyboard that I bought especially for her. Corina could keep herself busy playing the keyboard while Sonia and I talked. She was too little to understand our conversations or even to want to understand them. At other times she would draw, using a set of crayons we kept at our house. Corina seemed to be happy with whatever she was doing.

"Aunty Neli, I would like to be many things at once," she said out of blue.

And indeed, she was gifted enough that she could do and be many things at once. Michael was different than his sister, but I did not know as much about his childhood as I did about Corina's. Corina was talkative, and easily expressed herself. She always had a creative thought in mind.

Michael on the other hand, I learned from his mother, was brilliant with math and logic, but less talkative and somewhat introverted. It is too bad their father separated them in their childhood when they could have complemented each other. Time doesn't allow us to go back and do things differently, however, it often gives us opportunities to correct mistakes.

Even though I'm not a pediatrician, I still have many opportunities to encounter children. So, I know children. And I do believe that every child is sent into the world as a magnificent creation. Each carry, as a fruit-bearing tree, branches of genes loaded with promising gifts. I find it amazing how in the same family, from the same parents, one child will extract one set of gifts, and another will extract a different one. Inheritance is an inexhaustible treasure trove; the more you take out of it, the more becomes available. Endlessly and timelessly something new spills out from its hidden recesses, deeply embedded along the generations. I wonder who or what unleashes it and at what trigger? It is a mystery! As Sonia was, I was also fond of mystery. Mystery is just in everything, and we always find a reason to look for it.

Sonia told me about her excitement as she waited for her children to be born.

"It made me curious, extremely curious about the surprise within, about the features of the life branching out of me. It is a feeling hard to explain," she said.

Nobody comes into the world, we know, without gifts…it is a law of perpetuation.

Gil and I, we often wondered about the bedrock of Sonia's personality; she never looked-for excuses in the face of adversity, even though she faced so many adversities. I don't think she called them by that name, but referred to them as challenges, instead.

She believed in *will* power and so did we. We were big followers of Schopenhauer's philosophy, which viewed the world through the light of the will. Our club even bore his name.

Many pages of her journals are a testimonial to the *will*, as was her life.

In Sonia's journal, I came upon one of those days in which every moment had to be carefully scheduled.

This was 1985, before she left Romania. Her first stop was daycare

Blessed with Twice the Freedom

to drop Corina. off. Then she'd jump on the first bus she could find that was going in the direction of her work. Then she had many other chores, and on this day, a day off, for me, I was happy to be scheduled to pick Corina up from school for her. I loved to do it. I would immerse myself in the feeling I longed for: motherhood.

Around 5:00 P.M, the alleyway to Corina's school was crowded. There were people, mostly mothers, hurrying in and others already coming out and listening to their little ones' chatter. I cannot describe in words the love on their faces. I loved that picture of motherhood.

I had the opportunity to meet Stela, Corina's favorite teacher. Then I learned that Corina was also one of her favorites. Both Sonia's children were lucky to be her students. I had actually heard about this famous Stela, first, from my neighbor's children, who happened to also be in her class. They, too, said she was their favorite. One day I jokingly told them, "Hey, little neighbors, you make me jealous. I thought I was your favorite. When do I get to meet my rival?" And now, the opportunity to meet her arrived.

The children were right, she was special. All the parents would have liked to have their children in her class.

Sonia used to call her "Star" and not only because of the similarity between her name Stela with "Stea" which in Romanian means star. She was a real star among the teachers. She had a calling for being a great teacher. It was her talent.

The basics that the children learned completely in her classes will stay with them forever. At least this is what I got firsthand from Corina. Later, when I met Michael and talked about Stela, his remarks were the same-

Gil and I gave Sonia all the help we could not only with Corina but with food or other supplies. There were shortages of everything, so having a relationship with the providers was key to getting even the simplest things. I must admit that sometimes my patients spoiled me rotten. In return, I could get medications for them through Sonia.

But our first and foremost priority was Corina. We were happy

105

that Corina was like a sponge, learning easily and reciting freely. One day while Sonia was on duty, I offered to bring Corina to her piano lesson. One of the ladies who waited for the bus with us at the station approached me and asked,

"Your daughter takes ballet lessons, doesn't she?"

"Yes, she does. Do you know her?"

"No, I don't but I could tell by her movements. I teach ballet and I can notice those talents even outside the classroom. Anyway, I can tell, that your daughter is talented."

"I wish she was my daughter or that I had one like her. She is my good friend's daughter."

"It doesn't matter. I can see that you treat her like one of your own."

After a long wait, the bus finally arrived. People flocked to the door in a hurry. I stepped aside, I didn't want Corina to get crushed.

The driver noticed me playing it safe and without taking his eyes from me said, "There are children, elderly, and possibly sick people in the crowd, please allow them through the door first. I beg you to listen. Otherwise, I will not move from this spot."

Some who were first at the door started grumbling but soon stepped aside. Corina was among the first to board the bus, and I followed her. As she passed by the driver she said,

"Thank you, Uncle Man, you are a good man." She put a smile on every face.

I was proud of her and glad that such people were still around. Gil and I refrained from talking to her about leaving Romania, even though we both knew that one day she would be on her way to America and we would both miss her so much. One time as if she read my hidden thoughts, she said,

"Aunty Neli, I would like to take you and Uncle Gil to America with us, so much. If I can't, then I think I'll get sick from not seeing you."

Blessed with Twice the Freedom

I bit one of my lips, as I used to do when I had to cover a painful feeling with physical pain. I didn't know whether they would have even a minute to think of us after their arrival.

CHAPTER 20

1987 – An Angel Hidden in the Inferno

Sonia again, in all her cinematic glory:

"On my way home, I got caught in rush-hour traffic. I was glad I wasn't late to pick Corina up from school. Initially I had planned to drop her off at Neli's so I could run some errands alone, but it was too cold to walk up to our friends. After waiting too long for the bus in the freezing weather, I changed my mind. I decided to postpone my errands for a better day and just go home instead. No sooner had we walked in the door when the phone rang. It was the Security Office!

Just the word "Securitate," as it was called in Romania, froze my mind for a second and I could hardly answer. I knew from that moment on that my future was in their hands. I must do everything right or I would never make it to America. "Good afternoon, Comrade Cătușan, how are you? This is Officer Giurgiu." Of course, I couldn't honestly say how I felt after waiting an hour in the cold at a bus stop. Attempting an agreeable tone, I explained to him that I just got home. Maybe he looked at the clock as he said, "It is 3 o'clock now; could you see me at my office in an hour?"

"Of course, I will do my best."

"Please ask at the front desk to be directed to room 118. I will be waiting for you."

"Yes, I understand, thank you," I said, confused. Confused and afraid. Fear overwhelmed me as soon as I hung up the phone. A confused stampede of thoughts bubbled up in my mind. One straddled the next; nevertheless, I bravely managed to keep them under control. I kept telling myself: I can't make even the slightest mistake.

Every time I passed by the Security Service Building I got a strange feeling. I had never been in it, but there were stories about the atrocities hidden inside. I had to hide my fears from Corina because I would have to take her with me. I had no time to make other plans for her, and then I knew that whatever would happen we had to be together. A few minutes later I analyzed every word I had said on the phone, to see whether it was correct and in the right place. I felt like a little frightened mouse under an elephant's foot. I wished this could be easier.

"Who was the man on the phone, Mommy?" Corina asked when she saw me standing next to the phone, still and quiet. She guessed that it was a man; the conversation must have sounded very official to her. She was right. In interrogation services, the Securitate Service used exclusively men. We still had our coats on, and so we turned back to the road right away. For a moment, I considered taking the bus, but that was too risky. I might not make it in time. I could not be late under any circumstances. If I were late, there would be a price that I could not afford. A Security order was a very serious proposition and it had to be fully respected.

I decided to take the sidewalk. I knew that sidewalk – potholes and all – by heart. It was the only reliable way when running against the clock. Holding hands, Corina and I walked quickly, synchronizing our steps. We were both quiet. She might have been tired, and I was apprehensive, but on we strode. Here and there the potholes were filled with ice and Corina would slide on them ahead of me, making it easier for her to catch up to my steps. Other times she would have had fun doing that, but not now. It was very cold. Only our eyes were left uncovered, and like a sharp knife the cold cut through.

It does not usually snow when it is bitterly cold. Today, however, was an exception. It was not an intense snowfall, but flakes came down sporadically and wandered aimlessly. I was glad for nature's cooperation; I knew that Corina would keep busy trying to catch the flakes and let me keep the emotions of the afternoon to myself. I was right. As soon as she saw the flakes coming down, a flicker came to her eyes. She enjoyed the game of catching snowflakes. Each time she caught one in her hand, she considered herself a winner. When she opened her palm, all the flakes had disappeared. Her victory was nothing more than a wet hand. I could tell she was smiling by looking in her eyes. She didn't understand nature's game or where the beautiful flakes came from, but she continued to play over and over again.

Before we knew it, we had nearly reached the imposing building I had been ordered to visit. So many thoughts went through my mind. I remembered stories told about people going through that building's gate and never coming out. I also had heard about subtler procedures; like inviting people to sit on chairs with irradiating devices placed within them. I could not torture myself with these thoughts because I had to go inside that building to determine my future.

So, there we were, in the front of the building's large and numerous stairs. I glanced up to its many windows. I had a bizarre feeling that all the windows were eyes with their own mission. Once they fixed us in their sight they wouldn't want to lose us. Timidly we stepped up the stairs, leaving our footprints behind. There weren't any other footprints. I realized I might be the only appointment.

As soon as we opened the tall heavy door, a young comrade from the front desk took my personal information. Corina tiptoed up to the desk right away and looked at him with her playful eyes. She was waiting to be considered. As if he read her mind he said in a friendly tone,

"Hey little one... you aren't frozen, are you?"

"No, I am not cold at all, my mother has dressed me so warmly.

Do you know that I wear two pairs of pants?" Corina was ready to give more details until she noticed my sign, "Shh!"

The young man asked us to follow him. We were led down a long, gloomy, narrow corridor into the left wing of the building. At the end of it I recognized the room number that had been mentioned on the phone. I involuntarily took a deep breath before the young man politely opened the door in front of us. On the other side of the door a man with grayish-hair, not old, invited us in and then introduced himself, "I am Officer Giurgiu, who called you today. Please have a seat, Comrade Cătuşan."

While he talked, he offered me a chair across from his desk. I cautiously looked at the chair not knowing which of its corners it would be safest to sit on. "And who are you, beautiful girl?" he asked Corina, patting the top of her head before she came next to me and sat on my lap.

"I am Corina and my mother is Sonia." She had taken to introducing herself that way. She felt safer attaching her name to mine.

Then the man tried another interaction with her saying, "What a nice hat you have!"

"Thank you, my mom crocheted it," Corina said nonchalantly, looking at me and then to him. She felt that she owed him that detail. Or she might have remembered the hard time I had learning how to double the texture to make the hat warmer. That double texture protected her from the freezing cold.

I wondered why he took time to talk with Corina. He might have been trying to make her feel more comfortable in such an austere place. During his conversation with her, I tried to pin down the best descriptor for him. There was something unusual about him. I had the feeling that he was a great psychologist and a good mind reader rather than a resourceful Security agent who was looking for tricks to get the truth. However, the Security territory somehow intrigued me. There wasn't enough time for a definitive conclusion. No matter how tough or how many questions, I was ready to tell the truth and only the truth.

He had a folder opened on the desk in front of him. I was sure it was my file and my husband's. His questions flowed like a stream that started small but grew bigger. As I answered his questions he looked up from the file less and less often. About halfway through the interrogation I couldn't hold back my tears. Corina, still on my lap, hid her face in my scarf and did the same. He recognized how difficult this was for me and told me that it was too much for a child to be present. I agreed but also said,

"I intended to drop her off at my friends in order to finish my daily errands, but it was too cold to walk there. Then your phone call came and there was no time for any other arrangement."

I was sure he concluded on his own that public transportation was a problem. From all I told him, he could also conclude that I had no advance knowledge of my husband's plans to not return to Romania. I also told the agent that, on the contrary, Sabin had always been negative about the idea of moving whenever it came up in a conversation, and that he had said our age was an impediment to starting a new life from scratch somewhere else. The reason for his visit with his American family was, in fact, to get treatment for our son. As a mother, having a child debilitated by seizures, I would go anywhere, even to the moon, if there were hope of getting him treatment. I had chosen the moon as a reference point in a hurry. It was difficult to get there but it was still possible.

The interrogator pushed the file aside. I am sure that he knew more about my husband than I did myself. The entire interrogation might have lasted an hour. At the end he stood up, giving me the right to do so too. He concluded, "I am sure you'll do whatever your son needs you to do."

I answered firmly, "You must be convinced of this." I was surprised when he not only opened the door for us but also followed us out of the building to the top of the stairs. Outside it was still snowing, and the sun was setting. When Corina stepped down a few stairs

Blessed with Twice the Freedom

to continue her catching of the snowflakes, the man who had just interrogated me began speaking plainly. "Please do not look at me but listen. You were lucky that I was given your case today. And I am also happy for you. It would be a shame for you to suffer needlessly. Now pay attention. Starting today don't answer any strangers' phone calls, or better yet, do not answer the phone at all. Don't let the little one out of your sight, especially in public places or playgrounds. You understand what I mean. Now, good luck and keep this secret."

I was speechless. I looked in his eyes but couldn't say a word. I would have been sobbing if I did. My eyes were flooded with tears. Meanwhile I was glad that the snowfall had intensified, and the flakes whipped onto my face, melting there. It gave me an excuse in case somebody passed by. Even though some were happy tears, this was not the right place to let them out. I was truly lucky. Without this good man, as Corina called him, who knows what trap would have been set for us? I noticed that I was shivering. I waved to him secretly, as you do with a good friend, and then he left. I watched him enter the building and it left me wondering how he got into the Communist Security Service. My mother would say, "He must have been touched in his life by something so hurtful, that he couldn't let it happen again." Even in a service stripped of any kindness, he was a kind man.

Officer Giurgiu was chosen to be my interrogator today, to prove my innocence and to protect me from the pack of wolves that was ready to tear me into pieces. I called Corina, who to my surprise didn't interrupt my conversation with the man I would call an angel from now on. "Let's go, little chick," I told Corina, holding her hand tightly.

"That man was a good man, wasn't he?" Corina provided both the question and the answer.

"Yes, Corina he was extremely good, he was an angel!"

We were lucky to catch a bus back home without any stops. It would have been better to see Neli and Gil the next day. It was not only too cold, but the emotions of that afternoon were so crowded in my heart, that I'm sure I could not have made much sense to them. I was still bewildered. It was unbelievable what had happened, especially considering what could have happened. I was amazed at my good fortune.

It was still cold in the house, but it didn't matter. Corina and I nestled quietly under a thick blanket in a corner of the living room couch. I hugged her tightly. She guessed from my interrogation that we might be allowed to leave. She shared her thoughts with me. "I will be so happy to see Daddy and Michael. Maybe the good man will be happy too, don't you think?"

"Yes, my little star, the entire world is happy for you."

"Will you make me a strawberry birthday cake there, as you do here?"

"Oh yes, you will be gloriously celebrated on all of your birthdays to come. I will make a strawberry cake for you, and I will not have to worry about finding the strawberries. Remember how Neli alerted all her suppliers to find the fruit for your cake?" She held my arm tightly and let her little head rest on it. It was her way of showing that she was happy to hear it. She was enormously sensitive. How lucky I was to have her!

I decided to let myself get caught up in Corina's contagious happiness and to banish all my old doubts, if just for the day. My hopes had been renewed that afternoon. Corina, too, was still thinking about the moment when we would be reunited with her father and brother.

"Mommy, will Daddy have champagne for you, as we do in Romania?"

"Of course, my dear, he will have champagne and juices and all the goodies simply because we'll be there. Are you worried about it?"

"I am not worried Mommy, just asking."

"Yes sweetie, all four of us will be rewarded for our long wait and our boundless patience."

Blessed with Twice the Freedom

"Oh, Mommy I can hardly wait!" She had run out of words for the future she anticipated, and she became quiet and cuddled next to me, holding my arm tightly. We had a little snack before bed, even though I didn't feel hungry. My brain was busy, very busy with something else. I tucked her into bed with the promise that I would be in soon. But she fell asleep right away and I was again left alone with my thoughts.

I smiled as I thought about my strategy for the interim. I would turn that difficult period into paint. I would transform it on canvas into flowers and fruits. I would dress it with nature's beauty and my dreams. I could gaze at the delicate peach flowers of my garden's tree and imagine the ripe, velvety peaches waiting for me to immortalize them in oils.

The same flowers and peaches came and went three times before the two American and Romanian visas showed up, one set freeing us to leave, and the other one letting us in.

It was also very odd that the two people in charge of our visas – one from the American embassy and one from the Romanian Passport Service – had very similar names; Viorica Sas and Violeta Sasu; in Romanian Viorica is a diminutive of Violeta. I pondered the coincidence! And every spring now I remember violets and peach blossoms together.

CHAPTER 21

May I Be Happy Loudly?

It's been months since I came home from America. I still find it very difficult to accept the reality that my dear friend is gone. With a broken heart, I left my Sonia overseas, yet, I am comforted by the fact that I took a part of her with me; I do have her journals with her life in.

We were on different continents long enough to be used to not seeing each other frequently, but we heard each other very often on the phone. We were so used to it that I find myself reaching for the phone and even dialing a few digits from her number. Then a thought flashes through my mind and reminds me that her departure is real.

How lucky I am indeed, though, to have all her thoughts with me.

I run frenetically through the pages of her life. I clearly remember some of the events that she writes about – those we spent together. Then I find many pages about others, told in detail, giving me the impression that I was there or that she was just speaking to me from across the room.

I like best those pages where she can't contain her happiness but spills it all over. Here is a bit she entitled "On the Way to Freedom":

"For the longest time, I had no tears for joy, but I do now! I feel my breath up in my throat, stopping the words. What a paradox, to cry for happiness! It's a great feeling. This cry has been long suppressed. Pain and joy melt suddenly into the same tears. Could a simple phone call be so overwhelming? Yes! But not just any call. This call came from the American Embassy, the United States Embassy, the Embassy of the United States of America – such a distinguished resonance in those words.

Ms. Viorica Sas, the lady in charge of my file, spoke deliberately. She was bringing me good news. My way to the States has finally opened! There are no more obstacles! An approved visa in writing was on its way to me. I found myself saying out loud,

"Oh, my Lord, how much happiness you give me in this very moment!" Soon, only one physical day will separate us from our loved ones. Finally, we will be together as a family - after three long years of being separated.

Ms. Sas's voice lingered in my ear. I liked her way of pronouncing the letter 'r', letting it roll into the words, as French people do. It was not an affectation, it was how she naturally spoke. She had a good heart. Once she even dared to whisper to me, "I understand you perfectly Ms. Cătuşan. I am also a mother. I don't know how you have borne not being able to see your child for three years, especially one with health problems."

I said nothing. I was afraid of saying something that might prevent me from getting the visa. The comment could have been recorded and held against me. I couldn't spoil such a moment.

Now, still on the phone, I was jumping around in my son's room for joy. I couldn't cheer too loudly though because my walls had ears. Dancing alone and shouting gleefully about leaving the country doesn't have a patriotic tone. Then I began thinking of how to share my good news with others. I needed to share it. It was too overwhelming to keep to myself.

First, I called my Mother, but she was not home. I couldn't wait longer but called Neli, Gil answered the phone. Neli was at the hospital on duty. Anxiously I let him know that I would be stopping by with important news later that evening.

117

I am sure Gil guessed what was behind the call but said nothing about it on the phone. He knew the rule: secrets are not spoken "on the wire, for they could take fire".

Then I began looking for Corina. She was outside, in front of the house skating with the other children. The entire sidewalk and street was a sheet of ice. I called Corina from the window. I had to share the news with her. In minutes, I could hear her tromping up the stairs with her skates still on. There was not much left of her time outside, and she didn't want me to take away any of her precious play time. With a flushed face, she rushed into the house asking in a hurry,

"Mommy, Mommy what is it?"

"Little Bird," I whispered into her ear, "We'll be leaving soon."

Her eyes widened, and she replied dubiously, "Oh, yes?" But in that moment skating was more important for her than any news: skating was real. She had heard about the possibility of our leaving for America too many times. Now it was hard for her to believe it might happen indeed.

It is the middle of December and it is unusually cold for this time of year. The wind had started blowing unexpectedly, carrying snowflakes. Corina and I dressed warmly and walked along the street to Neli and Gil's house. We kept off the icy side of the road and found a path of hard snow instead.

The wind was northerly, and we could feel it whipping at our backs. I thought to myself, at least we are not going against the wind anymore. On the contrary, it seems that even the wind is in a hurry to throw us into a new future. We could finally see the light at the end of the tunnel.

As soon as we got to the front door, Corina raised herself on her tiptoes to reach the bell. Gil answered right away. With a jovial tone, he invited us in.

"Hey beautiful girls, I hope you haven't frozen in this cold."

Then he whispered anxiously into one of my ears,

"I am eager to hear your news."

Blessed with Twice the Freedom

"Oh, Gil today we wouldn't freeze, even if we were at the North Pole. Now even in this cold, the iceberg of our waiting has started to melt," I joyfully replied, looking down at my side.

There was Corina all ears. I knew right away, that she had a question to pose. Looking in my eyes, as she always did, she asked,

"Mommy what about the Surd Pole?" Before answering, Gil and I shared a smile. The fun part was that Corina, through a mis-association of sound, had just called the South Pole the "Surd Pole," which in Romanian means the "Deaf Pole."

Still with the smile on his face, Gill said,

"I agree, great news like this might melt both poles, North and Surd.

Then I tried to bring Gil current.

"We have to be careful how we share with Corina. She has a sharp mind and a large attention span. You might think that she isn't aware of what you say, but she catches every word. Then she gives the words that she doesn't understand meanings on her own. Listen to this. When she first saw lightning in the sky, she looked at me and then back at the sky in awe. She asked me,

'Mommy who is scribbling in the sky?' Hmm, I thought, what an amusing way of interpreting lightning.-'It is an unseen hand who does it, a hand that has also drawn you and me. You are one of that hand's most beautiful sketches", I replied.

Neli had not yet arrived. I still had the time to share with Gil another one of Corina's gems.

"Gil, listen to one more. One day a friend, Nina, came to visit us. Corina was sitting across the table from her, closely examining a birthmark on Nina's nose. 'Nina, what do you have on your nose?' she asked. Nina answered without hesitation, 'Corina, it is a talent mark.' Without taking her eyes from her friend's nose, my three-year-old touched her own little nose, and with a serious look, responded, 'I feel a mark growing on my nose too.'"

I had just finished telling this last story when Neli opened the door.

119

She had just worked a twelve-hour shift. She looked very tired; there had probably been more than one difficult case and she was drained after her long shift. Upon hearing our good news, her face lightened, and our good news erased the fatigue from her face. "Sonia, please tell me the news in detail," Neli asked impatiently, while handing a bottle of champagne to Gil.

"Gil, please open it. Sonia, please tell me, tell me everything, minute by minute, I would like to hear every detail!"

I gave Neli every detail, while Gil took care of the champagne bottle. Corina was right there, watching Gil's famous dexterity in opening a "trouble bottle," as Corina and I called it.

"Look at Uncle Gil! He did it just right! But you, Mom, you almost broke the ceiling with the cork on New Year's Eve!" Corina said, marking Gil's triumph and giving away my own lack of success.

While listening to me, Neli and Gil set up the table. All the food was tastefully arranged beneath the shining chandelier, and it magically transformed the dining room into a place of royalty. Corina was in awe. It was unusual for her to see all this food at once, so she asked, "Do you know Mariana from the grocery store also?"

Neli understood right away the child's innocent but relevant remark and answered her nonchalantly. "Of course, Corina we all know her, and we know the people in other grocery stores too."

Corina knew that I brought home such goodies only when the shop-girl Mariana called us. No further comments were made.

I suddenly wondered if it had been risky to take the extras from Mariana with Corina's knowing. It was always only in the dark and at back door.

However, food was not a problem for the Communist Party members, who had their own special stores, while ordinary people waited long hours in line. It was actually very sad. The elderly would bring small stools to sit on while they waited in line for hours at the grocery stores. Very often the food was gone by the time their turn came. Then there were some like us, who had a "Mariana connection",

Blessed with Twice the Freedom

and Mariana would work with us in exchange for our services.

Such thoughts filled my mind for a moment, but the hope that "The Golden Era" would soon be just a nightmare behind me, drove them all out as fast as they came in.

Gil put Corina at the head of the table. Then four hands raised their glasses to celebrate the great news. While the adults toasted with champagne, Corina toasted with sparkling water.

We got to the point that we pushed away all our fears and were so happy that we talked and laughed at the same time. Corina, quite confused, whispered a question in my ear,

"Mommy may I also be happy loudly?"

"Of course, my dearest, today and here, in Neli's house you can loudly exclaim your happiness, but not at our home though. Over there we still must whisper, remember? Nobody should know how much we love each other, it might create jealousy."

She was a bit confused at first, but the tumult of joy soon smoothed her confusion away.

Gil held her up to touch the ceiling. It was one of her favorite moments. None of us could touch the ceiling but her. We were happy to spoil her with love.

Neli and Gil walked us home because they knew there wouldn't be many occasions left for them to do that.

We could hardly wait to call the boys in the States. They were not home at our first attempt, and so wasn't Mom at our second.

Then we tried again and were lucky. The switchboard connected us to them right away. Other times we had to wait for hours.

"We are coming, we are coming!" I found myself saying without any introduction.

"Wait a minute, what are you talking about?" Sabin said grumpily at the other end of the phone line.

I was disappointed that he was not jumping up and down from happiness and I let him hear it in my tone.

"Aren't you awake yet? I don't hear your happiness."

"Oh, I am happy…" he said in an uncertain tone and left an empty space in the conversation.

Then I said, "I have already made the reservations. We'll be there on New Year's Eve!"

It seemed that he was not quite ready for us. I felt that our happiness didn't touch Sabin in the way that it touched us. He brought up irrelevant matters that didn't make sense at all. At that moment, a suspicion pierced my heart. I knew him well, but at that moment there was no room for doubts. We have already crossed our *Rubicon* – the point of no return.

CHAPTER 22

Sonia Follows the Sun

I could feel again Sonia's mixed feelings of joy and sorrow, in the same time.

"The winter holidays were behind us. It was exactly three years since my son and my husband left for the U.S. Now it was our turn to cross the same sky and finally have our family united on the same continent in a new world.

I would have liked to take with me some festive and beautiful memories of home, but unfortunately there was not enough snow at the time to completely cover our poverty-stricken land. Neither were the bare trees wrapped in snow. I would have liked to see them dressed in blankets of fluffy snow, just as in the fairy tales of my distant childhood. In contrast, everything was gray, heaven and earth coalesced in that cheerless color. The trees looked gloomy; black crows rested here and there, emphasizing the desolate look of a land that it seemed even God had forgotten about.

I had a feeling of unspoken guilt in my heart. I was breaking away from my suffering nation, under circumstances favorable only to me. I was ready to embrace a new country and for such an opportunity anyone from a Communist country would have been jealous. I was the lucky one. On the other hand, I was leaving my mother behind all alone, at an age when she shouldn't be alone. It had been three years since she lost my father, and in some way, she was losing me, as well. It would have been easier for both of us if she had other children, but we were all the family she had. One could read the sadness on

123

her face. Her black eyes had lost their shine, which would come back only when she cried, but I loathed her tears.

Before my leaving, we would often sit across the table from each other without saying a word. But I was sure that we both had the same thought in mind; departure. While I could hardly wait for it, she dreaded the loss of her daughter and granddaughter. I didn't understand her grief enough then. I had a child and a husband far away that I hadn't seen in three years. Yes, I was her child; but I was an adult. I had to take responsibility for my own children.

Yet, my mother, with her keen sense of sacrifice, would never have stood in my way. On the contrary, she would urge me to follow my destiny. I suppose it is normal for us both to have had mixed feelings.

Michael was only seven when he left Romania and he needed me more than anything.

When he was in that car accident, we almost lost him. He was only two when he was thrown like a ball from the backseat of the car out through the windshield. It was a true miracle that after such a blow, he was still alive.

Many times, I have gone back to that day of May 28, 1978. It was a day never to be forgotten. We were traveling on a European Road towards a resort for a few days of vacation.

An excavator, operated by a drunk driver, cut us off. He was very drunk; his blood alcohol was almost 0.3%, a level of intoxication easily conducive to a blackout. No wonder he claimed in court that he had fallen asleep at the wheel. That much alcohol would have acted like anesthesia on his brain.

It is hard to describe such an accident because it happened so fast, and in the very moment of it my awareness was not fully there. I only realized that something was going on when I heard, as if in a dream, my husband saying,

"What did you do, sir, have you killed my wife, sir, you have killed my wife!" Crumpled in a puddle of blood and caught between the hood and the front seat, my senses didn't give me any indication of what had happened to me. I didn't understand why he believed I was dead. I tried to open my eyes, but I couldn't see anything. Only at the hospital did I learn that my frontal bone was fractured. I could not see because the skin on my forehead covered up my eyes. Later I also learned that one of the windshield wipers was stuck in the top of my head.

As my senses returned, it was a while before I remembered that my child was with me in the car. I had heard my husband talking about Michael, and I began wondering where he was.

"The baby is okay, my dear, he is already at a Children's Hospital, do you hear me?" I had heard my husband saying.

"Yes, yes, yes…I do hear you," I said, as if I had forgotten there were other words I could use in that situation. It was like waking from a nightmare. I couldn't make much sense of reality.

I guess I started to become agitated when I emerged from the haze. The doctor asked my husband to leave the room. I assume, Sabin himself was still frantic, and the doctor thought that the transition I was going through required calmer. The surgeon was an elderly doctor. As soon as my eyes were uncovered, I saw his face. That face was imprinted in my memory and has remained there with all its detail, even to this day. It seemed that my brain had resumed its normal functioning and had started recording things, as if on a blank sheet. Those things I will never forget.

As soon as I fully regained my memory, I went back to that day, and I dissected it in my mind, piece by piece. Michael and I were in the back seat. At that time, there were no car-seats for babies in Romania. He fell asleep with his head on a little pillow placed on my lap. I remembered how blessed I felt by having him. His beautiful face and curly hair made him look like an angel.

Then I took a glance outside. Along the road, the green hills were coming to life after a long winter. Nature was bursting into a brand-new green. It was like a huge and beautiful landscape painting. I remember how my eyes were in a hurry to take in as much I could from the windows of the car and then store it in my memory. I knew that I could use that memory to escape to when presented with one of life's gloomier days.

With such beautiful surroundings around me, I found myself humming something from Schubert; "Oh World how beautiful you are." Meanwhile Michael woke up. He had just turned two and was no longer wearing diapers. He asked for the putty. While I was helping him, I took off my glasses, a very unusual thing for me to do. I had no clue that time was quickly counting down the seconds to something that would change our lives forever. Crash! The excavator hit our car! Good thing I didn't have my glasses on. I would have been blind today if I had. And if Michael had not been sitting on the putty, he would have died hitting the dashboard. Instead, he went flying through the windshield, which saved his life. I remember the quick sound of horror Sabin let out right before the collision, and after that, deep silence. I don't know if that silence was only mine or if all reality lost the ability to sound.

I am still amazed. It seems that, as if triggered by Providence, Michael had woken up at just the right time and that moment spared his life, just as having my glasses off spared my eyes. To that fraction of our destiny we should be indebted forever. Another fact came to strengthen our beliefs that Somebody was watching us. When Sabin took his shirt off at the end of the day, he noticed that a medal with the image of the Virgin Mary on it fell out from underneath. It had been hanging from the rear-view mirror, but it had landed – miraculously – inside his shirt. He was bewildered. We got that medal when touring the abbeys of Moldova, many years ago.

I picked up the medal and looked at it. It was unusual; I saw the face of the Virgin Mary on one side with a halo around her humble image. On the other side was printed, "May the Virgin shield you from accidents." It didn't specify car accidents, but with such a message on it, we had decided that the little medal should be hung on the rear-view mirror of the car. It was there for so long, we had forgotten about it. But our lives were saved that day. So, it may have been because of that accident – the accident that we think was the cause of Michael's seizures – that we were finally able to escape to America. That accident was a bridge over the many barriers that opposed our way west, to freedom.

CHAPTER 23

Is There an Orphanage for Dolls?

"The day before leaving, I preferred that my mother did not see us off at the airport; our departure would have been too painful for her.

Gil and Neli brought us first to my mother's house to try to say more than we knew how to say.

Before I left her house, she hugged us tightly as if it would be our last hug; I hid my tears under my glasses, but I could see hers splashing onto the top of Corina's head. Goodbye! Our visit had to be short and it had to look like our many other visits, to give the impression we would return soon. My mother had aged quickly in the past three years. Because of her compassion and generosity, she had eventually accepted my need to be under the same roof as the other half of my family. Yet our leaving affected her

"My dear girls, I will never see you again," she said at the end of visit.

"Mom don't say that. We are not going there to die."

"Not you, but I," she whispered.

Mother was right; she passed on before we could see each other again. Her last words still haunt me, as does the sad image of her waving at us that I watched until our car disappeared around the corner.

It was the day before the New Year Eve of 1987. In the evening,

Blessed with Twice the Freedom

we had to be in Bucharest for our early morning flight to America.

That morning, we had started our journey early, before dawn. The first stage of our trip had begun! This was the trip of our lives; we couldn't be late! All the radio stations were also up early and were loudly playing the traditional Romanian New Year's song "Plugușorul." I let myself indulge in thinking that those good wishes on that last day of the year were just for us. We needed this last blessing from the land where we had been born.

The last phrases of the song resonated profoundly and lingered in the air. I had heard them every year, but this year their meaning imposed itself differently. All four of us were listening to it quietly, maybe as an excuse to avoid talking about "tomorrow." At one point the silence became too heavy and Neli said,

"Hey you lucky girls, tomorrow will be more than a New Year's Day for you, it will be your first day in The New World. We will follow you with our minds on this long day to the West. Don't forget to call as soon as you get there."

"That's true," Gil added; "It will be a very long day for the two of you. We here in Romania will pass into the New Year seven hours before you." Then our dear physicist stopped. It was not a good moment to elaborate a theory of time. It felt wrong to be so abstract when our leaving was so real and our saying goodbye so close.

Corina, who up until then had seemed to be snoozing, woke up, as soon as she heard Gil's comment about the seven hours. She was not too happy to hear that her waiting would be seven hours longer than his, so he assured her that the world of time zones was only in our imagination. It was hard to explain such things to Corina so we changed the subject.

Just before arriving at The Romanian International Airport, Otopeni we all became quiet again. The greatest but also the most difficult moment was so close.

We would soon cross a line that would separate us from all our dear friends. It also would separate the Old World from the New.

129

An American plane belonging to the Pan-Am company was being readied to take us on board in a few hours. Then we would pass over the Atlantic Ocean towards America.

We hugged each other briefly without too many words, but there were tears in our eyes. Corina started to cry when she hugged Neli and Gil.

"I'd like to take you with us," she said, "I will miss you both so much." I think her little heart was, like mine, ready to break into two parts; one trying to stay back and the other anxiously waiting to fly.

Neli and Gil adored her and now it was hard for them to see her leave for good. We had known that such a moment would come to pass, but now the moment had come. They started joking around to make everyone more cheerful, but they had little success.

Gil grabbed our suitcases and let them slip through to the customs office one by one. Everything we were taking out of the country was in those suitcases. Only two per person was allowed.

We still, however, had all our priceless memories in our hearts, memories nobody could regulate or control.

No matter where you turned, you could see emotional flourishes revving up then dying back down as people lined up on their way into customs.

I turned to Neli and Gil to make one last request. "Please don't forget my mother."

"Don't worry, she has become like our own mother," they assured me.

I ruminated on how little we could take with us.

For the past three years, I had been learning how to give things up, material things as well as sentimental things.

First, they confiscated my house. They made me pay off the mortgage and then pay rent just to stay there. All I could do was humbly bow my head and do their bidding. And I was still indignant about the disrespect my husband had shown me, ignoring my human dignity by unilaterally deciding the future of our family. Instead of a discussion, a conversation, an entreaty, he had said,

"The pies had to be served cold to you, so they wouldn't burn your tongue."

Despicable! Those pies were not just cold, but bitter. They didn't burn my tongue, they made me bite it instead. I couldn't share my feelings with anybody at first. I felt like a puppet. And he knew more than anybody else how to pull the strings. In that regard, he should have been awarded a first-place prize for puppetry.

My mother couldn't get over it either. She couldn't understand how a husband could decide for his family without consulting his wife. And this was not just some small thing, but a life-altering decision. On top of everything, there was the ominous shadow of the Security Service. I did not want to be branded his accomplice and endanger my safety.

Romanians don't have the right to search for freedom. Romanians who dare to look for freedom are called traitors to the motherland. Traitors have no protection. Even outside of Romania's borders they are vulnerable. People blacklisted by the Communist Security Service are very carefully watched. Some of them disappear without a trace. Others are simply killed. Nevertheless, there are always people who are ready to give their lives for freedom. I was caught in the middle. Sometimes my feelings pulled me towards this great opportunity to be able to leave, and sometimes they immersed me in the sorrow and humiliation of the way that the news was served to me.

For my husband, everything was simple. He left Romania as a happy tourist. But I was left behind to face the consequences of being related to a fugitive. And not only that, but a fugitive with unresolved financial obligations. He could have at least shared a plan with me. But no. I felt that I was stripped of everything; both materially and emotionally. I never thought that losing my belongings, which I had nonetheless worked hard for, would affect me very much. When the time came to empty my house, Neli and Gil had sent me out for a walk while they sorted what was left and gave it away. I was grateful that they spared me that job.

The house had to be empty before the State Agent came to take the house keys. I remember how he took them out of my hand; it was even a little uncomfortable for him. He must have been a good man, but his was not an easy job. He looked at the closed door and to cover the difficult moment for me, he said,

"Ma'am, I wish you luck. Never look back." I was glad he didn't call me comrade.

Corina was quietly keeping up with the line's slow flow. I wondered what was going through her mind. If she were thinking about what she had left behind, then surely, she was thinking of her dolls. She loved them all but each one differently. Her dolls gave her a world where she had no fear of being hurt or lost. On the contrary, she felt duty-bound to love and protect them. No matter what was in her mind at that moment, I read a sadness too great for such a little face to hold. I said nothing. I knew her very well. She would snap out of it in a bit; she was overall a happy child.

Thinking of one of her more recent questions, a smile came to my own sad face. "Mom, is there an orphanage, for dolls?" She had asked me this as she looked over the crowd of dolls in her room. She knew that she could take only one of them. She had a difficult time choosing. But in the end, she had to decide. The lucky one was a doll named Zuzu.

Suddenly, I had heard the commanding voice and saw the frowning face of the customs officer. He asked me to show my hands so that he could verify my jewelry. Besides my wedding band I had two other rings, both with sentimental value. One was from my parents as a congratulatory gift when I had graduated from the Pharmacy School. The other one was a ring with a ruby stone, a gift from my grandparents given to me on the same occasion. Initially, the latter was my grandma's ring. My grandpa brought it to her when he returned home from America. It was the ring which renewed their vows after they had been apart on two continents for more than 15 years. When they passed the ring on to me, I knew the story behind it.

With the same imposing voice, the officer ordered,

"Comrade, take off the ring with the ruby stone. Such a ring cannot be taken out of the country." I looked at him and at the ring in disbelief. Such an order stripped me of more than the ring itself. I considered the ring to be my American and Romanian charm. I thought of it as a swallow, the bird that always finds its way back home. In my mind, it was a magic thing that I had in my possession. It was my "American chaperone" into the land of unknown that I was heading toward.

Obediently, I took the ring off my finger. I turned around to find Neli and Gil who were still watching us from a distance. I beckoned to Neli and she came in a hurry. She was confused, not knowing what was wrong. I gave her the ring and asked her to return it to my mother. In our last hug Neli managed to whisper,

"I will give it back to you when you return to Romania as an American citizen." Neli was right. I did get my ring back later.

The officer was still not done with me, though. In the same rude manner, he pointed to my jacket. It was a fox-fur jacket very in vogue in Romania at the time. He ordered me to take the jacket off and to leave it behind also; that it was too much to take abroad. I looked at him, puzzled,

"But it is winter cold outside; I cannot travel without a jacket". Frightened, I glanced at Corina. I was afraid she might say something as children often do in their innocence, that might, accidentally, infuriate the officer. I noticed not only the fear on her face but her attempts to cover up her colorfully embroidered vest. She held Zuzu over it with both hands. The vest was a gift from my mother. She had made it for Corina as a good luck gift.

Even the agent, tough until then, couldn't keep back a smile. Then he looked into my eyes, and I could read his; they were telling me that there was room for negotiation. The practice of bribery in places like this was very well-known. I had packed some Kent cigarettes for just this reason. They were hidden in my purse under a travel guide. Our eyes remained fixed on one another's as we wordlessly transmitted our thoughts. Nonchalantly, I pretended to look for something in my purse. I pulled out the book and at the same time, I placed the cigarettes under it. I let them both slide towards him. He understood the move and with practiced dexterity caught them before they fell from the counter. He kept the cigarettes and pushed the book back to me. Even though it worked, the trade left me feeling sullied. Then with a superior and sarcastic tone he said,

"Well, comrade I don't have a choice then but to let you have the jacket. I don't want you to arrive there frozen." He emphasized the word "there," smirking.

We waved goodbye to Neli and Gil one more time before passing through the door to freedom. I sighed in relief. I could see the Pan-Am plane through the window and Corina couldn't take her eyes from it either.

"Mommy, is this the plane that will bring me to my dad and my brother?"

"Yes, little bird, this is it."

"Mommy, we'll see them for sure today, won't we?" She whispered this in my ear, her face radiant with joy.

I had to remind her, though, of the old instructions. "We sometimes cannot show happiness the way we feel it. Remember?"

She looked at me like it didn't make any sense to her, then she asked me in a hurry, "Why, Mommy, why?"

"Because our happiness could easily be taken away from us." I couldn't tell her that security agents were everywhere disguised as ordinary travelers. Then I assured her,

"But do not worry, my little star. Today is a great day for all four of us. We're starting a New Year and a new life.

I read these pages from Sonia's journal over, and over again. They had no clue that in less than a year, they would find themselves alone again.

CHAPTER 24

Family, Living Treasure

As soon as I met Sonia's mother, Ms. Elena Sava, I had the impression that I had known her forever. It might be because she and Sonia were so much alike. I noticed especially that when assessing a situation, they did it in the same manner, making use of an intuitive gut feeling. When assailed by suspicion, they gazed intently into it, as if sending in a beam of light to uncover the truth. They easily read other people's minds and they let others read theirs. I liked that about them.

Ms. Sava was physically a tiny lady with noticeably erect posture. Her white hair was well kept and gathered into a bun. She always looked as if she had just come from the hair dresser. The clip of her hair bun was consistently coordinated with the color of her clothes. I could see her artistic sensibility from the first moment. Later, I would see her creativity in the garden as well. Everything there was simple. There was no chasing after effect. Everything was simple and beautiful. Ms. Sava was also a music teacher. Sonia must have inherited her love for color and music from her mother.

Like Sonia, Ms. Sava liked to talk about her roots and was proud of her native village. For almost a century that village bordered what used to be the Habsburg Empire. People from the border villages had special rights in exchange for their service to the Empire. Such privileges endowed them with a stoic and courageous character which over time became in- scripted into their heritage and passed on to successive generations. They were a stern people that never

Blessed with Twice the Freedom

bowed their heads easily.

Sonia's mother Elena was one of the three daughters of Papa Ioan, as Sonia referred to him. He was a visionary who wanted all three of his daughters be educated, which was unusual at that time in a rural village. He worked in America for many years and had not only brought back money but also a new vision. He could often be heard saying, "Education gives man wings to fly, in order, to get in the places where he cannot get by walking."

All three of his daughters not only got an education, but they also became educators themselves, passing the torch of learning on to the next generations.

At a summer camp organized by the well-known Romanian historian Nicolae Iorga, one daughter, a very talented student, made such an impressive literary presentation that she was offered a scholarship to study Romance languages in Rome. She became a linguistics professor. Because she spoke Italian, she also worked at the Italian Consulate from Transylvania.

Later, she became Mrs. Arrigoni, the wife of a gentleman employed at the Italian Consulate in Romania. When the Communist regime was installed, many of the Romanian intellectuals — who foresaw the depredations to come – fled the country en masse. The Arrigoni family was among them. As I had learned later from Sonia, her aunt's shunning of the Communist regime followed Sonia throughout her life. It was one of many "troubling spikes" in her file.

Her father chose to be a Greek Catholic priest – which allowed for married priests, unlike the Roman Catholic Church – at a time when God couldn't be mentioned publicly. So that was not a favorable page in her file either.

Father Sava, as the people of his church called him, was not only a fine priest but a deep thinker, and an erudite philosopher. Since, however, the only philosophy allowed to reach the Romanian people's minds was Marxism, Father Sava's cerebral bent was a problem.

He too came from a tiny Transylvanian village a step away from

Habsburg Austria's border". It was interesting to see the difference in mentality between the people of these two villages, whether holding their heads up proudly and bowing them down submissively.

Sonia was very attached to her set of paternal grandparents, the Sava side. I saw it in her talking and writing. Possibly, it was because she was their only granddaughter. Her other grandparents she had to share with many cousins. Perhaps, that's why I find more details about the Savas in her writings. Thus, here she goes...

"My grandfather or Papa Petre, as I used to call him, went to America for the same reason Papa Ioan went – to provide his family with a better life. He left behind my grandmother Ana with their first born in the crib, who much later grew to become Father Sava. By the time he returned home, the lad was fifteen years old. Besides her son, my Grandmother Ana Sava, reared five of her younger siblings because they had lost their mother – my great grandmother – to the Spanish flu.

Europe was impoverished by World War I, decimated by the Spanish flu, and was looking to find a way out of poverty. History documents the exodus to America of those poor Europeans. They felt they had no choice but to pass to the other side of the Atlantic looking for work. They called it the New World. My grandparents, like many other immigrants, left for the promised land, taking with them just their name and the hope that one day they could return home in good health and with savings for their family. I have never forgotten their sacrifice; instead I am grateful to them and have deep respect for them.

Later, when in America I could find the names of my grandfathers on the Ellis Island documents on the computer. I imagined them getting off the boat, disoriented at first, then stepping into the unknown, and looking for work. How hard it must have been to take such a long journey over the sea, how hard to be away from family for so many years. At that time, there were no phone connections or fast postal service. It must have been unimaginably hard.

Blessed with Twice the Freedom

I am sure both my grandfathers would have been proud of my courage to follow their path into the unknown. In fact, my both grandfathers became good friends in America. When they returned home to Transylvania they continued their friendship and through their visits, my parents Elena and Mihai Sava, first met. I am more than happy for such a coincidence. If my grandfathers, hadn't decided to go to America at the same time, my parents would likely never have met. I ponder this often. We depend on events, which are strung together like the beads on the thread of destiny. If one bead goes missing, then all the others change places and the pattern is quite different.

One day, Gil heard Neli and I talking about the play of coincidences in one's life and added something interesting,

"Yes, my dear ladies, all things belonging to earth are governed by the Law Cause and Effect. Only God and subatomic particles do not obey it. For them, that law dissolves into nonexistence."

I couldn't help but say,

"How beautiful! Not only the law, but everything, at one time or another, can dissolve into nonexistence, and transcend manifestation, can't it?"

I enjoyed talking with Gil about the secrets of physics. We could go on and on about it. Neli was not as passionate about physics as I was. Yet she let herself be amazed by the subtlety of it.

Because in a world where non-Communist ideas could not be expressed, we looked to the magic of science for freedom to think. I got a taste for the subtleties of the unseen world from my father. Of course, God's realm couldn't be mentioned in a classroom.

Unfortunately, Neli and Gil didn't have a chance to know this side of my father, who died shortly after we met.

The years my father spent in the concentration camp had ruined his health. But at least he didn't die there, as did so many.

The regime was reluctant to call the place a concentration camp, because of the association between the word "camp" and the Nazi camps. Thus, they simply called it "Concentration."

The goal of Concentration was to get rid of all the people who were suspected of non-allegiance to the regime.

The Concentration recruiters were empowered to pluck people from their homes, without explanation or warrant. This was a thing they did only at night, using the darkness as cover. In daylight, nobody, could discuss it, or speak a word of resistance. Though they had no basis in law, they did not need a law. Their power went beyond the law.

I have no recollection of the night they came to get my father. I was at my grandparents' house. But afterwards, I looked for answers – even though everyone told me told to be quiet, saying that otherwise my dad would suffer even more. Ever since, suffering has had a profound impact on me. I suffer silently. When I am hurt, I muffle my tears.

In the so-called Concentration places, people were compelled to do hard labor under risky situations – these sentences were often in fact death sentences – where the communists/killers were free to get away with murder.

The most dreaded place of all was the Danube-Black Sea Canal. Almost 20,000 political prisoners were concentrated there. The labor imposed on them was very often more than they could complete, and under the most inhumane conditions. Those who were behind in their work were punished by missing meals or being mocked and beaten. Many never returned home. The canal was rightly called the Canal of Death. For the Communist regime, the plan was a success. The Canal was built. However, for Romania it was a page of the most tragic history.

My father was lucky. It seems inappropriate to talk about luck in this context, but my father returned home. He was very fragile, but he was home. I remember how ecstatic we were to have him back home. Maybe I should say again that he was lucky. He was placed in a different camp that was both smaller and not as brutal as the Danube

Canal. My father never spoke of it. I don't know how much of his silence was due to him forgiving those who trespassed against him or how much was him not wanting us to know what he had gone through.

There were several reasons for the regime to hate my father, and all of them groundless. First, he was a priest and because he respected God's laws, they believed he was subversive against the new class of the proletariat, whose laws stood opposed to God's. His father's time in America was also a mark against him. For the Communists even mentioning the word "America" created hostility. My grandparents had prospered through honest work and sacrifice, not by exploiting others. But also, perhaps it was his wealth that damned him. In the end, being wealthy was a cause for suspicion. Everything was unfairly snatched from them and turned into property which belonged to all. It was the regime's attempt to level the differences between the social classes. Nothing could be done - we had to follow orders. We never found the precipitating cause for his arrest and gave up looking for it, indeed. Instead, we were happy to have him home and alive.

My father and I often wondered, what makes some people go to find the truth, like the pearl divers do, disregarding the dangers separating them from their goal. My father was a man in a continuous search for the truth: who we are, where do we come from, and many other questions. He would say,

"The answers to these questions are not easily found, unless we have recourse to heaven."

No doubt, he was correct and obstinately kept his beliefs unaltered, regardless of the outside pressure. He was very happy with my decision to study chemistry under all its aspects, and more than that, to do it as a service to help others, as a pharmacist.

I was not only honored to do what I love but I was able to research and find answers to my own many questions. Chemistry shed light on things for me that up until then, were still in the dark. The more I would study, the more I could see with my mind's eyes the unseen hands behind creation. I acknowledge a Creator – One who exists in everything and reveals Himself through its creation.

In a Communist country we're indoctrinated with the idea that matter is supreme and no such thing as spirit exists. We are told that nothing exists beyond Mendeleev's table (as we call the Periodic Table).

Its elements are samples of the stuff that composes the universe as we know it. They are arranged in groups like family trees. Everything is there – from A to Z. But even the table has its own fascination.

Science dissects one by one every element from the first square to the last. First, they found that the atom, which was thought to be indivisible, that in fact has its own components. Next, they found that the laws inside of the atom are different from the laws outside of it. Inside, I told my father, there were sacred laws, similar, to the laws of God.

To such a theory, my father answered thoughtfully,

"I think that the essence of the periodic table that you are talking about is nothing more than the alpha and omega, the Everlasting Eternal.

In the beginning was the Word, a word that was more than a few letters put together, it was wisdom itself. The first spoken words were **'Let there be light'** or as the Latin translators of the Hebrew book said, 'Fiat lux.' Then every speck of the universe, every atom as you call it, was subjugated to those words and incorporated the light of Wisdom into it, to become the elements of the table you are talking about. We still don't know whether such a table exists in other places in the universe. Wisdom is boundless, just like the infinite universe."

I let myself indulge in these kinds of conversations with my father very often, but especially during an unexpected turn in my sentimental life.

My five-year relationship with my first love, Adrian, had suddenly ended. It was not our decision to end it, but that of the Communist Party, which ended it for us. The Communist Regime controlled every move in our lives, inclusively whom we were allowed to love. We were put under surveillance. This was not the kind of problem I could solve like a math equation. There were too many unknown terms. So, I had to put my love aside for a while."

Now I understand Sonia even better. She is a person of strong principles; as she would herself recognize, maybe sometimes, too strong. I call that integrity. I learned a lot about her love for her family; no wonder she became a dedicated mother, a devoted wife, and an equally grateful daughter and friend. For her, family was a living treasure. I liked how she sometimes compared the ties within a family to chemical bonds. I guess only a chemist could make such an observation.

"See Neli," she said, "Just as atoms cannot be taken randomly and forced to form a stable molecule, the same is true with couples starting a stable family. There must be an affinity between parts based on the principle of give and take. The secret of such a principle of attraction resides deeply inside molecules as it does within people. Judging by the nature of people, perfection probably only exists theoretically. Nobody is perfect. No two humans are, exactly, the same. They fall short or excel in different ways. But such differences cannot stand in the way of a strong relationship. Instead they may be leveled and smoothed harmoniously by the dynamics of the resilient rule of give and take.

Nobody comes into this world empty handed. Everyone is given a gift. But the gift is wisely wrapped, stirring the curiosity of the receiver. To make the search irresistible, the gift is first presented as a tiny germinating seed. Information about what will grow out of it is vague. Only by nurturing that seed can the in-born talent be developed into a passion, which actively turns then into a mission. Passion doesn't let us stay passive in front of what comes with life's flow. Its forces move us forward to avoid stagnation.

Just like the ocean continuously sends tides to and from the shore, Eternity sends messengers with each generation to solve the mysteries of the unknown, one by one. However, not all the messengers landing ashore are clear about their mission. Some of them, rise and fall, like the tides do under the will of celestial forces, lacking their real purpose."

I let Sonia finish. I didn't say a word. Other times, when talking about passion, she would cite her father. We both liked what he had to say.

"Without passion there is no bravery. Only passion can leap over very high barriers. Nevertheless, passion doesn't reside only in a grand pursuit, but also in a person's everyday life. I have seen with a child's eyes the passion of the plowman who could hardly wait until dawn, to go to his field, to turn the soil and till it into a furrow, burying the seeds of a future crop. This is the passion for life itself, everyday it yields its real gift. And how many times are we are ready to throw away a gift before we even open it? Isn't it such a life given in vain?"

I learned from Sonia that the little church where Father Sava served was always packed. From every sermon people took something home. Every sermon was a life lesson. People were starving not just for food but for knowledge. They wanted to learn how faith, truth and hope work together. He would illustrate this concept by reference to the pool of Bethesda, one of the Bible's parables. I myself like to contemplate this parable. How often do we feel paralyzed by the heaviness of our problems, how often do we wait for somebody to jump to our rescue? And only to find out that the rescuer resides in us. There is our Faith.

Because of her father's passion to spread God's word, he was pushed further and further to the outskirts of city. The Communists feared his strong influence on people. Young people stopped attending services in the churches at the heart of the city because students who were caught in church were ridiculed in the mandatory political student meetings. Surely, they failed their Dialectical

Materialism exams, also a mandatory course in both high school and college. Anything opposed to Dialectical materialism was considered an impediment to the young generation as they grew within the Communist spirit. But no matter where Father Sava was moved, his followers found him.

So, Sonia's father was a metaphysician, looking for the unseen beyond matter. Her grandparents admired America. Her aunt left Romania for Italy. All, of these things, weighed heavily on Sonia 's file. She didn't have to do anything to attract political suspicion, it was enough that she was born into a family which was marked by communists.

Sonia dared to confess these personal things to us only after we knew each other very well and after she learned that we shared the same ideas. It was our big secret. Had our subversive nest been discovered we could have lost our jobs in the most humiliating ways. Or worse.

CHAPTER 25

A Frontier Between the Old and the New

We finally left Bucharest and arrived in Budapest, Hungary at 8:00 AM. I had a strange feeling crossing the border. To me, it was more than a simple line of demarcation. To me, it was the first bite of a "fruit of freedom."

Corina and I were happy that our little belongings passed, in the end, through customs, all except for one of my rings.

I used to repeat the word "America" in my mind; it had a special resonance for me. Maybe because for such a long time it was a taboo. And now I wasn't just saying the word, I was going there. And I was thrilled that soon the word "comrade" would stop being a part of my vocabulary.

In the beginning there were just a few people in the waiting area, then slowly the crowd grew. Only a few were speaking Romanian.

After a long silence, Corina snuggled under my arm and said,

"Mommy I would like to whisper something into your ear." She knew that our secrets couldn't be shared publicly, and we had so many.

"I am so glad that he didn't take my vest," she said in a hurry and then went on to add,

"Dad will be so happy to see us dressed beautifully, won't he?"

"I think so, little bird."

I couldn't say firmly, of course, because I had a feeling about it

146

that I couldn't share with anybody. It was a fear that I didn't want to admit even to myself.

Until we boarded, Corina was rushing up to whisper to me again and again. It was her joy, that she couldn't keep still.

"Mommy, on this very day I will see my dad and my brother, won't I?"

Because I had just been nodding my head, yes, to her questions, she asked me whether something was wrong.

"I know we have a lot of secrets today, but people around us might think that we're talking about them and we don't want to make them upset," I said softly.

"I see Mommy, let's not talk about them anymore," she said, her playful eyes taking up the joke.

After the torture of customs, we both felt relieved. What a magical brick the imagination is! With it you can build anything! In our minds, we were on top of the world!

A small group of people boarded the plane in Budapest. I wondered if they, like us, were lucky to be leaving Communism behind. I wanted to shout out of joy, yet I had to be quiet. Even in a Pan-Am plane, we had to exercise our discretion. Everybody knew that a Communist security agent was always among the passengers going to the West. We were still Romanians and couldn't make any questionable moves. We could have been turned back at any point. For that reason, I often had to put my index finger on Corina's lips and say, "Shush." She finally rested her head on one of my arms and fell asleep. She didn't wake up until our next stop, Frankfurt, Germany. We could get off the plane because we had a long layover.

This was the first time we had stepped out onto free ground. There were a lot a people walking past in a hurry and others having breakfast or shopping. All of it made the airport inside look like one of the main streets from our town that we had just left behind. The only difference was that everything here was shiny and bright, and there was an abundance of food and other goodies that we had never seen before. No matter where we turned, tempting displays made us feel as if we were in a dream after going to bed hungry.

"Mommy, look, bananas! May I have one?" Corina said anxiously.

"Sorry, little chick, I don't have dollars, Deutschmarks, or any money at all. But don't you worry chickabiddy, your father will spoil you with many of those and many other goodies, as soon as we got there." Then a smile of anticipated joy radiated throughout her entire face as she relinquished her craving.

For me though, it was another reason to think about home, about Romania, which we left behind just a few hours ago. Hard currency in a Romanian's pocket without any proof of innocent origins could have created problems, and we couldn't risk even a penny's worth of trouble.

The long lines in which we waited for a few paltry bananas or oranges were still fresh in my mind – and, also the barren and dusty shelves in the stores. But I had to let these thoughts vanish quickly and replace them with thoughts of the bright future that was laid out in front of us. And little Corina seemed to be hatching the same thoughts,

"Oh, Mommy if you only knew how happy I am."

"I am too," I said it, to be agreeable, while the nagging thoughts of Sabin caught at me, like the empty and dusty shelves. At one point I felt even annoyed that couldn't banish these images. Why couldn't I snap out of it? It was New Year's Eve. Finally, I let a wave of celebration engulf me, like a willful fire.

The earth was close to finishing its 365th rotation and was not stopping before the next. Why couldn't we let ourselves be a part of it? Every moment we left out would be our loss.

The plane from Frankfurt to JFK was packed and ready to take off. After everyone had found their seat and settled down, the boarding crew delivered the required instructions and wished us all a Happy New Year. Even though there were people of many languages it seemed that they understood each other, and also, understood the

Blessed with Twice the Freedom

flight attendants who, shortly after, hurried through the aisles to serve the first meal. Corina spotted bananas on a food cart in the aisle and she beckoned to me, whispered into my ear. It seemed that she was not yet over her craving for the bananas she couldn't have in Frankfurt. Like a bird attempting its first chirp, I dared to ask an attendant in English whether my daughter could have a banana.

"Oh yes ma'am, of course. She can have more than one if she wants. I shall be back in a minute". I wondered if she could see that we were coming from a country where bananas were a great treat for a child, but it didn't matter. She came to us smiling, bringing a plate of four bananas. She said, "Ma'am, you can have some also, and please let me know if you need anything else."

"I am all set," I said, "Thank you much."

Then we even chatted a little. I don't know how I put together all those words so quickly. I had just had my first conversation with a native speaker of American English! No matter how simple it sounds to others, I was as thrilled as if I had just passed an important test. I was shy with my English. In school I had studied Russian and French. English began to interest me only after I learned about Sabin's decision to not return to Romania. I had known that studying English was a must. But there was so little time that I could take from my overloaded schedule. I had my full-time job as a pharmacist, then my parenting job, also full-time. Then there were Corina's many activities: piano, swimming, ballet, and other creative activities. She was like a sponge when it came to learn, and I did not want to neglect any of her talents. Then there were all those stressful bureaucratic tasks -- appointments with the police, and the passport and customs offices. All this and unreliable public transit, too! At the end of the day I was exhausted.

My only leisure was when I visited my mom, Neli and Gil, or when our "Englishwoman" as we called the English teacher, came to our house. She taught us the rudiments of this language that I found very difficult at first. I wondered if she would have been proud of

149

my first English chat on the plane.

After the first meal the plane became quiet again. Even though it was before mid-day it was time for siesta after our copious New Year's Eve meal. Anyway, our day had started earlier than usual, so it really did feel like siesta time. I had already set my watch seven hours ahead, and it would stay like that for the rest of my life.

Meanwhile Corina captured the attention of a lovely Romanian couple Mr. and Mrs. Răduţ. They were going to Pennsylvania to visit their daughter's family. They also had a granddaughter around Corina's age. I could easily understand why they got so attached to Corina. I was glad that she was busy with them and I could compose myself and hide all the emotions swirling in my head. I hardly could wait to see my family a whole again.

We got closer and closer to America. A happy feeling stretched all around. You could read it on everyone's face. It was like a wave of happiness that didn't leave anybody out. Everyone was happy that the plane touched the ground safely. Until the full stop, the plane sang two songs we were hearing for the first time. First was God bless America. I had never heard the name of God spoken in public before. That was a very touching feeling, it was my first touch of freedom. Then there was another song; something like our Romanian song "La Mulţi Ani." This was "Auld Lang Syne," which Americans sing just for the New Year holiday. I liked it very much, it had something very European to it. Later I had found out that it was brought to America by the Irish. The song invited us to lay the past to rest and welcome the new with open arms. The song fit us perfectly!

As soon as we landed, I saw people covering their hearts with their right hand and heard them singing the American national anthem. They were Americans. We were happy to do the same, drinking the American spirit in. Deep inside I was grateful that America's anthem was to become mine.

We were lucky to have the Răduţ family to initiate us to an airport as huge as JFK. Without them we could very easily have gotten lost. They knew all the rules; they had taken many trips to America before.

Over the years, JFK Airport was always the start of my visits to Romania, but every single time I went there, I remembered my first day at JFK.

I would find the same unstoppable bustle of the crowd. I would still try to catch a word, without much success, from the many languages spoken around me. I would see the same rigid faces at customs; and then my first day here would come to my mind again; except that I didn't carry fear anymore. I had become American.

On that very day, we were given our green cards, with the right to reside legally in the United States, but as Romanians. We felt we were not just in a seventh heaven, but a ninth!

After a long walk through crowded corridors, we finally got, to an end where a lot of people were waiting for the coming passengers.

From a distance I could spot faces I recognized. At first, I couldn't believe my eyes, it was like a dream. Corina dropped off her little luggage in front of me and ran as fast as she could to Sabin and Michael. There was my dearest son, my husband, Sabin's twin brother, and their mother. They didn't welcome us with flowers, as Romanians would have. Instead, they had brown paper bags in their hands. I was intrigued. What could they be drinking from a bag? But I put aside my question. It was not the time for questions.

Finally, we were facing each other, but we had no words. Our emotions were stronger than words. Michael, my baby, had grown a lot in three years; it was an age where the years made clear differences.

He was confused, not knowing whom to hug first, his sister or me, so he hugged us both at once.

Sabin was detached. He avoided my eyes and gave me an awkward hug. I could hear a weird sobbing sound on my shoulder, which really annoyed me. I freed myself from the hug and asked,

"What is all of this? Aren't you happy to have us here?"

He didn't answer, but his brother Dan did, sneering,

"Of course, he is happy, how could he not be?" His mother said it too.

I knew right away that something was hidden from me, and that all three of these people knew what it was. Sabin and his brother were experts at concealing the truth, so I had no hope there.

And the mother was like a person with Parkinson's, a face without expression. So, she would be no help either. When dealing with her, I had often wondered whether her feelings were locked up somewhere inside or if she simply didn't have feelings. I remember the day after the car accident that had almost killed me, when she came to the hospital to see me, she apologized for not being able to show the affection she had for me. She said, "I love you, but I don't know how to show it." I felt kind of sorry for her.

"Don't you worry, if there is love, it will shine," I replied. Perhaps I had been wrong.

Then I couldn't help myself from asking, "What are you drinking and why from paper bags?"

"It is beer, and beer is not allowed to be drunk in public from a can, but it's not a problem if the beer is in a bag," answered Dan without any hesitation and in Romanian.

They could read the disappointment on my face right away.

"That is deceitful," I said, "and not a good example for Michael. It's also not something you should be proud of." I said it with no remorse. I knew from home that drinking was a problem for Dan, and it looked like it might have become a problem for Sabin as well. And again, I was sure, at that moment that they were hiding something more than the beer in a bag. By any means, this was not the welcome we had hoped for.

CHAPTER 26

Falling Off the Cloud Nine

"Although both children were thirsty, there was only beer in Sabin and Dan's cars. They had each brought their own car. Sabin rushed us to his.

As soon as we got in the car, I learned that apparently, somebody was planning to pay him a visit, and he had to be home in time. I was too tired to ask any questions. His brother and mother left first, and we followed.

Our children were in the back seat, unexpectedly quiet; in the front seat, we were quiet too. The heaviness of the silence made me very uncomfortable. I broke it, asking if we were, allowed, to talk in the car. Back home we had rules.

"Come on, honey, don't be sarcastic, say what you mean."

"I'm just refreshing our memories: In the car we don't speak unless we are spoken to, we don't touch the driver's seat and we don't eat, remember?" I said the last word looking not at him, but back at Michael and Corina.

They completed the phrase in unison, "… if we want to reach the destination." Yes, they remembered it. Sabin didn't react to our teasing.

I was trying to cover up Sabin's awkwardness and, in some way, Michael's also. Corina stopped chirping, as she had been doing all throughout the trip. Looking quickly at Sabin's face, I imagined a sign that read "Do not disturb." I felt alone. I still had some joy left in me from the excitement of our trip because it was hard to let that go, but

Domnitsa Uilean

I remembered the Romanian saying, "You cannot escape your fears."

Suddenly, I had the impression that Corina and we were nothing more than Sabin's poor relatives, people he was rescuing from the Communists. I cringed. I felt alienated and humiliated. I felt as if I was in a cab taking us to an unknown destination. I guess at this point, Sabin, felt my unspoken distress. Staying true to his musicianship, he came up with an "impromptu" pretending that everything was normal and would only speak now because it was his turn. He started emphatically,

"As soon as you step onto this land, you have to leave behind any Romanian habits. You must assimilate this very different American lifestyle.

You will find that the Americans are a cold people and are not eager to hold the door open for foreigners. You'll never make friends like you did in Romania. And one more thing: do not be surprised to learn that the divorce rate in America is over 50%."

I don't think he breathed in and out more than three times while delivering this news to me. It came out like a package of instructions.

"Why should we be worried about the American divorce rate? We have each other and our children now, don't we?"

The expression on his face did not change, but I could feel his arrogance coming through. Then I took another look to our children. Michael was holding Corina tenderly in his arms; she fell asleep with her head on his lap. It was an overwhelming day for her and I don't think it was any different for Michael either. I wish Sabin and I had tender feelings for each other, the way the children did.

"Hey, Michael what would you say about …" I didn't have to finish the question. He completed it himself, "…the Scandal Seed?" That was Corina's nickname. It was given to her because of her boisterous nature. She always wanted to be first. She even questioned why she had been born second! We all had a good laugh. We let ourselves catapult for a moment back to Romania, to the good times.

Again, there was a break in the conversation. There was not a

154

word about our trip or about my mom or the others left behind. However, Sabin didn't forget to ask about the plum brandy I had been asked to bring.

"Of course, my dear, I have brought a bottle for each of you."

Sabin was not an alcoholic like his brother, but he always enjoyed a good drink. They were fraternal twins and it was interesting how they divvied up their parents' patterns. Sabin took his physique from one parent, the other parent gave his character to Dan, and vice-versa. Even though they had spent their first nine months together and were nourished by the same blood, they were very different people.

All four had something in common, but the popping up of recessive and dominant genes of the twins was not totally harmonious and dealing with the extended family was exhausting. I tried to avoid such gatherings.

Even though it was just a little past noon, it was dark outside, too dark for that time of day. I thought to myself; I wish the weather was on my side and not as gloomy as my feelings. I was tired, I wanted to fall asleep like Corina, and upon awakening, find everything changed for the better. I dared not say another word.

I let my eyes wander over New York City. The skyscrapers of Manhattan were real, but from the distance they looked like a page in a magazine.

After less than two hours driving, which seemed like an eternity, we finally reached the front door of our new address. Eagerly I waited for the door to open and for a bountiful table full of goodies and flowers to be revealed, a welcoming celebration. Mrs. Cătușan with some awkwardness and a deliberate slowness unlocked the door. I followed behind her, holding my children's hands. Sabin and Dan were to bring our few belongings in. To our painful surprise, there was nothing on the table, nothing. I was embarrassed that I had encouraged Corina to believe in a special welcome.

I had the feeling that my mother-in-law, instead of opening the door to our new home, had opened instead a Pandora's Box full of evils. I knew that I would need to connect with Hope from now on.

No sooner did we get in the house than Corina let me know that she had a secret to whisper in my ear,

"Mommy, we shouldn't have come here, it was better at home when we were waiting."

"Yes, my little angel, you are right, but we are here now, and we must stay here for good," I said with a choked voice".

These fragments from Sonia's journals were much like the contents of her many letters to us. Gil and I could hardly bear the weight of her news. It was like an illness that we couldn't talk to anybody about. Nobody but us knew about the trap our girls were caught up in. For almost a year we kept the secret sealed – the truth would have been more than unbearable for Sonia's mother. First, we had to prepare her; otherwise the shock could kill her. Sonia was everything she had. I remembered Sonia's last request in the airport; she had begged us to not forget her mother.

After Sonia left the country we called Mrs. Sava "Mama Elena" as Sonia herself did. We always reminded her that she could count on us and that she should not think of herself as alone. My own mother reached out to Mama Elena after Sonia's departure.

I will never forget Sonia's first letter. We had been very apprehensive. We had made her promise to call as soon she got a phone in her hand. Sonia was not a person to ignore a promise. All New Year's Day, we kept our ears and eyes on the phone, but there was no call from America. The ring from overseas never came. We became genuinely worried. Towards the middle of January, the mailman handed us a registered letter. Gil and I had a gut feeling; both of us had our hands on it but didn't dare open it yet. We were right; it was not a letter of good news. Hastening to find the truth we went directly to the end of the letter. And this was the way she concluded,

"I don't know what tomorrow brings for us. I have become more patient than my nature allows me. But as you know, I do not give up

Blessed with Twice the Freedom

easily. Even though I'm having an unbearable time, I like to believe that I am not forgotten. Although reality doesn't seem to favor me right now, I still believe that I am one in God's favor, and I hope that at the end of this odyssey, I can see Him, turning this trap into my stepping stones".

"Oh, this cannot be true!" we exclaimed simultaneously. Because that day was more than an ordinary day, Sonia would rehash it in many other letters and in her journaling. She would describe and re-describe Sabin's cold welcome, the lack, not only, of a celebration dinner but of any dinner whatsoever! Here's one of those takes:

"In between two phone conversations, and seemingly irritated by the conversations and less concerned by our presence, he told us to check the refrigerator if we were hungry. Surprisingly, it was as empty as the one we left behind. The children had cereal. I myself couldn't have eaten anything even if the finest food in the world had been put down in front of me, it was all too much to swallow. I felt like I was caught in the jaws of a steel trap. Scared, I waited for his next move.

His brother and mother were still there, waiting for the plum brandy. As soon as they got it, they were in a hurry to get home. Their cat Coco, they said, was all alone. Half joking, half serious Dan said, "It is New Year's Eve for Coco also, isn't it?"

" Yes, it is," I said with sorrow.

I stepped into the other room, pretending that I was looking for something in my luggage. I beckoned to Sabin, asking him to follow me so the children wouldn't hear our talk. I tried my best to remain calm while stressing every word.

"Please tell me what is going on or what is bothering you? Can you please give me an explanation? Is there something specific I should be worried about? Ever since we entered this house you have been on the phone. Your phone calls are more important than your family? Please, tell me, tell me! I am pleading for the truth. Corina has already whispered into my ear, that we shouldn't have come here.

And she is right, we shouldn't have"

"No, nothing like that, your place is here, our children have to grow up together."

"Oh, really? That doesn't feel like the plan." I said it with disappointment.

He blurted out that he had invited a former co-worker to pay him a visit that evening, but, it seemed, she had turned down his invitation. She had moved out-of-state, but had come back for the holiday, to see her grandma, who just happened to be Sabin's landlady. I didn't say it, but I thought that the lady he was waiting for had more common sense than he did. What I said was,

"How can you let yourself be bothered by such an insignificant event and take out your frustration on the biggest event of our lives?"

He didn't answer. He grimaced. He stared at the ceiling and said in an impersonal tone,

"Honey, I don't how to phrase it, but from today on, our lives will proceed separately, but in parallel."

At first, I was more incensed about him calling me "honey" than I was by the content of the phrase itself. I said, "You call me "honey" in the same breath that you eviscerate me? How can you strip that word of its meaning? You don't choose to run "in parallel" with a person dear to you. Leave me alone! I can't take any more from you today! Leave me alone!"

Without any sign of remorse, he stepped back into the other room.

I was too tired; I couldn't listen to his nonsense anymore. Corina was right; we never should have come here. But again, there was Michael with his health problems – for him I had to come. It was a must! Emotionally I was numb. A rush of adrenaline pushed me past the tiredness from the long trip and the early rising. One single day had brought so many changes at once, to me; changes in space, in time, and now in my heart.

I grabbed one of the suitcases where I had packed our strictly

Blessed with Twice the Freedom

necessary items. Swiftly I took out everything I needed for Corina and me and then prepared the children for bed. The children and I shared the bed. Sabin slept in another room on an old, ragged sofa. I was not critical about the poor furniture per se, every beginning is hard, but hadn't we come here for a better life? Sabin had always been stingy, but this stinginess felt intentional.

We were in that house only for a few days. The landlady, it seems, didn't want to renew his lease. A move to another town was planned for the first week of January. Absurd as it sounds, I fantasized a little about flying straight back to Romania. It was something unconceivable, How, could I go home? I had to put that thought to rest for now. Instead I chose to lovingly prepare my kids for bed, just as I used to do when I was back home. I lay between the two children. Corina started to weep silently as if something was hurting and she didn't want to talk about. I moved her between me and Michael, and we held her little hands tenderly while reassuring her that we loved her and that everything was okay.

They both fell asleep. My mind was again spinning and was far from winding down. I had too many questions, but the answers were with the man sleeping in the other room. Parallel lives? Disappointed by a rejected visit? A cat more important than Corina and Michael? Very strange!

If we hadn't had children, it would have all been very simple. I would have asked for our marriage to be dissolved the moment I learned that he had been dishonest with me. He had made me feel insignificant, like a thing to be managed. Back when we struggled to get visas for America, we had talked things over. We both agreed that at our age – we both were 43 – it would be hard to start all over again. If I remember correctly, he was the first to say it. However painful it is to have your hopes crushed, at least I was an adult. I worried for the children, though. I wanted to go into the other room and shake him awake and demand all the answers he owed me. But at that point I was beyond exhausted, and I realized that what I needed most was

159

sleep. More than twenty-four hours had elapsed since last, I closed my eyes. I found myself praying,

"Oh, my Lord, give me, please, a moment of relief and chase away all these thoughts which are tormenting my mind now. Please help me sleep, please help me!"

Suddenly I felt that all my thoughts halted. They could do nothing but let sleep take over. Towards morning I had a strange dream. It was short, intense and clear, like a real event:

In the dream, it seemed that I was not on the earth but somewhere out in space. I had an urge to talk. Suddenly, a microphone landed in my hand. I somehow knew that, and elf had given it to me. I knew my time was limited and that I was, allowed, to say only one word. The word was "Whyyyyyyyyyyyyyyy?" I shouted it long and loud to be heard throughout the heavens. My word sounded like thunder, followed by a moment of deep silence, the same silence that I had "listened" to after the car accident. But it was more than just silence, it was also emptiness. It is so difficult to explain. Then I heard a calm, austere voice, reverberating softly. "Do not doubt his love, (he was not called by his name). When he met you, he loved you more than anything in the world. But he doesn't have enough substance in his soul to keep a marriage alive. Flatness replaced love. Then your three years apart made even that disappear. There is nothing left, nothing."

"Nothing, nothing is left." I spoke these words aloud to assure myself that I understood the message.

I woke up feeling that I had had a conversation with a counselor. It was all so real. It was like rain coming too late to a field already scorched by burning heat. Fully awakened, I tried to go down the dream's trail step by step. I wanted to pin down the time when love was flattened.

"It came when your children were born," said a voice inside me.

That voice was right, but I had always thought that through love I could fix anything that stopped working. Unfortunately, it was not possible with this one. I ran back through our twenty years together and analyzed all, of the stages we had gone through.

We met at driving school, where we had the same instructor. My lesson was after his, but from the first lesson on he would wait until I was also done, so we could go back to the city together. I hadn't considered it a big deal or seen it as more than simple school collegiality. Every Thursday for the three months that the class lasted, we followed the same routine. One day he invited me to have coffee together and to continue our conversation. We talked about just everything, and we seemed to be aligned on many topics. We enjoyed each other's company. Even the instructor noticed it and said, "Miss Sava, I think Sabin has a crush on you."

"Really? You said crush not crash, right?" I said.

We both passed the exam and with an entire group of newly licensed drivers, we celebrated at the Continental, a swanky restaurant in the city. He asked me if he could walk me home. But I said, "Another time, OK?"

He was not happy with "another time" but I was not yet prepared to bring him into my life. So, he found my work phone number and started calling me there. Sometimes he even showed up at my work. He was a musician and played violin with the City Philharmonic. All, of my friends, myself included, thought that in addition to being good looking, he was charming and had a good sense of humor.

My friends also knew the sad love story of my former love and how it ended. Although, it has been more than two years since the Communists took control over our lives and split us apart, Adrian and I still, remained a couple in our hearts. I didn't continue talking to my friends about Adrian, because the relationship was forbidden, but it was hard to let it go. It was like a death I had to recover from, without being able to mourn.

Life goes on, and mine had to too.

When Sabin came into my life, I was ready to leave the past aside and embrace the present again. Maybe his persistence made the transition easier. He was very pleasant company and I could talk with him about all the things I was interested in. In that respect he was much like Adrian; an erudite guy. That, in fact, was the basis of our friendship.

My social background was not a problem for Sabin as it had been for Adrian. On the social scale we were on the same step, as were our files from the Security Service drawers. Nevertheless, our relationship was not grounded in complaints about the government. That wouldn't have been romantic at all.

Before, I went to musical concerts often, but after I met him, I didn't skip a single one. When he performed, in the brief pause before he began to play, he would look out at me. I could feel it on my face as a warm sunbeam, yet it also gave me a pleasant chill. That was our first secret. He was happy that he had found a fellow music lover.

And one day he told me I was his soul's music. I found it very flattering! Our friendship slowly slipped into a relationship. I was happy, thinking that I was very lucky to find again the man of my dreams. It was around that time that I said, "Yes" to his proposal. It was a long time ago…

Now I am left wondering; how and where did the love disappear? What about the inadequate level of "substance" in his "soul" that the dream referred to? It did indeed seem like there was nothing left for us but the children. I turned around and watched my children deep in their sleep. I found myself smiling at their perfectly synchronized breathing. They were as much a part of him as they were a part of me. Yet, we were not synchronized anymore, or as Sabin would say, we were on parallel paths, on different wavelengths.

I was still in a stage of numbness when Sabin woke up. I had nothing left to say to him. He was as strange to me as the room I was in. I got out of the bed and looked around that strange room to find a little corner where I could crouch hoping to gather easier my thoughts, which were hovering frantically over my head. My heart was still heavy, and a cry was ready to burst out, so I rushed to get into the shower and let it. After I finished sobbing, I crouched back into

Blessed with Twice the Freedom

my corner. My hair was still dripping wet when Sabin came in. He came over to me and, lifting a strand of my hair, asked me whether I would like a coffee, as if nothing had happened only hours before.

"No," I answered briefly, without looking at him.

"You know Sonia, I don't know how to explain this to you," he started,

"We are not on the same wavelength. It is not your fault that we are so different, that we have different ethical values, right now, maybe it's because of the two different worlds we've been living in."

I listened to him, for a while, without trying to read between the lines as I usually do. It is nothing left in his heart for me, and that explains everything.

Suddenly, the other break up, the one, I went through with Adrian, entered my mind. The wall that had kept Adrian and me apart was Communist Regime. That wall a temporary wall. It meant to last only, if the regime itself did. But the wall between Sabin and me was different; we ourselves were the wall, and that made it impassable.

With a gesture implying that I would like to end the conversation, I stretched my right hand to turn on the radio, which was on a stand next to me. At the first turn of the dial, I came across of a piece of music as fitting as if I had ordered it. It was Chopin's Piano Concerto No. 1. Absorbed by the music I let myself stare at the ceiling. I imagined the music's refrain making steps back and forth. It reminded me of the oscillating steps I would have to take, until reaching stability.

The children woke up and came out to me. They embraced me. They knew that I was sad.

"How have you slept my little birds?" I asked them. They didn't answer right away, so I didn't persist. I was afraid that Corina might speak up about her disappointments. She was good at speaking her mind. I was not as worried for her father as I was about Michael. He had waited anxiously to have us here. Sabin had told me that lately he had been crying because he missed us.

163

Corina cuddled under Michael's arm and he was happy to show her how a protective big brother he could be. Sabin decided to take a picture of them; I still have that picture, and every time I see it, it reminds me of our awful first day in America. I can read the sadness mixed with fear on the faces of my children. Only half of me was in the picture, I think it was done intentionally; I was cut off in the picture just like I was cut out of his plans. Even Sabin could feel the children's repulsion as he awkwardly tried to draw them into conversation, but they didn't change their positions or really, even look at him. To smooth over his children's indifference to him, he made us all aware that we would have to start packing soon for our next move. He didn't get much traction with that theme either. Our bags were hardly unpacked.

Again, the children had only cereal until later that afternoon, when he brought home some Chinese food. I wondered if this was our first lesson in not getting used to the abundance that America was well known for. Or was it to show me that he hadn't changed his mind about us living apart?

In fact, on our first day in America, I saw very little of him, he was gone for most of the day.

The children went out to play; they were glad to find a fluffy new snow had blanketed the small back yard overnight. I listened to them talking about plans for a snowman. I was happy for them. They were too little to understand our grown-up problems. I was alone in the house. I was no longer floating in the ninth heaven that I had imagined just a day before. I was, falling, fast as with a parachute that wouldn't open.

Throughout our first day together, in the short time when Sabin was home, we were silent in front of the children. Nevertheless, if the children were not around, he would come up with a short remark to emphasize his decision.

"Each of us, in the future, can live our lives separately, but we can still raise the kids together."

Blessed with Twice the Freedom

Was he losing his mind? What kind of future was he talking about?

Ultimately, Sabin and Michael had come to America for the very real reason that Michael needed to have an MRI test. Unfortunately, three years later, that test had not yet been done. So, I could not go back to Romania yet, no matter how long I had to wait or how much I wanted to leave.

Three days after we arrived, we were moved to a new town. The children and I traveled in a car with Dan, and Sabin drove a U-Haul. I didn't want to talk with Dan about anything. For one thing, it was hard to catch him sober. He was a professional engineer in Romania, but his American job didn't require any higher education. I don't want to criticize first jobs, though. I knew that all of us must start from the bottom, until we can manage to achieve the equivalent of our education from Romania. That achievement would open the door to better opportunities.

Dan, to break the silence, tried to mumble something about Sabin's crisis being the result of the stress he was under. But as we say in Romania, "everything was sewn with white thread," meaning that the truth can't be hidden.

Sabin was afraid that I would have never followed him to America if I knew his real plan. He was right, I would never have followed him, because he was not a man to rely on.

Dan was just making small talk, and I tried not to listen. I knew that the plan was being directed by the Cătușan family and that Corina and I were not part of the plan. I had a feeling, though, that God was watching over us and that He had another plan for us. Things always turned around in my favor, I only needed to endure. It didn't matter to me how long it took. We had already endured three years. Dan talked on and on. Finally, he, said,

"You have to be patient, everything will be fine."

"What do you mean? I think things between Sabin and me are very clear."

I made it clear I had no more to say and wanted to hear no more.

165

The children did not need to hear the rest of this conversation. I was incensed.

We got to our destination; it was a very old house with many things not working, but it was roomy enough. Sabin was already assigning rooms. He and Michael were to share the bedroom going into the living room while Corina and I would get the bedroom with an entrance from the kitchen. No one had any objections.

Two days later, Dan and I met with the principal of the school where my children were to attend. I let Dan do the talking, my English was not at the level of such a conversation, neither was my understanding. Nevertheless, all the people in the office were nice. They smiled at me and I smiled back as if everything was fine. Corina was going into the second grade and Michael into fourth grade. We left them there like two lambs in a large flock of sheep.

That same day Stacy, whom Sabin had introduced as a co-worker, came to visit us. Her family owned the house we had moved into. She came with one of her children. I have learned that she had four. Stacy was short and stout and looked old for her age, which she disclosed to me without my asking. In fact, she did most of the talking. At that time, even in Romanian, I could find no words to express my feelings.

I was surprised that during his co-worker's visit, Sabin didn't participate in our conversation at all. Had a co-worker visited us back in Romania he would have been totally different. I knew him well. He was always interested in making a good impression. And I wondered why he wasn't doing it now? It felt weird. But there was already much weirdness, that one thing more, or less, didn't matter. Much later, I learned that Michael had confided to Corina that the visiting woman was their father's girlfriend. So much for our different "ethical values"!

I don't know how; Eurydice and Orpheus myth came to my mind; Orpheus devotion and love to Eurydice pushed him to try almost the impossible to save her from the Underworld and bring her to

Blessed with Twice the Freedom

life. On contrary, my "Orpheus" would have like rather, to throw me Underworld.

I was left in the New World to rescue myself.

To make it in the New World, first, and the most important it was to learn English. I spared no time but doing it.

I devoured my Romanian- English dictionary page by page. Superstitiously, I kept the dictionary under my pillow while I was sleeping. If I ran out of time during the day, I wanted the words to come to me in my dreams while I slept. I wanted them stored in my brain and then to be at my fingertips in any conversation. Back home all my study was sporadic – there was not enough time in a day to do everything. Nevertheless, before we arrived, I had thought that I was doing OK in English and that my husband would be proud of my accomplishment. But that was not the case at all. He couldn't have cared less.

In time, the iceberg of fear and panic started to melt. I was like a person coming out from a coma. I had to learn everything all over again. I was lucky to have Michael as a tutor, because his English was perfect. Even Corina helped me; her English was also better than mine. Every morning before breakfast they verified the English I had learned the day before. They gave me spelling quizzes and taught me the American pronunciation, which were sometimes different from the British English I had been working on. I struggled to learn fast and to not disappoint them. We, the three of us, were a great team helping each other. Sabin was not enthusiastic at all of this, he was grumpy when he was home.

I knew he would get jealous quickly if one day I got ahead of him.

In my marriage there were no any signs of improvement, in fact the tension continued to grow, until it became harder and harder to be accepted.

When spring came, Sabin started going to outdoor concerts on Saturday nights. I was more than dismayed to see his parents encouraging him to take some time off and enjoy his life, after he had been "condemned" to spend three years alone with Michael. Had he brought me to America to be a babysitter? I couldn't understand where his head was at. We were as poor as church mice, but he spent time and money looking for fun, instead of trying to provide a better life for his family. Why had any of us left Romania? Little Corina couldn't understand all of this either. Once, when I was ironing a shirt for him, she bluntly told him, "It's not very nice of you to go to the concerts while mom stays home to work for you." This startled me,' and I burned one of my hands on the hot iron. I got a blister and then a deep scar that is on my arm to this day and forever reminds me of that one."

I feel Sonia breathing through the pages. I am often tempted to browse randomly through her journals, as eager and curious as a child who is looking for something new in a book, that is almost known by heart. Then I let myself get trapped in one story or another and revive it in my mind.

Sometimes in her writings she explores death, a concept that intrigued us both. After Gil passed, she explored death more than once.

Now, both she and Gil know what is on "the other side," and I am all alone, arguing with words on a page. She told me, "Neli, don't look for Gil in the cemetery, only his physical body is there. The body is the part that obeys the implacable law of the return to ashes. The body is just a thing the soul borrows. The soul uses the body as a temporary temple, to manifest itself."

I imagine Gil smiling at this kind of talk. He, as an expert physicist, would have termed it double-talk; but on an abstract scale there is a similarity between this metaphor and the theory of light – which can behave both as a wave and a particle, but not as both at the same time.

Oh Gil, you who were an expert on the laws of physics you who now knows heaven's laws too, please don't be too hard on my humble beliefs, which cannot be proved by science. Let me indulge in my belief that the soul finds its temple at birth and breaks apart from it at death. That's why we dare to associate Light with Death, I think, and why we put them together in one piece. We believe that there is a light that comes into the soul from above, and that it enlivens the body during the period marked by the two endpoints "birth" and "death." The way this happens exactly is still a mystery for us and far from being deciphered, but for you, Gil, it is not a mystery anymore.

I remember the way Sonia explained the passing of Mrs. Sava to Corina. She described the grandmother's death as a transformation into a beam of light, which is the only way to reach the faraway Eternity. Sonia didn't touch only Corina with her explanation, she touched me as well. I choose to believe; thus, I find continuity between what we see and what we cannot see. I smile to think that I am only a speck of both particle and light left behind them.

Both Sonia and Gil visit me in my dreams, but they have never explained the mystery to me.

I met Gil while I was still a student in medical school. Gil was at the Atomic Physics Institute of Bucharest. He was from Transylvania and he convinced me to establish my practice in Cluj after finishing school. For both of us, it was love at first sight. I didn't think twice before I decided to follow him. I would have gone with him to the end of the world.

Like Sonia, I sometimes think about the unknowns in the equation of our existence, and about the random events.

If a friend of mine hadn't suddenly gotten sick, I wouldn't have had a chance to go in her place to a concert. It happened that Gil had a ticket to that concert too. Our seats were in the same row, close enough to one another. We looked at each other during intermission, and our smiles matched our eyes' glance. We started talking about the concert, and we both also wished the intermission was longer, so we could keep talking. We both mentioned that we would eagerly attend the next concert. "And that was it," as Gil liked to say. We were meant to meet each other at that concert and then be together for life. We met Sonia the same way, on a predestined day. Sonia easily became a part of our family as did Corina, the child we never had.

We spent time with them mostly at our house because hers was most likely under surveillance from the moment it became known that her husband fled the country.

We knew Sabin and Michael only through pictures. I learned though that Sabin, a violinist, wasn't terribly in love with his profession. He was always looking for something new, even to the point of choosing to use a variety of aliases. Only Sonia consistently called him by his real name. He used a different name with every group of friends.

Between the pages of her journal, Sonia preserved a greeting card that Sabin had sent her for her birthday during the first year he was in America. Under the picture of some red roses were his words, "I didn't look for these roses, but I found them, and I know that you like roses. Don't expect any other words of love because that's all over between us. Happy Birthday, Sabin."

On that same card was her annotation, "Too bad!"

So, she had known all along, she just wasn't able to believe it. This denial affected Corina, too. When Corina visited us, she preferred to play her little keyboard or read from her favorite children's book, The Three Fat Men. At first, I wondered why that book. It was about the adventures of three fat men trying to get slim. It was funny, though, and she enjoyed it. I also found it really. funny. At that time, Corina was not yet enrolled in school, yet she already knew how to read. I think they both tried to keep their minds busy in order to forget some of their own distress.

One day, after we had our dinner, Sonia without saying anything, sat in front of the piano and we were surprised with how much refinement she played a part of Chopin's "Andante Spianato." She turned to us and smiled. We were amazed and gratified by such an unexpected recital. Her face was calm, her eyes were bright, and her characteristic smile played on her mouth. It was like looking at a portrait on a living room wall.

CHAPTER 27

Resilience!

"I arrived in America on New Year's Eve, 1987, with two suitcases, an eight-year-old girl on my tow, and nothing else. However, I must add also, my dreams of a better life for my family, reunited – finally – in one place. My American dream. Then the dream was turned into a nightmare. Less than one year after my arrival, I was facing an ugly divorce and fighting for custody of my son.

I was not used to being defeated. I thought that only weak people lost battles. I did not want to give up, and at times I felt panicky.

I felt like, I had fallen from the sky into a new world that put me to a test that I was not at all prepared for.

I didn't speak the language. I never imagined that the inability to communicate could have such a strong and debilitating impact on a human being. The isolation I was experiencing was unbearable. I realized that the English I had learned back home was less than satisfactory. The turmoil I was in, made me forget not only the English words I had recently learned, but sometimes even the old Romanian ones. I was left without words to express myself. And the words I needed were a whole new vocabulary of despair, that I had yet to acquire.

Americans talked very fast and used a lot of slang, making most encounters truly intimidating.

Everything was so foreign to me; even my husband was not the man I thought him to be. Nevertheless, I had to find work and make a living because I couldn't depend on my husband for anything.

171

I could not envision the future. Some days I wanted to vanish without a trace or to be blown out like a candle in a relentless wind. But running away from difficulties was never really my strategy. I had to prove to myself that no matter how relentlessly the wind blew against me, I would prevail.

This is when one of Gil's wise sayings came to my mind,

"Heaven doesn't give a man more than he can carry."

I wondered if heaven had forgotten to stop adding more.

Both Neli and Gil had said they saw in me a will of steel. I had to find that will in me again and hold on to it tightly, for the sake of the children. I was at the end of my rope…

Suddenly, I heard chirruping like two little birds, my beloved children. I hadn't heard their happy chatter for a long time. But now it came like a miracle, reminding me of my great responsibilities. They were my reality; they were all that mattered. First was Corina's voice, clear as a little bell, saying,

"Mommy, do you know that I miss you even when I am in school? I can hardly wait to come home and see you." How could I have dismissed that?

Then Michael came to me holding a card in his hand. It was my first Mother's Day in America. They had both drawn their little hands on the card as their signature. It was an award from them, declaring me the most wonderful of mothers. It was the perfect cure for my broken heart. Truly, their love was the salvific miracle that dissipated my dark thoughts like the sun burns off fog. Their voices and their love pushed me out of my despair. They gave me a reason to fight and to survive.

I started working, walking three miles to work on weekends when there wasn't public transportation. I never wept. I was glad that I had a place to work and the good health to walk. I chose to work weekends because I was paid extra, and I need the extra. I was finally free. But this freedom was totally different from the freedom of escaping from a communist country. This one burst from my inner self. It helped me confront rain, snow, and cold when walking to work. It helped me look far ahead and to see past obstacles. I was a new woman. I had been reborn and was given the gift of resilience".

***

When I read and reread these thoughts of Sonia's, it feels like I'm watching a good friend run the steeple-chase. I am ready to cheer her on and support her. "Bravo! Bravo, Sonia, you are a winner! All of the others are behind you, don't look back!"

We knew each other for a long time, Sonia and I.

Even though she is not around anymore, I still like to think about what she would say when I have my own moments of frustration. When confronted with a problem, I remember how Sonia would close her eyes halfway, and rummage through her mind for answers before sharing. She always tried to see things from all angles and to find a balance within. She understood the power of forgiveness. She did not believe in hatred, envy, and revenge. She never put herself first, but rather others.

In the cluttered and uncertain years at the beginning of her time in America, her focus was on her children and her career. She even made a joke about it, saying, "When God shared the duties of motherhood, I raised my hand more than once and I have no regrets. I am honored to accomplish those duties. The same with my profession; no matter how many times I am asked, my answer is that I want to be a pharmacist. I like this profession."

I don't know too much about Michael. I did meet him on several occasions when I visited Sonia in America. Even though he is fluent in both English and Romanian, he always chose to answer in English. His sentences were short and often followed by a hard-to-define smile, a smile somewhere between witty and timid. He has Sonia's features except his serene, blue eyes. No wonder his mother called him her "patch of sky."

Corina, of course, I know very well. We became friends, as we often joked, watching those snowflakes turning into water on a window pane, together. It was fun watching those stubborn droplets struggle to push themselves back on the running train's window. With the eyes of a little child, Corina watched them as if they were alive. Later, when she was old enough to understand, Gil explained to her that far from being stubborn, those droplets were just complying with the laws of inertia. So, the mystery was solved scientifically.

Corina was the child we wished we had. After she left for America, we still, remained close. She sent us notes with her grades and told us about the events at her school. She wanted us to be a part of her life as much as we wanted her to be a part of ours. She was an extraordinary child. Her teachers were amazed by her passion for studying. But she would confess to us that there was more than one passion.

"Auntie Neli, I would like to be many kinds," she used to say in her Romanian, already touched by the influence of English.

For Sonia, her children's birthdays were her own holidays. Gil and I had, luckily, caught three celebrations of Corina's birthday before she left Romania. She came into the world at the beginning of summer. Sonia saw this as a great favor from above. She would comment on it,

"I got my little bundle of joy, at the same time, that nature gets its own bundle of the most beautiful flowers. For me it has great meaning."

Corina's first birthday in the U.S. brought a great sadness to us. At that time Sonia didn't have access to a phone, so she wrote us a detailed letter about that day.

"I wish my little girl had had a birthday filled with happiness, as she did when we were still in Romania. Her birthday falls on Father's Day, but we did not celebrate that in Romania, and had not planned to do so here, either. She has turned 8.

Blessed with Twice the Freedom

She invited some of her friends from school to share a strawberry cake that I made from scratch. Here it was not a problem to get the ingredients. Remember last year, how lucky I was to have you bring me the strawberries just in time? As always, Mariana came to our rescue. But this time, having plenty of strawberries was not enough to make Corina happy. Her father, chose to go to another party for a Father's Day celebration instead. She said,

"Dad, don't you want to stay home on my birthday?"

"Sorry sweetie, I am invited to a party at my work. It is Father's Day, today."

"But you are my father. I am the first to celebrate you. And today is my birthday. And I want you to celebrate with me."

He left without answering. Even though the other children were happy singing and having the eight candles from the cake flickering on their faces, Corina's face only showed sadness.

At the end of the day I said,

"Corina please save a piece of cake for your father, you know how much he likes strawberry cake."

"Mommmm?!!!" she cried. "What??!!"

Little by little the children understood. Mom and Dad were running in opposite directions. Sabin preferred to call the directions "parallel" so that the parents' separation would sound less negative to the children. But the children did not understand "parallel." They did understand, though, that there was nothing they could do to fix their broken family.

Corina stopped asking Sabin questions. Even as a little child she was tough on him, but now she withdrew. Michael however, persisted. "You know, Dad, if somebody hurts Mom, they will have to deal with me."

Sabin was annoyed. He replied," What do you mean?"

I was surprised by Michael's concision. "I mean what I say," he responded.

Sometimes their attempts to make sense of our new normal, made

175

me feel uncomfortable. One day, Corina stood in front of Sabin and asked,

"Why don't you love Mom anymore? Don't you see how beautiful she is?"

He didn't look at her, but I did. I looked, into her glassy eyes, drew her aside, and said, "Maybe your mom is not worthy for love… maybe she has to beg for it?"

"No, neither thing is true. He doesn't treat you right."

"Honey," I said, "Don't worry too much about it. I have your love and Michael's love and that means everything to me. Let your father stay in his world; don't push him to come back into ours. One day he may want to return but it will be too late. Unfortunately, these kinds of things happen. And believe me it is not your fault at all."

It was hard for them to understand but in the end, they did, and there were no more questions for Dad.

As the days passed, we tried to not get in each other's way. I wish I could have moved out. However, I had only two choices; either be homeless or live in a shelter. We had come to America to have a better life, but we were restricted, for now, to those two dreadful choices.

I had to think practically. I had to be on my own. I started with a few hours a week as a pharmacy technician, based for the time being, on my Romanian pharmacist license.

Then one day, Sabin brought some work home for me from the company he was working for. For that work I didn't need English. These were electronic pieces that had to be assembled according to a certain design. Every piece from that panel carried out a specific function, therefore they had to be placed correctly. I was happy to do it. It cleared my mind. I wondered what piece was misplaced or missing in Sabin's panel. There might have been more than one.

At the end of a few months, I was paid about eight hundred dollars. It was my first big payday in America. I was so proud and happy. However, I never saw a penny of the money because Sabin

Blessed with Twice the Freedom

took it and put it into his account. Unfortunately, when tax time came around, he also refused to file as a family, so I was asked to pay taxes on money I never saw. I knew very little about taxes, but my American friends made sure I understood the IRS. There was no room for bargaining with the IRS. I had to borrow money from my generous friends Lee and Gary – who never accepted my repayment – to pay the IRS.

Before I knew it, our first summer had come. The time for vacation was not far away. Sabin prepared his car for it. I learned that he would take only the children on this vacation, that there was not enough room for me. My mother didn't know anything about my drama so far. I kept everything hidden from her. She wouldn't have been able to endure it. Back home, he considered my car, solely his own. Anyway, they were ready to go to Lake George, which I had heard was a beautiful vacation spot in New York State.

Corina was not happy to leave me home alone. She offered to stay at her teacher's house during my few hours of work. But Sabin packed her up and pushed her into the car. She cried.

I stared at the car as it left, unable to wave.

Corina called me every day when she was away; she could hardly wait to come home. I, too, felt very lonely without the children. I could hardly wait to have them back.

The day they returned was Sabin's birthday. I tried to prepare a somewhat festive meal for the occasion, but he didn't even look at it. And instead of a thank-you, he made a quick rejection of it. "You didn't have to," he said.

"I know that," I said. "I did it for our children; they might like to celebrate."

He had no comment. He was in a big hurry to leave because he had a "business affair" to go to. Let him go, then, to his affair. I had my own affairs to take care of. My first affair was to learn English. I was lucky to be around Americans, even if only a few hours a week. I could learn English at work better than from a book. I enjoyed working with those people and I learned more English every day. I was also learning about American pharmacies. I knew that one day I could be a pharmacist again.

My first contact with an American pharmacy was an extraordinary event. It seemed that not only had I passed over the Atlantic but also through a tunnel of time. The concept of pharmacy on the two sides of the Atlantic was radically different, almost as different as heaven and earth. They had only one thing in common – the healing power of the human body.

I was fortunate to work with wonderful people. Sabin had said that it would be hard to make friends and that Americans did not like foreigners, but that was never true for me. The two pharmacists, and the two trainee students, all became my good friends. From them, I learned a lot of things, especially words pertaining to my new world and my daily life. They say that a language is learned more easily if one is immersed in it. That was true, my English was learned and mastered from among the Americans.

Seeing my eagerness to learn, the pharmacy manager brought me information about getting my American license in Pharmacy. I took a look at it, and didn't let it overwhelm me. Instead I tried to remember some old Romanian sayings of encouragement. First my Grandma came to my mind. She used to say to me, "Always follow your dream closely and don't let it out of your sight, otherwise it could fly like a butterfly from you, and disappear faraway."

I knew that it was a long road ahead of me and not an easy one. Great changes in my life had hit me once, but I did not let them beat me down.

My age was not very much in my favor, but I ignored it. Inside I felt younger and I nourished that feeling. I had to think like a student again. When I first stepped into an America pharmacy, I looked around on the shelves and found some drugs that had the same names they had in Romania. I was so happy! It was as if I had found old friends. Before I left Romania, I had never imagined that such a simple thing would be my first bit of happiness in America.

CHAPTER 28

Is There Still a Great Moment?

Throughout Sonia's diaries I have enjoyed her many dialogues with my dearest Corina. I found fewer dialogues with Michael, though, because he mostly grew up with his father. His sister, however, asked enough questions to make up for the them both.

One might wonder how a little girl could come up with questions so full of significance on her own. We called her a prodigy because she really was one. I read a page of their conversation, and I go back and read it again. To this day, her voice is still vivid in my mind. One such conversation took place shortly after they arrived in America. It might have been 1988.

"Mommy, very often you told me that we were waiting for a great moment to come. Are we still waiting for it?"

"No, Corina we aren't, it is over. It was much different than we expected. Yet, we can still call it great, because we get to be with Michael."

"But why doesn't Daddy want to live with us anymore?"

"I really don't know. One day we might find out his reason, but probably by that time neither the question nor answer will matter. So, let's not bother with that now."

"Mommy, let's go back to our house in Romania."

"We don't have a house there either. But please come here and look in my eyes and listen: I promise you and Michael that we'll have a house here and we'll call it Our Very Own House. You know I never make a promise without keeping my word. Do you remember what I used to tell you and Michael when you were given chores? Remember that Romanian saying? 'A promise given becomes a clean, clear duty.'" But as I expected, Corina had a question to clarify my Romanian saying,

"But could a promise also be unclean?"

"Yes, it could, when you don't keep your word."

"I know what you mean; Daddy's is dirty, isn't it?"

"Let's have a clean-clear promise now of not talking about Daddy's promise."

I was trying to dodge a subject that was too difficult for kids to understand. However, children don't want to be left out or have their opinions ignored.

One afternoon, Corina and Michael had two friends from school over. Just like us, they were new in America. They came from India, a country even further away than ours. I enjoyed seeing them play and laugh, busy with children's things. They were exactly my children's ages and I noticed their similar interests. The boys were talking about science. The girls were taking care of dolls. I met their loving parents who were also happy to have my children over in return.

One day, Sabin entered the room like a triumphant rooster and almost stumbled on the children sitting in a circle down on the floor.

"Hey, you, what are you doing?" he asked, complacently.

Before the others could answer, the little girl, Aadrika without looking at Sabin and somehow in an angry tone said,

"I don't like you, because…" and she paused for a few seconds, "you have two wives."

While the other children looked down quietly, I was afraid of what would follow. The blame would fall on Michael who dared to let that part of the family secret out. Aadrika was right. Our marriage was a little too crowded and I had to step out of that crowd. The simple paper of a marriage license cannot keep a husband and wife together. In the end I wish our marriage could have been torn apart as easy as ripping up that document.

Unfortunately, our divorce took a long time to finalize.

To my surprise, Sabin said nothing back to her, but instead left the room like a scolded dog with its tail tucked between its legs.

The children resumed their play as though nothing had happened. I am sure Michael heard more about it when he was alone with Sabin. This was one incident of many that were hard to forget and hard to heal. Michael and Corina went through counseling and therapy for a while.

My work schedule and many other responsibilities prevented me from getting counseling. Instead, I had to unravel the tangled things on my own. I had one single word in mind: survival.

My healing was to go back in time and rummage through my old Transylvanian memories that I had kept enshrined in my heart. I found everything there: my grandma's great words from her simple prayers, my father's wisdom and subtle understanding, my mother's unshakable calm in the face of distress, and my grandpa's philosophy of generosity. He would say, "Give and you shall receive tenfold." And my Transylvanian fields were there to teach me endurance. I realized that I was not alone and that I had nothing to fear. An unseen hand miraculously helped me either to get up or to keep me from falling. I was frequently asked,

"How did you do it? What did you do to succeed?"

"I don't have an exact formula, I just did it," I would explain. "Success and failure are part of life. I don't look at success as an event but as a process. Very often I use music to match the kind of day I'm having. Rough events soften at the sound of music. I cannot imagine a deaf world or having the music locked in my brain so that nobody could hear it. Today I am longing to listen to Rachmaninoff. Nothing fits my feelings better than the murmur of his Cello Sonata in G minor. Sometimes I like to read Rainer Maria Rilke or Rabindranath Tagore. Their deeply reverberating words push worry out of my mind for a while.

"Or I would take a paintbrush and play with colors or take a simple walk in a quiet place. All of this, lets me get caught in beauty's subtlety so I can ignore the things that seem hard to solve, at the moment. I challenge myself to explore new things, letting time unwind old problems. In difficult times, you must let go of tensions. My grandmother used to say, 'Time heals and unravels everything.' I've found a lot of truth in that."

Eventually, time unraveled to me that the abyss between Sabin and me started with a fissure from the time of our children's births. In his opinion, I was too devoted as a mother. He was right, I had to fill in and compensate for his absences. I didn't have time to coddle a man who wouldn't walk on his own. My kids came first. So, he looked elsewhere for support, over, and over again, using his smooth tongue and gentle face.

My greatest disgust wasn't with what he did in the three years we were apart, but with what he did when we lived under the same roof.

When Michael's seizures reoccurred, Sabin's escapes did too. He would claim to have more rehearsals that all ended later than usual. Then there was a new affair. For him, Michael and Corina were problems, but for me they were treasures.

One night before bed I read a story about a wild gosling that had a broken wing. It was late fall and the geese had to prepare for their departure to warmer climates. As though they were at a family council, the geese decided that the mother goose should not leave the wounded gosling alone. Both my children were emotionally touched. Corina, as always, quickly found something to say about it. "Oh, Mommy that goose was like you, a good mom."

"I am glad that the goose was like me and not me like a goose," I replied.

Then they went to bed at peace, knowing that the gosling would not be left alone. They fell asleep right away. However, I sat up, thinking about the gosling and the mother goose. It was the mother's

Blessed with Twice the Freedom

instinct not to abandon her offspring, but to take care of it. In addition to that same instinct, human beings are given the ultimate gift: a conscience. But what happens when one uses neither instinct nor conscience?

CHAPTER 29

Terrible Means Terrific in Romanian

"Another great opportunity in our favor came through Corina's lucky streak. She got into a class with a teacher who was absolutely heaven sent. Lee O'Neal, Corina's teacher, and her husband Gary, were destined to be our friends much like Gil and Neli in Romania. We needed to belong to a family after being excluded from ours. At the time of our first beginning in America, the O'Neils' generosity and affection reawakened our love and our will to hope for the future.

One weekend we were invited by Lee to meet her family.

When we arrived there, I was in awe. For the first time I was seeing a house like in the American movies. It was like looking at a glamorous film. My command of English, however, was" too weak to convey the overwhelming of the house's impression on me. I said, "Wow, what a house! All the rooms look like restrooms!" What I meant was "Your elegant house is like a vacation mansion." Lee, thankfully, understood what I had been trying to say rather than what I said.

After all, when I first met her, I had said, "Oh, Mrs., you are a terrible teacher! Corina talks about you so much at home and she loves you very much." "Terrible" in Romanian means "terrific." Lee smiled kindly, then too, knowing that I must have meant the opposite. That was the way our lifelong friendship started. Lee and

Blessed with Twice the Freedom

Gary became the family we were craving for.

It was Sabin who dropped us off at their home after receiving their kind invitation. As usual, he left and went about with his own business. I spent all afternoon with Lee, and I managed, in my broken English, to confess to her everything I was going through. I could see that American people were totally different than those described by Sabin and his family. Lee and Gary could hardly believe Sabin's perfidy. From that moment on, Lee and Gary decided to help us in any way they could. With their kindness in mind, they surprised me at the end of the summer with a party on my birthday. Lee invited all of us and a few of their friends to celebrate my first birthday in America. I was 47.

I remember the beautiful gifts I got from them. The presents were wrapped in beautiful paper, the likes of which I had never seen before. When opening the gifts, I was very careful not to rip that paper. Instead, I wanted to save it, by folding it carefully, to keep it as a part of the gifts. The Americans looked curiously at me as I neatly folded the wrapping paper. I am sure they had never seen something like that either. As in Romania, I tried to recycle it.

We would remember that day and talk about it for many years to come.

By this time, Sabin and his family started to worry. They knew that my finding emotional support might be just the "flip" I needed to get me back on my feet again. They were right; the O'Neals' friendship stirred my determination to stand up for myself. I imagine that in the Cătușan family council this was their first concern.

The tension at home grew each day. Every morning when the children were still asleep he started calling me out, like one would rebuke a servant, for not doing the job right. He didn't want any witnesses, so he did it before the children were up.

"Please pay your part of the rent or out!" As he said the word "out," he would point at the door.

The first couple of times it happened, I just stood there, speechless.

185

I could not find the words to say. Finally, one day I found the courage to speak up.

"You are not reasonable. Don't you remember all the unpaid debt you left behind when you fled Romania? I paid it all as if it were mine. Don't you think that you owe me that? I didn't ask to come to America. You didn't tell me anything about your intention to not return home. Don't you think that you have a responsibility for the fact that you brought us here? Is this a better life for our children? Corina was taking piano lessons at home and now you tell me piano lessons are a luxury. You are a musician. You should be the one to help her follow in your footsteps." Not that I would want to have her follow in his actual footsteps." Why did we come here? What was your reason? Please tell me."

He didn't answer any of my questions. Instead, the next day he started up again with the demands and the threats. I knew already the entire repertoire. I knew that the best thing for me was to move out, but I had no place to go. I was in the middle of nowhere. Also, for some reason – and it is hard to explain – I held out hope. But I noticed that he was no longer wearing his wedding ring. I was still wearing mine. Clearly, he was planning the divorce.

For almost ten months now, I had been hiding the truth from my mother. I was afraid that the tough reality I was going through would have been too much for her to bear. But I couldn't postpone it forever. Besides my mother had always been my confidante at the decision points of my life. I could always look to her for the best advice, even when we both had nothing left other than our beliefs and our faith. We both believed in a better tomorrow, no matter how harsh the present. I needed to hear that from her once again and I could no longer keep the imminent divorce a secret from her. My attempts to change Sabin were over, as was my time of despair. I could not lie to her. She would have heard it in my voice, which is why a phone call was the right way to deliver my news, even though overseas phone calls were forbidden. I dared to call her when Sabin

Blessed with Twice the Freedom

was not home. It was only this once. It was a must. I needed to hear her voice.

I knew that she wouldn't be crushed by my story, if I cited her stoicism and I was right. She did not say, "I told you so." She never claimed to have all the answers, or the final say. Even though she was at first more than shocked, the next moment she was looking into how to help me. Right away, she assured me that nothing of what had happened was hidden from God.

"He has a reason to let you go through all these tribulations, so in the end you can be delivered from Evil, as our daily prayer says."

I understood what she meant, and I felt an enormous sense of relief. Nothing calms an injured child more than a mother's hands tending the wound. She reminded me that the right people, who came miraculously to my rescue out of nowhere at exactly the right time, was a sign that I was not forgotten. Then with trembling voice, she said, "My dear child, my heartfelt prayers shall be with you." She asked me why I had delayed telling her this news.

"You know me." I said. "I didn't want to give up on my marriage. Instead I tried to offer him chance after chance to redeem himself. But I am still looking for the truth."

My mother didn't wait long to reply, "I shall pray for the truth and only for truth. For now, make sure you take care of yourself and the children. You gave this man too much time and too many chances to find his lost soul. Please do not wait in vain anymore. I wish I had known all of this when it began."

I had been wrong to think that my mom wouldn't be able to handle my bad news at her age. As soon as I heard her words, I felt stronger. After that we communicated strictly by mail that I had her send to Lee's address, so, as to make sure that the letters were not intercepted – Sabin had gotten into the habit of opening my mail.

I learned that my mom had started a six-week fast and prayer, to force the truth to come out. It gave me a great feeling of safety that I was not alone anymore. The last week of her fast coincided with the week of American Thanksgiving. She didn't plan it, but that was the way it happened.

For Thanksgiving, we were all invited to the O'Neals. My children and I were delighted to spend such a holiday with an honest-to-goodness American family, whose traditions were rooted in the beliefs of the first settlers. It was an honor for us to be with them.

Lee and Gary had hoped that Sabin would someday join us at their home, but it never happened. Corina insisted that Sabin spend Thanksgiving with us, but he told her he, unfortunately, had a conflict. He had plans to go hunting with his friends. But here's how the truth came out:

The children finished their homework and had supper. Michael went to spend time on his computer in his bedroom. Corina on the other hand, was on the bed in our bedroom preparing her Zuzu doll for sleep. She noticed her father hiding the portable phone under his vest as he went down to the basement, and she brought it to my attention. I picked up the extension in the kitchen and turned on the speaker. The three of us could now hear Sabin and Stacy's conversation. He, with a low voice, so not to be heard by us, and she, giggling from the other end of line, were making plans for the "hunting trip." At the end of their conversation I said, out loud, "Good bye." They were stunned. The truth had been unveiled!

He came in furiously, blaming Corina. "This is your fault; don't you see what you have done?" That was his style he always blamed somebody else for his own mistakes. Without looking at him she firmly responded, "The fault is yours and not mine."

I wanted to be alone. I went to the bathroom and locked the door behind me.

I stared to myself in the mirror after I learned the truth. An unexpected inner peace rushed over me and I could see it in my eyes as I looked in the mirror. It was weird at first, but then it was a relief. I was at the end of my long fight. Even the stress that had almost broken me down had subsided.

I began to take refuge in music, a lot of music, as if there were no other sounds in the world. I let what was left of that stress dissipate amongst musical notes.

Sabin and my broken, unfixable marriage were totally removed from my agenda.

I was lucky that Anthony, one of the pharmacists I was working with, was also fond of music; he himself played the piano. I also learned that he had a great collection of classical music. Anthony was born in Italy, but he came to America as a child. He fell in love with Corina as soon as he met her and was happy to learn that she had taken piano lessons in Romania. Corina was happy to meet somebody like Anthony as well. To show her respect and admiration for him, she gave him a recorded piece of music she had learned to play back home. It was Beethoven's "Fur Elise," a very well-known piece of music that most beginners play. Anthony learned that we were as fond of music as he was, but the music was not at our fingertips. He didn't wait long until he bought a radio-cassette for his new little friend as well as a pocket cassette player for me.

Corina couldn't have been happier, and neither could I. Every day, he would give us a new cassette to listen to. That music helped me to regain my strength and then to heal from the pain of my bitter ongoing divorce.

My favorites were Mozart and Beethoven. I never found such a healing effect in music before. Especially in the morning, I listened to Mozart's music. Some say that his quick notes can reinvigorate the brain.

His Eine Kleine Nachtmusik always reminds me of the last days of that winter, with its snow melting away. A warm sun shone through the window of our bedroom, in the afternoon. We could hear a song heralding spring in the water droplets hurrying down the eaves. It gave us hope. I like to think of Mozart wrapping himself up in such a light and listening to the gentle music of the raindrops.

I felt the unfairness of the last part of his life, of his death, of how he was thrown into a common grave among the poor and unknown. Though he had no place of his own on the earth to rest, he was given all of heaven through his everlasting music. He was a rich man who left behind a wealth of music. His grave does not speak to his true value. But whose grave does?

One day, Mozart was asked, how could he compose such great music? He answered simply, "The music was in my mind, my duty was just to deliver it." And he did that like no other.

On the other hand, Beethoven let his music go into the depths, where his pain could softly vibrate. Nobody before him could dress suffering in such a heavenly robe as he did. Beethoven began to lose his hearing when he was still young. At the end of his life he was cut off from what he treasured most of all, sound. Nevertheless, the music inside him was heard by the ears of his soul. Because of his deafness he was a loner, and sometimes mischievous children would mock him. Just the thought of it makes me sad. Some days I could only listen to Beethoven.

These titans didn't let the vicissitudes of life stifle their creativity. Instead, hardship inspired them. They created music of incomparable beauty. More than that, their music soothed the hardships and broken hearts of others like me. I was ready for a life without Sabin. I had a feeling of relief. I didn't stumble anymore over his rigid and nonsensical rules.

I was a pharmacist in Romania, and I knew that no study would be too much or take too long if I could become a licensed pharmacist again. I had my degree, and I just had to figure out how to make that degree apply here in America. As they say: first things first. I started with English. I couldn't study at home. I didn't like that house at all, but it was not just the physical house itself, it was the tension. So, I found a secluded place within walking distance on the bank of something called Steel Creek. It was an open space, a clearing, with greenery all around. Nobody could see me from any of the sides, only from above. The best part was the pleasantly noisy little

Blessed with Twice the Freedom

waterfall across the stream. In a world of hostility, this place became my sanctuary. I could hardly wait for each day that I was able to go there.

Against the hush of the waterfall, the birds chirped and flittered about. I didn't know if they were looking at me as an intruder or if they were cheeping, "Welcome!" Soon enough we were accustomed to each other.

I had my routine, which I respected as a ritual. I brought Anthony's mini-cassette player with me, so I could listen to a piece of music before I started studying. It was Trumpet Concerto in D by Leopold Mozart, father of the great Amadeus. That's what I would always listen to first, because to the sobbing sounds of its rhythms I could add my own, if I had to let them out. The music, the waterfall, this was my safe heaven.

A thick, low branch that had been bent by a storm served as my chair. Next to it there was an older tree that I could lean comfortably against while studying or admiring the sky.

My children were amazed by my progress in English. I almost knew my English book by heart. Learning a new language in one's late 40s can be a challenge, but for me it was delightful. This is not to say that English grammar never gave me headaches! I was too used to Romanian's rules and when I was tired, the Romanian rushed in. When taking a break to look up to the sky, to try to connect the word sky, with all that pertains to it – its color, its immensity – it took a while before I could spontaneously say "sky" instead of the "cer."

I knew that in time, I should be able to master my new language and then both the word and the image of what it represents, would arise in my brain at the same moment. At first there was a gap in between, just as there is between thunder and lightning. But my great desire to get out of a deaf and dumb world, as I used to call it, helped to bring that gap to a slit and then to no gap at all. I was finally able to communicate again...

Unfortunately, there was more thunder at home. After the

"hunting" incident our clashes were more frequent and sometimes even violent. Corina started putting a chair in front of the inside of our bedroom door at night. I often stumbled on that chair but never asked why she did it. I assumed that she wanted the old door closed.

One morning, before the children woke up, Sabin ordered me again to leave the house. His eyes had a bizarre look and words I had never heard before bursting out of his mouth. The previous day, he had actually threatened to kill me. I hadn't called the police because the children were just outside, and if police came to the house they could have been scared. But that morning it was clear his anger had not yet dissipated. His deep voice, deepened further by the usual hoarseness of early morning, sounded even scarier. He said, "Do you know that yesterday you were a step away from death? Do you know that?" He emphasized the question as if it was difficult for me to understand the Romanian language.

"Why, please tell me the reason?" I responded.

Without looking at me and in the same rumbling voice said, "I don't know why, but I feel like killing you. Disappear! I don't want you in my sight."

In the midst of this Corina cracked the bedroom door open, pretending she was thirsty. She came to me and hugged me tightly, and then looking into his eyes, begged him, "Please do not hurt my mom; I have nobody else in the world." She was crying. Sabin was more than furious that Corina had witnessed his threat to me. In the same rough voice, he demanded that Corina to go back to sleep. But who could sleep after assisting such a moment?

I told my co-workers at the pharmacy about the threat, even though I was pretty sure that it sounded more serious than it really was, that it was just to scare me out of the house. They, however, felt that it was indeed serious and shouldn't be ignored at all. Not to frighten me more, but to make me aware, they told me how some people do lose their minds and commit all kinds of unpredictable acts. They were worried about my safety and helped me find and visit

Blessed with Twice the Freedom

some support groups. I even visited a domestic violence shelter with Lee, not to move in, but to see that I was not alone. But above of all they helped me find a lawyer.

"Where there is faith there is no perishing." I remember this saying from both my parents. It became a shield for me: I still believed that I was a favorite of heaven.

Then it was December 6, 1988. Our first year in America was ending and so was my marriage. For Romanian children, December 6 is St. Nicholas's Day, a forerunner to Christmas Day. That morning the children were looking for gifts in their shoes, and they found them full of candies. It is something similar to the tradition of a stocking. I followed the Romanian tradition that year in hopes of bringing some smiles to their faces. It was a year that had brought such sadness to all of us, especially to them. They didn't understand what was going on with their parents. I was still with the children counting candies when Sabin let me know in an official tone that somebody was looking for me. That somebody was an official document server, who handed me divorce papers. Sabin had taken the first step. Triumphantly, he looked for my reaction. To his surprise, I received the papers unemotionally, telling him that my lawyer would be taking care of things. He couldn't say any more than two words,

"What lawyer?"

He didn't know that one of the best lawyers in the state had taken my case pro bono. My mother was right. God had not forgotten me.

Shortly after I had to learn how to get to the courthouse by bus; I didn't have a car yet. But for my first appointment with the lawyer I got there by cab. She would often mention that she had never had a client get to her office by cab. But now she did! Anthony, my pharmacist friend, had called a cab to the pharmacy to take me for the first time to meet my lawyer, whose office was in another town.

Sabin was the plaintiff and I, therefore, was the defendant. It was so strange; two Romanians who had waited three years to be together were getting divorced.

My first day at the courthouse, I approached the doors timidly, but afterwards I got used to it. My English was not yet strong enough to defend myself in the courtroom. My lawyer, Julia O'Day, well-known for her devotion to the truth, had to get a translator in order to represent me. She found Mr. Moraru, who over the years became not only an American citizen but also changed his name to Mr. Miller. He was a very nice man and had a job with the church. He had an accent when speaking Romanian. He stood close to the stand to be able to hear and understand me and vice-versa. I listened to his translations carefully to insure, that I was being heard and understood correctly.

In the end, the court decided that our children should be with their mother and their father would pay child support. But Sabin didn't stay defeated for too long. He got another lawyer. Then he put pressure on our eleven-year old to go back to court and ask for a change to the order. Sabin promised Michael a computer for his service and convinced him that I wanted to kidnap him and bring him back to Romania. Michael still needed special care and he and I were both in America to obtain that, but facts didn't matter to Sabin. Then, as if to drive this point home, Michael had another seizure. Nevertheless, the court respected the wishes of the eleven-year-old child to reside with his father and to see his mother and sister every other weekend. My sorrow was not as great for not seeing Michael every day, as it was for the threat to Michael's well-being. We were dragged back into court, along with a cohort of witnesses. Even Michael's school teachers came to plead on his behalf that he needed special care; however, the computer won.

As if it wasn't enough to split the family, Sabin – in his despicable way – had to split what our children enjoyed the most: being together. They had already missed each other for three years being on two continents. This separation came to be not only longer, but deeper. Corina couldn't forgive her father for the longest time after this. In some ways she even blamed Michael for letting himself be foolishly deceived.

Blessed with Twice the Freedom

During the entire divorce we still lived under the same roof. It was the most uncomfortable time of my life! Outbursts were imminent at any moment and without a real reason or prediction.

My lawyer and Lee were looking to find a safe place for Corina and me, but before we found it, Sabin moved out. While I was at work, he and Stacy loaded a truck taking almost everything from the house – including Michael – and moved to a town about an hour away. He informed Lee, rather than me, because Lee was known for being calm in all situations. Still, Lee couldn't believe Sabin's selfishness and what he was doing to Corina and Michael and me. This was the only time I ever saw Lee really, angry. Lee and Gary give me a ride home from the pharmacy that day. They had Corina with them. It was the middle of April and still cold, but the heat was already cut off in the house. It was empty and cold. I had left one empty house in Romania and now I found myself in another. The very next day I got an official notice of eviction, and on that very day Lee found us a new place to live. The landlord was one of her former students. The deal was done without any of the formalities necessary with a lease. Lee and Gary assured the landlord that if there were any issues with the rent, they would cover for the shortfall.

Fortunately, there was no need for that. At the same time, and also through one of Lee's connections, I got a new job in a hospital pharmacy at double the pay. It was hard to believe that the tide was really turning in my favor.

But as my Mother said in one of her letters, "My dear Sonia there is so much to be happy for, all except your son. With patience Michael will come back to you one day. It might take a longer time than expected but you must be patient and never lose your faith." I cut those words out of her letter, and I stuck them on the kitchen cabinet, so I can see them every morning, almost as soon as I open my eyes.

Suddenly one afternoon, I got bad news from the school nurse. Michael had had another seizure. By the time I got there, he was already in the ambulance. They were waiting for me to go to the hospital with them. It was the second time I had to see my child lying on a stretcher without him knowing what happened. If only he knew what was in my heart. Ever since, I have a strange feeling whenever I see an ambulance. I always have a thought for the person inside.

The school also called Sabin at work and he arrived an hour later. Here we were in the hospital, one on each side of our child, speechless. Our child was the only thing we shared, otherwise we were two strangers.

I didn't let this setback cancel all the positive things that were happening for me. I sought balance. I would have liked to take all my son's burdens upon myself and carry them, but unfortunately, he was not living with me and I could not. Michael was spending more and more time alone with virtual friends on the computer. He was bereft of the social skills that are so important to a growing child. One of my friends, who knew our children well, pointed out, "With his problems, Michael could have used four parents, but he had almost none."

She was right. Michael became a loner. He didn't have any friends to visit him or others he could have visited. Nor had he good examples to follow. I wondered how Michael understood his life style. By the end of high school, Michael was anxious to move out from his father's; he had had it. Before he went to college, he moved back in with us. A new court order was not necessary because Michael was already 18.

Sometimes, I would intentionally pass by the house I was evicted from. I liked to do that, so I could measure my achievements by comparing the situation of where I started from to where I was presently. Sometimes I let memories of the past sneak in. I liked to re-encounter the events that shaped my will. It's true; what doesn't kill you makes you stronger.

We were on our own. Without saying anything, Corina and I hugged long and tightly as soon as we stepped into our new place, both of us thinking "no one is going to be asking us to move out of this place." This apartment was beautiful and above all safe. Also, Lee and Gary not only helped us move what little possessions we had, but they brought everything else we needed to settle in. I mean *anything* somebody just starting out would need. We were so lucky to find such kind people. They must have been sent from God. If Michael were with us, I would have asked for nothing more. Our world would have been perfect.

Looking back, I could see that though the times were tough, in the end everything fell meaningfully in the right place. I always liked things I had to fight for. Maybe that was the reason I was granted so many opportunities. That was how I looked at tough times, as opportunities. My only worry was my son. He was too little, and he lacked the experience to turn scars into stars.

Many years have passed since... Many relationships have also passed through Sabin's life, too many to remember. I could compare him to the wind, which rustles and disappears. This last is more than a literary trope. Sabin disappeared from the living. He stepped across to the other side a year ago, suddenly. I don't know if thoughts of regret had the time to rise from his heart; I don't know if he was at peace. Or maybe if he had one more moment to live, he would have used it with the selfishness he was known for.

Words of apology never touched his lips; even when he knew deep inside that he was wrong. He was still fighting between who he was and who he was posing as. I had the opportunity to know both men without fully understanding the mechanism he used to slide so easily from one to the other. He was more than cunning in doing so. When all is said and done, I don't think he knew who he really was. But today I feel pity for him. He was given multiple talents, but unfortunately, he didn't use even one of them to good effect, but only to hinder others.

Happiness is a state of mind that cannot be stolen but can be killed by malice.

Sabin was a musician, and by its nature music is known to nourish the soul. Instead he listened to the music of treacherous sirens and let himself be lured into a deep sea of misery. He never understood the joy that rewards a job well done.

Understanding true joy is a duty which is given with the gift of life. That joy is more than raising the ego up as a trophy, it is to contribute one's own drop to the ocean of humanity and its riches. No matter how vast an ocean is, it is made up of drops; a truth hard to visualize, but still true.

CHAPTER 30

Family Is More Than Blood Ties

"In America a car is not the luxury that it is in Romania. Still, for the first few years I was in America, I relied on public transportation. The buses have air conditioning and, more importantly, they run on time! They feel more like limousines than buses. However, the buses didn't run on weekends where we were living. In good weather I liked walking to work and in bad weather I didn't mind. Americans couldn't understand how I could find walking pleasurable. I recommended that they spend just one day in Romania riding the buses!

Every Sunday morning when I was not working, Corina and I would get dressed and go to church. Our new friends, Ricky and his wife Sandy, would take us to church. I could hardly wait to hear the choir singing "Hosea," my favorite hymn. It means "Salvation." I felt like saying, "Here I am my Lord. Only you can save me." This church was very different from the little one my father served in, but in both I found the same God. He understood my prayers, whispered in Romanian. For Him there is no language or suffering he can't understand. My still-broken English was no hindrance in church. We learned that the American church has not only ears to listen, but also hearts full of love. All our friends — these people who wouldn't cast us out to live on the streets — were a part of it.

When my mother passed away and we had to get home quickly, they gathered around us like a family.

199

We were included in all the American holidays and were invited as family to celebrate with our friends.

Sabin and his family were the only people I knew when I arrived in America. Even though they are not my family anymore, they were the reason that I was forced to re-invent myself. Without the great pain they caused me, I might not have been spurred to succeed so quickly. Sabin had his own pace, which was much different from mine. I had accepted the difference for too long. I had done so unconsciously, so as not to hurt his feelings. But, his ego was larger than his spirit. The latter was always in the shade of his ego. Like a plant deprived of sunlight, he grew frail and spiritless. Like a beetle trying to climb on a wisp of grass, he would fall when there wasn't enough support. He never stood tall on his own and he always found ways to put me down.

We are inclined to believe that heaven forgives everything. But there is still free will, which often drives us to punish ourselves. We ask God to repair what we have willingly broken. We depart from or violate God's great rules, and then blame God for His wrath. God throws bread to us and in return we throw stones. The act of forgiveness at any scale, even that of forgiving ourselves, cannot be fulfilled unless it is followed by a commitment. I realized that Sabin's understanding of forgiveness was discordant with such a principle. That's why he continuously made mistakes.

One Sunday my children and I were invited to the O'Neals. Sabin had forbidden Michael to visit the O'Neals, because he considered them his enemies for the simple reason that helped me. They had helped us out from under his thumb, after all. But Michael's happiness was blended into ours, and Sabin's heart bled with envy.

Anyway, on one of the summer weekends that Michael was with us, we did go to the O'Neals to enjoy their pool. The children were having fun playing water polo when Sabin called to check, only to discover that his son was having fun in the swimming pool. He became enraged. He made the long drive in the scorching heat to

Blessed with Twice the Freedom

the O'Neals, and furiously pulled Michael out of the water. We all stood there in disbelief and Michael was thoroughly frightened. We could only imagine what Michael would endure on the way home, as Sabin could be verbally venomous. The other children stopped in the middle of their game and the rest of their day was ruined.

It was another incident that Corina added to the wall she was building between herself and her father. Although that was a weekend that the court said was mine, Sabin still had the power to ruin it.

Unfortunately, this was not the only incidence of that kind. For example, there's the story of Michael's birthday. My children knew that their birthdays were thought of as holidays. And this one was no different. Or I should say that it was somehow special. It was the first birthday I had been free to celebrate for my child without having a "supervisor" over my personal bank account. I was excited to prepare all the best of Romanian cuisine for this occasion. There were flowers, gifts, and of course all our new friends. Surprisingly, we got a last-minute phone call from Michael telling us in a sad voice that he couldn't make it. I knew right away that it was Sabin's cruel mind that had devised this scheme. My distress in particular, was a source of happiness for him. So, I was sad but not mad. It wasn't fair to create more sorrow on my son's birthday. I just said,

"I am sorry, my dearest, but for now I will just tell you happy birthday on this day which means so much to the two of us. All the presents will be waiting for you and you'll have them on your next visit. And of course, there will be your favorite cake. I love you." I stopped there.

However, Corina added another brick to her wall. And here was Sabin's logic: Michael had to hold the ladder, so Sabin wouldn't fall when trimming trees. Pathetic! "

Enough, Sonia, enough with this man, I cannot read another page about him. I wish Gil and I had our own set of a Corina and Michael. It was not meant to be. We were blessed to be able to adore Sonia's children instead. I often wondered why Gil and I were not able to

201

have children. We would have loved them more than anything. It did not make sense to us that people like Sabin were given the gift of children, but it was not for us to ask why. Instead, as Sonia often did, we continued to count our blessings.

But maybe there was a reason from above. Sabin's "free will" generated a slew of consequences, which were reflected in all the people's lives he touched. He was a great provider of tough lessons to be learned.

When Sabin left the physical world, he left behind a lot of baggage filled with distress for others to handle. I truly believe in the Law of Justice from above. So, did Sonia. She would often mention her father's thoughts on it, quoting him,

"We are given the freedom to choose our way, yet we are responsible for how we choose it. On the journey there are symbolic signs to guide us, so we don't get lost. Cinderella, with the pristine ingenuity of a child, sprinkled ashes on her path in case she had to retrace it. Similarly, a wise man sprinkles good deeds on the road, to keep himself on the right track."

CHAPTER 31

Thoughts Still Lingering in Memory

It seems that Sonia liked this song from the moment she heard it, for the first time, on the plane which brought her to America. Later, she understood its words, and liked it even more. I could see it in her note, one year after...

"Should old acquaintance be forgot, and never brought, to mind?" I heard this for the first time when I first stepped into the New World. Even though I didn't know the song's words, I guessed them and later I translated them and learned them by heart. It was a New Year's song, about the old and the new.

Of course, there was no doubt in my mind, that I would never forget the land I left behind just a little more than a year ago. So, at the beginning of each year I would always drink a cup of kindness to Auld Lang Syne.

"Memories shouldn't be reminders of hardship, but rather impulses to move you ahead." I can still hear my grandmother saying these words.

But today, my thoughts are stuck on some memories of difficult moments. Yet, I should keep close to my grandma advice.

However, the day began apprehensively, not knowing in what kind of spirits it would find us in. Everything felt uncertain. But still, having my children together made me happy and was a big part of my dream coming true. And at school, the children were enrolled

203

in support groups with a counselor whose job was to help the little ones, cope with transition, and sometimes this included the pain of their parents' divorce. It is so unfair to children to be dragged through things beyond their understanding!

One day, when I picked my little one up from the school, she had tears in her. I was very concerned until I heard the reason behind them. She refused to go after school counseling, a program which was set up for children like mine; having a hard time understanding their parents' divorce. She argued:

"Mom, every time, we get new students in the group, and I have to hear their new stories which I went already through. I don't want to hear it again. I want to forget it, mom," And she started sobbing. I tried to console her;

"Don't cry my little bird. You don't have to join the group anymore if you don't feel comfortable". Then I heard the word *healed* coming out of her mouth. Even the word, carries o positive message within, I felt sorrow in it also. Corina shouldn't have to go through this.

For me was different I have heard the same story every day. In addition, I had the tools of a grownup to oppose stress and expect *healing*.

I kept myself busy and live in the present.

I tried to do that even with my children; keeping their mind busy with other things than those coming out of a bitter divorce. I made them feel important. Their English was much ahead of mine. I let them believe that they are my English teachers. I remember how they praised me, that every morning I did a little better on my spelling tests. They got a *job* and they were serious about it.

Already I heard them speaking English when they were playing. I had my doubts that I would ever speak English as well as I spoke Romanian. I was overwhelmed by my fears; I was not young anymore.

Routinely, before they went out the door every morning, they hugged me goodbye. Those hugs would remind me to stand tall all-day long. Then they both moved ahead, carrying their school bags like two little ants carrying their burdens. I watched them with misty eyes until they turned the street corner.

I find myself smiling at one of Michael's questions, "Mommy, are tears the brain's perspiration?"

"Yes, darling, I think they are. When the brain is working hard to find an answer it perspires." And then I thought only to myself; yes, that's right, sometimes we might get drenched. How endearing, to give tears a more pleasant meaning! As I continued to analyze this simile, I decided that Michael really was somehow right. Excessive tension or pain gathered in the brain and the heart dissipate more easily after a good cry. A good cry is called "good" because it clears the mind of the inexpressible. Sometimes I wonder if something in the brain changes physically when you cry or laugh, as do the muscles of the face...

I watched my children going to school every day, their little routine; Michael would make a playful leap before disappearing beyond the school's fence and then the little one, as usual, copied her brother. It made me glad to see that they were still children, even though sadness clouded our home.

"Yes, my dearest Granny, you were right. I should never forget these days. They are a reason not to give up".

After the children left for school today I had an important task on my agenda. One of the pharmacists from work thought that a counselor might help me with my troubled marriage. He also thought that a church might be the best place to look for help. My friend made an appointment for me at a church whose denomination I did not know. It didn't matter to me; all churches serve God. I went early in the morning and had to walk more than two miles to get to this place. The morning traffic was heavy and there was no sidewalk, so I didn't have any other option than to walk in the grass, which at that hour was still thick with dew. If I could, I would have taken my shoes off and gone barefoot, but I didn't want to look strange.

Finally, I reached my destination. First, I stopped at the rectory. A plump blond woman with a cold look in her eyes showed me the way to the counselor's office. I got there a few minutes early. The waiting room was a long, dark corridor. I glanced around without taking a seat. The door opened and suddenly a middle-aged, bearded man stood before me and briefly introduced himself as Scott.

Timidly I entered the room while he held the door open for me. His office was not only darker than the hallway but also colder. It would have been helpful for the people going there in distress if the room were a bit brighter and friendlier, I thought. The gloomy room was not helping at all. It was even more difficult to find the correct English words to describe the problems I couldn't resolve on my own. I didn't know what to begin with, because I was still unsure of when the problems in fact, started.

I knew that the time I had with Scott was limited, so I started at the beginning. I was born in a family where I learned that the truth had to be expressed simply and didn't have to be demonstrated. I was also taught that the truth, a noble gem, should shine by itself – no polishing required."

It was not easy to put all these words together, but I did my best to make them sound understandable. Then I got to the point: "My husband and my son came to this country three years ago…" Then in my broken English I unfolded the most important parts of my story, ending with, "I am going through a terribly hard time. I need help. I am looking to find some good-hearted people who don't owe me anything, yet who would still have mercy on me." At that point tears flooded my eyes. But Scott didn't show any sign of counting himself among those merciful people.

Without saying much, he handed me tissues to dry my tears. Then finally he said, "You must make friends, as many as you can." To me, he sounded like a robot without feelings.

I said, "To make friends is a good thing but I must stand on my own two feet first. Right now, I am at my lowest. My true priorities are my children and my profession, nothing else is more important

Blessed with Twice the Freedom

than them."

He stood up – which I took as a sign that our session was over – and handed me a bill for $35.00. He knew that I took home $75.00 each week from my part-time job, yet he charged me $35.00! My jaw dropped. I couldn't believe it! Thinking that the fee was there to enroll me in a program, a series of sessions, I agreed to another appointment. Unfortunately, the second session was not much different than the first, and he charged me for his services again. I don't remember what words I used to tell him that I did not need any more appointments with him, but I told him. It was not worth it.

My pharmacist friend, Bob, helped me to get set up with a different social service organization run by a different church. These sessions cost more than Scott's. Bob was outraged and picked up the phone to speak his mind. I heard another new word I had to look up in the dictionary. It was "ludicrous." He was right, the fees for these services were ludicrous. Then he concluded, "You tarnish your church's reputation as beacon of hope for souls in distress. Now, please delete that charge, before I go public with this story."

I had never seen Bob so upset. On the other hand, I was sorry for putting him through it. In some way both counselors were right; I needed friends. Anthony and Bob became my first friends along with the two trainee students; Lisa and Michelle. They helped me tremendously. And beyond their and even my believes, we got our pharmacist licenses at the same time. I look back and I don't know how I did it. It was for me as a miracle!

I was lucky that these people came into my life, not because I was looking for friendship but because they had hearts that didn't allow them to see a human being in distress and do nothing.

They cherished the Ten Commandments and applied them daily in their lives. The counselors, however, did not seem to practice the Ten Commandments.

Little by little, though, Corina and I did make friends and America did become our home, because with very few exceptions, the world is full of very good people. And I truly mean that. I began to realize that there was a silver lining to my husband's abandoning me like he did. It made room for the good, kind people of the world to fill my heart and my life. If I had stayed with Sabin, I would only have had room in my life for his moodiness and his complains.

And how could I forget my first summer in America? That was when we met the O'Neals. I remember how impressed I was with their beautiful house. One day, Lee in her soft voice put hope in my mind saying, "Sooner than you think you will have a house of your own." And she was right. In a few years, that dream came true.

Their house was large with a huge in-ground swimming pool that mirrored the blue sky and with the surrounding flowers. It looked like picture of heaven. I had never seen such a house before. All of this lifted my spirits from the ground up. Both my children adored Mrs. O'Neal, the teacher. And as soon as they met her husband, Gary, they became attached to him as well. They missed having a father figure. Corina even made Gary a Father's Day card, and I noticed that Gary put it out on display.

"Dear Gary, I love you so much, that if you asked me to fly, I would try to do it for you."

The O'Neals' son Andy was close to my children's age. They became buddies right away. When the children got together, the entire swimming pool was full of their energy. I have never seen a father take such enjoyment in playing with his little ones before. Gary taught my little duckling, Corina, how to swim. I remembered that Sabin used to go to the pool without his children. Gary and Sabin seemed to be opposites. Lee and I floated on swimming chairs in a corner of the pool, talking and talking for hours.

Lee had a special sense of humor, always graciously displayed. After getting to know her better, I told her that the unambiguous calmness of her thoughts was the secret to her not having wrinkles. She would listen with the same calm that she talked with. Thus, she became my best counselor not only during my hardships, but

Blessed with Twice the Freedom

throughout my life. I found in her to be my best confidante because she had a golden heart.

Sabin had no clue that my first day with the O'Neals gave me the key to many doors which I have since opened. That was the day where my American Journey really started to bring me to where I am today. These were times when money was scarce; we did not have enough to make a living. Because our rented apartment was on Lee's way to school, she would frequently stop to visit with us and to check to see whether we needed anything. She would secretly make a list of things she thought we needed. The next day Gary would bring us whatever was on that list. I couldn't stop thinking about heaven's blessings because Lee and Gary could only have been an intervention from above.

One night, before our first Christmas in America, they brought us a tree and the ornaments to adorn it with. They also brought hot chocolate and cookies. Our children sang carols and enjoyed the goodies. We forgot about all the awful things that had happened to us. We had a joyous, beautiful evening that I will never forget. I still have some of those ornaments and keep them as treasures. It was the first sign of a holiday in a house that otherwise was so sad. It was before we moved out to our new place.

Gary surprised us with a cassette of one of the most beautiful Christmas songs I had ever heard, "The Sleep of Infant Jesus" by Henri Busser. It was a tender song, kind of a lullaby; we all came together around the cassette player to listen. It made me think that there is no other holiday as uplifting as Christmas. The music filled the air with a sound that spoke about the peace hovering over our heads before settling into our hearts. Christmas music, like all religious music was not allowed in Romania. For us, it was a piece of Heaven.

For Corina and myself, that first Christmas in America provided us with the healing that we needed so much. In one single year we had suffered so many traumas for which there was no medicine other than music and gratitude. I remember how moved I was the first time

I heard Christmas carols at work. I had to hide my emotions so as not to appear odd. When I heard "Silent Night," it reminded me of one very particular Christmas Eve in Romania.

I was in college. One of my roommates had a little radio that she got from her relatives in Germany. Emma Froehlich herself was of German descent. With her radio we could catch broadcasts coming from Thessaloniki, Greece. They broadcast the "Voice of America" throughout Europe.

With the door to our room closed, we hid under a blanket and listened to the radio. The song we listened to was "Silent Night."

Listening to music like that was a punishable crime. If we were discovered, we could have been expelled from college. We were so bold back then! We turned on the radio shortly after a team of UTC (Communist Youth Union) went from room to room checking for any *wrongdoing*. They were looking for any signs that anyone might be celebrating Christmas and would have reported anyone who was, but we had hidden *everything* pertaining Christmas until the UTC team was gone.

When, suddenly, my memory made the connection to that long-ago night in my dorm, I was surprised how my memory brought it so clearly back to me. It must have been the intense emotion associated with that music.

No matter how much the Communists tried, they never controlled our hearts. They had a very sophisticated Security Service, always looking for any little cracks in the façade, but it was powerless before the human spirit. I still count the blessings of my being here and being free.

That Christmas my children got more presents than ever before. The presents were not from the stingy Cătușans, of course. They came from our new American family, who spoiled us and who, like us, found joy in giving.

Just before Christmas we were honored by another benefactor stepping in. It was my lawyer, Julia O'Day. She came to help me

Blessed with Twice the Freedom

defend myself from my husband, the plaintiff. To this day I don't know what I did wrong and why I should be the defendant in a divorce proceeding, but I am also no longer interested in knowing.

Julia O'Day was the best lawyer in the area. She charged me nothing to serve my case, but her work value meant a world to me.

I count Julia as one of the many blessings given to me in that first year in America.

Also, our first Christmas in America was surely a time to be grateful. It was perfect. I got that phrase from Lee. Whenever something was pleasing to Lee, she would say, "It is perfect." It is a phrase I began using a lot.

CHAPTER 32

Every Life is a Song

What really made me want to cry was that Sonia's diary contained contributions from Corina. Some of them were clumsy lines of poetry and others were drawings. They were her pure, deeply felt emotions. Oh, my dearest Corina I wish I could have had you back home with Gil and me until the storm was over.

In one of Corina's drawings there was a wounded heart and in another a rose. There were tears dripping from them both. In uppercase letters with what looked like a trembling hand she wrote,

"They are crying for my mom."

Corina had tried to convince her parents to stay together, not understanding what "parallel" lives meant. She was afraid of the family being separated again. She also wrote an awkward little poem on the same sad theme. I keep this poem in my purse like a talisman and I show it to couples I know who are looking forward to having children. As they read the touching phrases of this child's thoughts, I ask them if they are ready for the responsibility of shared parenthood. I read their response in their moist eyes.

I think there should be required classes for parenting, especially for those who show signs of being self-centered; nothing more important than themselves.

Personally, I never met Sabin and I had no desire to ever meet him. I still feel disgust thinking about him, and I don't know how Sonia put up with him for so long. However, at one point, when we were *splitting the hair* on this issue, she had an explanation for her endurance; "until our children were born he was a husband, every woman in the world, would have liked to have. Even he changed, considerably, after that, I still, kept dearly in mind the man he used to be, hoping that one day he might be back. Then, for the sake of our children to have a father home, I have endured more than a wife would decently have. Plus, in a family like mine, of Greco -Catholic believes, a divorce is prohibited." This being told, I understood Sonia reasoning.

Then she would farther argue… "And even if, the past couldn't be changed, somebody shouldn't be stuck in it, but it seems, that I was one of those. For that I have, to forgive myself. Then I turned the wheel at my will. The clarity opened again in front of me allowing me to see far in the future.

I have known from my father many sermons, that one's deliverance comes only by forgiveness. It can untie us from the past and help us move ahead.

No wonder forgiveness, is believed to be, the gatekeeper to Eternity.

It frees one from all the bitter grudges, desire for revenge. The instructive phase; *turn the other chin*, would stop the thirst for a perpetual fight.

Even though the memory diligently sorts out, and stores all the things which touch it, there is a need of consciousness work, to process the artifacts of memory, in order, to cut out and throw away the parts of the past that disturb the present.

Forgiveness is essential to our faith. "Forgive and you will be forgiven" is a common motif in the Bible. I could see that Sonia's faith played a crucial role in her forgiving those who at first sight seemed unforgivable.

Left to fester, revenge can become poisonous and, even when directed at an enemy, can destroy the one who hosts it.

Through our faith we say, "Forgive us our trespasses as we forgive those who trespass against us."

But faith is not just for the frail – as some are prone to believe – just as forgiveness is not just for the naive. So, I told myself if Sonia could forgive, I should forgive too. Those who hold true faith in their hearts never get lost in life or pretend to be someone who they are not. They don't need alcohol or drugs to numb their discomfort or to stir their feelings up. Sonia, often, compared faith to an orchestra's conductor:

"Under its baton, events arrange themselves side by side like musical notes, an adagio, or an andante, brought to a tumultuous fortissimo, without ever losing melodic content".

Finding a melody in every life must be considered art, and truly there is; composers, are great artists.

Now, I can explain to myself and other may too, how in only one decade, Sonia achieved the dream every American would dream of.

She freely and humbly admitted that her success was due not only to her strong determination, and a freedom beyond the freedom of politics, that allowed her to be herself; but all of this under the effigy of faith.

It is true that America is the land of opportunities, but the true happiness given by such offers, is reached only by those who are looking for them with both eyes and heart

I was glad Corina followed on that same path as her mother.

She excelled in everything – in the classroom, on the field, and in the arts as well. I was so proud of her. I can't even describe the pride her mother felt.

That girl, who once blinked at every grace note struck from the piano's keys as she listened to the Appassionata, became a master piano player – and Beethoven's music became one of her favorites. She would bring up feelings of turmoil and peace, struggle and victory, the same way Beethoven had felt them in his heart.

One day, I was amazed, to hear Corina's statement.

"You see, Neli, no matter how strange it sounds, I dare to say, that I was *lucky* to be born in a Communist Country. The hardship, taught me many things.

Pursuing a goal, becomes more avid, when obstacles are in front of its reach, than when it is given for free. It is the beauty of the way of reaching that goal, and the lesson how to get it. That brings the happiness of achieving. I feel sorry for people that look differently to it". I should say like mother, like daughter…

In Sonia's journal, I found her persistently transforming despair into purpose. But I'll let her tell the story in her own words,

"I remember those first day in America … they seemed to be part of a trial, no matter how much subterfuge Sabin cloaked them in.

I knew, that what I needed the most, was patience. I had to find serenity in turmoil. And so, I turned to music. Every day I brought home a cassette of classical music from my friend Anthony, our "musician angel," as we called him after he passed away.

Corina and I would withdraw into the little room that served us as a bedroom. She could hardly wait to snuggle under one of my arm, so I could hold her tightly next to me. Everything in that room was improvised and all around had a temporary look, reminding us, that we were not staying there, for too long.

The cassette player, also from Anthony, was in between us, so we could quietly listen to the music. It was like a prayer.

About the same time Sabin bought a computer for Michael so he could play his Nintendo games. Sabin would do just anything to keep Michael away from us, and that was hard for both of us. Corinna and I would always have our little chats before bed and the music helped us to not feel so alone. Music didn't ask me to look up the notes, in the dictionary to understand it. With music we closed our eyes and could feel at home.

"Mommy, what it is the name of this music we listen to so often?"

"It is the Appassionata, sweetheart."

"Mommy, what does Appassionata mean?"

"How could I explain it to you clearly?"

"Say it in your own words. That is the way you ask me to explain

215

things, isn't it?"

Instead of immediately answering I squeezed her under my arm dearly. Then I started to find my own words.

"The word you would like to know comes from another word: passion. Passion is a strong overflowing feeling that covers the heart and mind at the same time. These musical notes gushed out from Beethoven's heart and mind simultaneously. If I say that you are in my mind and in my heart simultaneously, I mean that there is no way I could love you more."

She was confused by my theory of passion and pointed that out by saying,

"Mommy, but you are in my heart and in my mind more than I am in yours."

"Really?" I said looking at her questioningly.

"Mommy, it is because you are bigger than me."

"You are totally right, sweetheart. Exactly. I will do everything passionately just to see you happy."

"I understand you, and I passionately love you," she said. I wanted to let her understanding of passion rest, but it seemed that she was not done with the subject.

"You know, Mommy, one day I would like to play this music passionately for you."

I answered her first by another squeeze and then I said,

"I am sure you will one day. You already play the piano so well and you love it."

"But, you know, he said that I have to wait until we have the money."

"You mean your father, don't you?" She nodded her head.

"Don't worry about that, sweetie. You know that together with a strong will, passion can always find a way. You know what Mrs. O'Neal says, don't you?"

She mimicked her teacher, "Where there's a will, there's a way."

"That's right; it is the best encouragement, isn't it?"

Blessed with Twice the Freedom

"Do you think I could find a teacher as good as Mrs. Gina Voicu?"

"Certainly, just have a little patience."

"Oh Mommy, I love you passionately," she said again, closing her eyes halfway. It seems that she liked the new word and hadn't exercised the limits of its profundity yet. She repeated,

"Oh, Mommy I love you passionately."

"I know you do and so do I, but we have to go to sleep now. It is late and tomorrow we'll have a lot of things to do".

"I know but please may I ask just one more little, little question?"

"Sure. But this is the last one tonight, okay?"

"Whose music is this?"

"It is ours to listen to now."

"Not in that way Mommy, I mean who wrote it?"

"Then you should say, 'Who composed it?'" I corrected her, and without any further detail I said, "Beethoven."

"Oh, yes Ms. Gina told me that I would be introduced to Beethoven when she was getting ready to teach me "Fur Elise.""

"I remember." I said, smiling. It was funny. Corina had been waiting for Mr. Beethoven to pay us a visit, so she could meet him.

"You see, he visits us very often through his music," I said, with tenderness.

"I know. I was too little then," she said, which made me smile again. That was only four years ago. Four years is more for her than for me, of course. I sighed heavily to signal that we were at the end of our conversation and that I was tired. I guess she didn't understand because she had another little question.

"Where is he now?"

"Corina, darling, he lived long before us and has already left this world."

"Where did he go, Mommy?"

"I wish I knew myself."

That was indeed her last question of the day. A little Romanian rhyme was her sleeping pill.

217

Sleepy little birds to drowse,
Toward their nests guide their flight,
Hide themselves amidst the boughs,
So, good night.

It had once been Michael's too, but he had been given all those gadgets for his computer and had been lured into a virtual world very different from ours. He had forgotten all about the rhyming sleeping pill from his childhood.

Corina fell asleep before the "Sleeping Little Birds" lullaby was over. She must have been tired. I was tired too. I used a lot of energy remembering all the joyful events of the day so that there wouldn't be much room left for grief.

Corina was doing, more or less, the same thing. Her frequent questions were, for her, what the joyful moments were for me. We both had our strategies for dealing with overwhelming emotion. I could not, though, fall asleep as fast as she could. I was left to reflect on passion, not so much its definition as about how it could be lost. I wondered if passion was ever real or just a flash in the imagination.

As I thought of our past, Sabin, my confusion grew. Once, you looked, into my eyes, and said,

"No matter where I would be cut, instead of blood, you would gush out of me" Was that reality or was it a dream? The contrast between those words and what I hear from you today are like night and day. Now we are two strangers with nothing in common but our children. You replaced me with a series of other women. I tossed and turned.

One day, I confessed my bouts of insomnia to Anthony. The next day along with a new cassette he offered me a set of headphones. The music became my sleeping pill. I used them after Corina was asleep. Anthony was right when he said, "You know Sonia, sleep is a prescription from heaven." I learned to bury my questions in my sleep, so that by morning they brought answers.

My questions didn't start with "Why" anymore. They started with

"How."

A torrent of new ideas, followed by new plans, engulfed me. I scrounged up the material I needed and then launched myself into an intense study of both English and the Pharmacy Board exam. The zest of my youth returned. The doors of a new life opened for me…I heard and was inspired by the expression "The sky's the limit."

Anthony made sure I wouldn't get bored with the same cassette and every few days brought in a new one for me. Little Corina enjoyed the music as much as I did. The music delivered us from a world of war to one of peace.

As wounded soldiers we could heal only off the battlefield.

Not long after this, Anthony found a piano teacher for Corina, and Lee offered to pay for her lessons. Another lucky day came when Corina's keyboard was replaced with a real piano. One of Corina's teachers from school thought that his piano, which was only used sporadically by his grown children, would be of greater use to Corina. He noticed that Corina would practice piano, before a school show, on her recess.

Somehow, our gloomy days turned into bright ones. Sometimes I was in a state of total disbelief. I found myself saying, "It must be a dream, it cannot be true." We were not used to getting so much goodness all at once.

Then we learned how to reflect on it. We found that there was even music to help us doing it. It was as if Antony knew how to coordinate the music he gave to us with our state of mind…One day I brought home "Consolation in E Major" by Franz Liszt. After I have explained to my little one, every word of the name if the tape, she concluded;" Like us mommy, doesn't it" I was moved by her thoughtfulness, and felt replying: "That's true my little Angel. Every life is a song with its own rhythm and cadence."

Luckily, our new American friends were messengers from heaven who improved our adagios and helped us to adjust to the syncopation, in front of us.

Anthony was hospitalized a few days before Easter. A few months earlier he had been diagnosed with an aggressive form of cancer and he had been in the hospital many times already. We talked to him on the phone on the day before Easter and promised him a visit the next day. As I used to do on all holidays, I prepared some delicious Romanian sweet bread, and was ready to share it with my American friends, of which Anthony was one. But before getting to the hospital on that special day, we learned that Anthony had been called home earlier in the morning. He never got the opportunity to hear Corina's many solo piano concerts.

I am sure, all the angels of heaven recognized Anthony as one of them; he had been an angel on earth. We were sad at first but then we were comforted by the thought that he would continue to watch us from heaven.

Corina had once sketched a few drawings for him from postcards he had sent us from Italy. He loved Italy, the country of his ancestors, and he would visit every summer. He not only visited, but he also took classes in painting and music, sometimes from very famous masters. He never stopped learning and he was never satisfied with what he had learned – he had to keep going. He was the best example of age not serving as an impediment to learning. His spirit was young well into his eighties. That spirit was reflected in his eyes, which were like two open windows.

When Corina gave him her sketches, I could read in his eyes how touched he was. Close to tears he said, "Corina, I knew that you were talented but not in such a way. Your sketches depict those places better than the postcards themselves. I cannot believe it." Then turning to me, "Sonia you were blessed with a multitalented child. I truly mean that."

I *felt* blessed. The One who had given me this blessing must have known how much I needed to be blessed.

Corina confessed to me later that it was the first time a person's

Blessed with Twice the Freedom

joy in her gift resonated within her. I was glad she got the message: talent is not something one keeps to one's self, it is something to share. It is like a farmer who throws out handfuls of seeds and then reaps the bounty.

We moved ahead slowly but surely. I got my first car and for us it was a big step towards independence. Soon the city bus became just a memory. The very harsh days of our first days in America began to fade.

Corina and Michael began planning short trips on the weekends and they had friends to discuss these plans with. Slowly, we were becoming more American, and we were so happy when it was noticed!

Then I'd get sad at the end of the weekend when I'd have to bring Michael back to his father and wait another two weeks until I could see him again. I knew that my son didn't have the care he needed, and yet I couldn't do anything about it. That indeed was the most difficult thing I had to rise above.

CHAPTER 33

Virtue Triumphs Over Wickedness

"Miraculously, the gate I had been knocking at just a few months ago had opened wide before us. The fear of being put out onto the streets with my daughter was gone. We could finally breathe a sigh of relief.

Lee enlisted so many people to help us! She spread our story through the school and to her many other friends. People I never met before swung by our place and dropped off presents – everything we needed for a new start. I was overwhelmed. Lee's network of churchgoers and true believers made the Church a living edifice for us. People didn't just give us tissues to wipe our tears, but through their kindness they kept our faces free of tears in the first place. Instead of passively watching our struggle, people chose to give us a hand, people we will never forget. I felt a desire to personally thank God for them in His house: the church. Lee introduced me to her other friends, Rick and Sandy, who waited every Sunday morning in front of our house to take us to church, when we could get there only by walking.

Ricky was also a pharmacist. He helped me to get work in a large hospital as a pharmacy technician, based on my pharmacy school credentials from Romania. Then down the road he also helped me work towards getting my pharmacist license. I don't think Ricky's assistance was random: I saw God's hand in it. At the new job I

Blessed with Twice the Freedom

was blessed to earn twice as much as I did in the public pharmacy. And I had extra time to study for my Boards. Moreover, the hospital had up-to-date medical technology, which made studying easier than learning strictly from textbooks.

My desire to become a pharmacist again pushed me ahead through all obstacles. There was so much to assimilate, though. Every day, I would stand in front of a computer not knowing its "language" at all and not knowing enough English either. Sometimes the pressure was unbearable, but I refused to collapse. It was hard work and very tiring, but in the end, I *was* licensed in the U.S.

I learned that in this country every state has laws specific to it in addition to the federal laws it must follow.

Unfortunately, the state where I built my nest was among the states that require a foreign pharmacist to have their last two years of college credit from an American school before applying to take the Pharmacy Board exams. Such a requirement was almost impossible for me to fulfill. I feared moving out of the state and being alone with my little Corina again. There were so many changes lately in my life that I couldn't tolerate even one more. I had met so many wonderful people that I fervently believed that the best people in the world were in this state. I didn't think they could ever be replaced by anyone anywhere else. But that was a very real option - to move out of this state to and into one where I could obtain my license and then move back, hoping it would transfer. I did not like that option.

I had just dispatched the nuisance that was Sabin, but now I had two more obstacles to overcome: my English and the Pharmacy Board exams. Then there was also my age; I was not far from fifty. I, definitely, couldn't do anything about that. The voice inside me was always saying, "Hurry up!" So, I listened.

My strategy was first to pass all the required exams in a neighboring state, and then ask the Pharmacy Commission in my state, to more closely align its requirements with that one. I was lucky, or better said, very lucky. The Chairman of the Pharmacy Commission was

223

truly heaven sent. He accepted my application, which in fact made my plea easier when facing the legislators. Through one of my town's representatives, the legislators learned of my story before I made my plea at the state capital.

My new friend, Ricky, traveled with me to the capital and we appeared in front of the legislative commission.

I remember the imposing legislative office building. I timidly stepped into the Legislative Auditorium and suddenly I had all those lawmakers in front of me. Everything around the room resonated gravitas. Feelings of admiration and respect left me speechless. My eyes moved from one end of the semicircular legislators' row to the other. Across from them there were many rows of people sitting and waiting for their turn to speak. We knew the order we'd speak in by the numbers we had on our tags.

I have always admired good speakers but I myself have always refrained from speaking to big crowds in most situations. I was always self-conscious when it came to delivering speeches. Plus, I had grown up without the freedom of speech. But, finally, it was my turn to state my case. I was taken by surprise. I misplaced my hand-written paper and began to speak freely.

My first words were, "Qui transtulit, sustinet," the Latin motto of the Connecticut state flag, which translates to, "He who transplants us sustains us." I felt that this motto was written specifically for me. Then I argued my case. I don't know if it was because of my accent or the emotion in what I was saying, but everyone paid very close attention to me. I concluded with the old English saying, "Where there's a will, there's a way." I had a feeling that without a doubt my proposal would be accepted and without much debate the law would be changed. And it was!

It was my big victory in America! I shall be forever grateful to the Pharmacy Commission's Chairman and to my town's representative. Without them, this achievement would have been more difficult.

CHAPTER 34

Open Doors to Opportunities

"From beyond the horizon, opportunities morph into dreams and rise up as the sun does. My excitement about my new future built up a great desire in me to be driven ahead. It is something I have never experienced before. Like the legend of the magical Phoenix, I came back to life after being crushed and burned into ashes. Anything is possible in the Land of Freedom, along with a strong Faith.

"She is right, and she proved it," Gil and I commented on Sonia's letter. "Her triumphant voice reveals a new side of her. She is no longer held back by a government or a husband's chicanery." As if she anticipated this assessment, her next line was a response to it: *"There is nothing greater than being allowed to be yourself and not to be afraid of that."*

We were very happy for her but our road to that kind of freedom was not yet paved. The Revolution of 1989 left behind a lot of confusion, everything happened too fast. We still didn't know who was, but we had impression that many of those in power had merely switched chairs. We were still apprehensive. The fear bred into you by the Communist Era cannot be eliminated overnight.

Only a month ago, even a simple gaze towards a comrade, could have been considered political defiance. One could easily be convicted of anything. The Communist Regime had owned us and our rights – freedom and hope vanished. It would take more than a single month to erase all that fear. We were happy about the revolution, but

225

freedom could only come slowly.

As a people, we did not know what freedom was, and it would take us some time to get used to it. At least we were, at last, able to openly talk about it.

Sonia was dealing with her new-found freedom in a free country, at the same time that Gil and I were dealing with freedom in Romania.

We easily let ourselves get caught up in Sonia's optimistic thoughts, which nourished us.

We reflected on her letters and wondered how many people go through life without taking advantage of all of their opportunities. These are the people who complain about having no luck or who blame others for their misfortune. Positive thinking is often the reason that opportunities are realized, while selfish and negative thoughts squelch hopes and dreams.

When touching upon subjects like this Sonia would always cite her father,

"There is a divine spark in each of us; like a lantern it illuminates our first steps into the unknown. Then the flickering light of that lantern, becomes a shiny light in us, by letting the Faith to set in. and for us."

She treasured her father's beliefs and made them her own. She always had a propensity for words of wisdom. And there was a lot of wisdom in the American melting pot. One day, she was very enthusiastic, to tell me about an American saying, which she just had heard. It was about enthusiasm; and she was ready to deliver it in the heart bit. It was one of her favorite feelings.

"There's no better way to boost your confidence and enthusiasm, than to count your blessings".

I pondered on it, and I found in it. a source of inner peace. But before I grasped it totally in, she came with another one, with the same subtly wisdom.

"When the going gets tough, the tough get going."

I like that. In a few words, it tells an entire story. Doesn't it have

Blessed with Twice the Freedom

an ecclesiastic flair to it? I couldn't help but asked. Then she told me that, she wrote phrases like these in a bold hand and displayed them on her kitchen cabinets. They filled her mind with their inspiring messages first thing every morning.

CHAPTER 35

Reverberations

Sonia called us with a great news…she had gotten her American pharmacy license! We were so happy as she was!

She wanted to be sure we told Mama Elena. There was no bigger joy for Sonia than spreading joy. Since Mama Elena's phone was not working, so we drove out to see her. We brought news of Corina too, who was still in the top of her class. Michael was doing well too, in spite, of his seizures. However, Michael and his health were a constant worry. Mama Elena said, "Except for Michael, everything is perfect."

I tried to soften her feelings about the dent in Sonia's happiness by saying, "At this time there is not much she can do about it. We must be glad, that she herself has managed to keep her mind intact, after so many shocking events…

" Mama Elena's eyes were heavy with tears, and she tried to hide them from us. "Don't be sad, Mama Elena," I said, "Sonia has put the hard times behind her and as you say, 'What doesn't kill you, makes you stronger.' And Sonia is much stronger than you think. I can imagine the sparkle in her eyes; many of us believe, as she does, that she is a favorite of heaven's. How could she not be? Look how things have turned out in her favor! And from you, she learned, that gratitude brings peace and eventually happiness. So, she is grateful. She is happy thinking about the day she'll come home to Romania with her two trophies – American citizenship and an American pharmacy license."

Blessed with Twice the Freedom

That day came sooner than we would have thought.

Unfortunately, Mama Elena passed away before Sonia could return to share with her the great moments of her life.

Mama Elena had experienced, suddenly, a severe gastric hemorrhage which without postponing, imposed, an abdominal surgery. The surgery went well, and the tests were done to rule out cancer. She was scheduled to be discharged a few days after the surgery. Sonia was ready to come home, but we all encouraged her to wait until Corina got out of school. Meanwhile, Mama Elena developed a high fever. Everything, was tried , but regrettably, nothing worked. The decision was made to open her back up. Unfortunately, she suffered a septic shock and her heart gave up. It happened very quickly and left us all in a state of disbelief. Mama Elena was gone. Her last moments will stay with me forever. She looked at me and, barely whispering, she said, "My girls," and drew her last breath.

I felt guilty because Mama died on our watch, and though we tried, we were unable to find any antibiotics or anything else to save her. Even worse than that, we stopped Sonia from coming home. We had no idea that things would take such a turn. Mama Elena was tired. The last five years of her life, being without her girls, and learning also, about all they had to go through, had worn her out.

Now that her girls had found love and success in America, she was finally at peace when called to go to the other side.

I tried desperately to get a hold of Sonia but couldn't reach her immediately. I wasn't looking forward to giving her the sad news, but I had to talk to her as soon as possible. When I did finally get a hold of her, I learned that she was working second shift and to let Corina stay at Lee's.

It was 11:00 o'clock at night her time. As soon as she heard my voice she asked me, frightened, "It's about Mama, isn't it?"

"Yes, Sonia, it is. I am sorry, deeply sorry. She passed away yesterday afternoon."

Then a heavy silence fell in between us. There wasn't any crying,

229

but I could feel a deep, smoldering cry hidden in the silence. There were no words for it. She was the first to resume the conversation. She would have to think overnight and make all the decisions for her first trip home, quickly.

"Tomorrow, as early as I can, I will call you. I must get everything in order, and I cannot do it alone or at this very moment. I have, to make all the arrangements at work. I have, to get an emergency passport. As you know I got my citizenship only a little while ago." Her voice was soft, yet strong, like a person, who had fallen down, and had to get up again.

"I understand. In the meantime, Gil and I will do everything that has to be done here. I will be waiting for your call."

Instead of "good bye" she added,

"I appreciate and thank you for being there for me, so that Mama was not alone."

It was the most difficult phone call I ever had to make. It was 4:00 o'clock in the morning here. She still had half of the night ahead of her there, and we would have another day to fill in here.

A mixture of emotions filled our hearts. One minute we were happy anticipating Sonia's return and then sadness would fill in again. Sonia confessed to me, that she had the same rollercoaster of feelings.

We were going to see Sonia and our little friend Corina for the first time in five years.

Sonia hadn't changed much but Corina was now a teenager. What a difference five year make in a child's life! We never thought that their first visit home would be to Mama Elena's funeral.

Life is full of surprises and some of them come as devastating bombshells.

"A tree that sways in the wind is less likely to perish than a stiff and rigid one," she said.

"I see. You mean that flexibility and the ability to surrender are key." And she did just that. Mama Elena was her pillar, yet the time came to let her go. That pillar was the template for what Sonia became

230

for her children.

"It's not an end but a continuation," she added.

I looked at her and I could see her eyes were weary from weeping.

Unfortunately, she couldn't take more than a week of vacation. A week was too short to cover the five-year hiatus of being apart, but we made the best of it. We had so much to share. Even Corina, who would have liked very much to be around us, understood that we should be left alone so we could talk freely. She had access to Gil's computer and his attention, so she didn't feel left out.

Among other things, Sonia learned about the affair her ex had been having before leaving Romania. At last she understood the reasons for his peculiar behavior during that time. She forgave Gil and me for not telling her about it then. She agreed that it was for the best at that time. She even recalled seeing him with the other woman once.

"They were coming out of a coffee shop. It was shortly before he left for America. Nonchalantly, he introduced her to me as one of his co-workers. I trusted him. It never crossed my mind that she was my replacement. That was such a critical time for our family and he was thinking of just himself."

"I know, Sonia, I know."

"Now, it doesn't matter anymore what he did and why. Even the truth about him doesn't matter anymore. I was blessed with the parents I had. They created in me a person who never crawled after learning to walk. They taught me to stand up for the truth no matter how tough it might be".

Impetuously, I felt the need to say, "Oh, Sonia I could see all of this imprinted on your face. I don't see the worries and the fears I saw on your face before you left for America."

Then she made me smile by bringing up Pinocchio's Paradox, a philosophical statement about binary truth.

"Neli, people's physiognomies, do display their character without their even being aware. The continuous repetition of the same

231

grimaces and wry expressions leaves an impression on the face. One's actions imprint on the person residing inside."

"In other words, the truth from our minds, sooner or later, asks to be displayed."

Then we found ourselves looking at each other and smiling, realizing that the accord between us hadn't changed at all. But her smile turned sad as soon as her gaze fell on the picture of Mama Elena that I had displayed on the piano. She said softly,

"Forgive me, Mother, for not fully listening to you. You saw more clearly than I could see at that time."

We cried together for a bit, remembering how much we loved Mama Elena. Our time together was short, and our emotions ran from one extreme to the other.

We talked about life in general. We discussed people who have what seems to be an insatiable void, a void they vainly try to fill, and which they then transform into pain, and finally they spew that pain all around them. We wondered why it came to that. Our minds were tuning into each other's as if we were still living on the same street and were no longer separated by an ocean. Our talks went back and forth from truth to denial and everything in between.

Our connection was extraordinary and more than a simple coincidence. I see it as a destined arrangement, a blind date between destinies. It was as if a magnetic force had brought us together and then guided us. Until this day I can't find any other explanation for it than Providence.

CHAPTER 36

Wishes Sent Out Through a Window

"When the time came to buy my first house, one thing was non-negotiable: the house must have at least one window with a panoramic view of the surroundings. I wanted to start each day by looking out into the world, no matter the season. That would be my first contact with the world and with heaven. No horizon should limit the strivings of my will. I thought of that window as a "wish delivery" counter. I would send my wishes out as if placing an order of things, I was longing for. But I have, always, ended my prayer list with: "Your will be done."

And this was the right thing to do, as it turned out, God often had to *edit* my wishes.

Gil, the physicist, came, to my mind on this. He, often, tried to argue scientifically that there was not a hiatus between the unseen and seen world, but a difference of their manifestation in different hypostases. "God can only be reached in the present moment and always offers the right picture of the moment." That could explain how my daily prayer is accepted every time as a brand new.

Then I remember, my grandma's short plea; "God please help and heal our helplessness." I pleaded that many times on my journey's bumpy road. And also she would tell me; "Where there is faith and desire to be whole, there is no need for crutches." This is the meaning of her succinct prayer: crutches are addictions and shouldn't be options.

I don't want to present a dissertation on faith here, but I do have a few things to say. Even in Communist Romania, where I was condemned for it, my faith remained a big part of who I was and who I am today. I need to believe that there is someone out there I could trust. The world around me in Romania was not only hostile but hypocritical. Yet, Faith was my strength. I couldn't renounce my belief in exchange for more societal and worldly comforts.

My faith was like a steel rod from head to toe that didn't allow me to bend, no matter the nature or power of outside forces. That steel rod was made of my principles. Some might say I was peculiar, but I preferred that name instead of a hypocrite.

I have no regrets for trying to stay whole at all costs. I had role models in front of me that were worth following. My parents and grandparents left behind a valuable legacy of living in the truth. They were my templates.

I have always been fascinated by the fact that every cell in the body carries the template of generations coexisting with one another. I imagine the tumultuous trade between the genes' DNA deciding which to stay dormant for a while and which to be dominant and determine our uniqueness. All of this happens under rigorous laws that we still don't fully understand. No less fascinating to me is the power of thought. As our friend Magdy used to say, "Imagine, believe, and make it happen." These three strong verbs are like a lifeline to me. Keeping my target in my sight, I carefully tend to my priorities one by one until the task is done. For me the journey to success is very often more valuable than the success itself. I don't like to have unfinished projects cluttering my mind.

When the unconscious mind is too crowded with suppressed or unsolved problems it becomes a minefield. It can explode unpredictably. According to Freud, these unresolved issues must be brought to the surface, decoded, filtered out through the consciousness, and acknowledged one by one. In a much simpler

Blessed with Twice the Freedom

way, that might have been the original purpose of confession. Sins acknowledged before the Great Judge were forgiven, and the soul was relieved. In this respect, Grandma talked to me often about the benefits of letting go, and letting God heal."

Oh, Sonia, I can't help myself from saying here, "I like how you see and understand the world. You can find an explanation even for all that Sabin has done with his life. He was a person who carried heavy hereditary luggage, and yet did nothing to lighten it. He even hid some of his extra luggage from everyone's sight, although there was no way to hide it all forever. It is too bad for him that he came into this world poor and left it broke.

All of this made me think of my own heritage…

My grandparents came from the monotonous terrain of the Bărăgan Plains. My grandfathers had the "gift" of drinking, as one of my neighbors called it. I learned stories about their rough lives from my parents. Even nature was not gentle with them. There were no slopes, no climbing hills, no Sub-Carpathian forests to promise them shade or enough water to quench their summer thirst. No matter how far you looked you could only see the lowland plains. Later, those plains became the main fields to grow grain in Romania. No season was easy for them. They went into the fields to work in spring, worked through the hot summer, and came out again in the fall. Winter was not easy. It kept them trapped inside with snowdrifts building up to the eaves of the low houses. Sometimes, the houses were buried in snow.

The Bărăgan people' way of that hardship was to drink the way through the winter. It was completely different from the beautiful Transylvanian Plateau that I jokingly call "Gil's Land."

Because of its climate, Bărăgan was considered the most inhospitable area of Romania. For this reason, it was used as a depot for mass deportations during the Communist Regime. More than 40,000 political prisoners were relocated there in hopes that before adjusting to the harsh land they would die. Every time I heard about my Bărăgan's ancestors' hardship, I felt sad and at the same time lucky that I came a few generations after and I didn't have to walk in their shoes.

They used the grain they harvested in the summer not only for their daily bread but also for their alcohol. Brewed and distilled beverages lifted their spirits during the harsh winter. Because there were no TVs, phones, or even electricity, these people craved their daily dose of brandy. Unfortunately, one drink paved the way for another until one had drunk too much. Being able to drink continuously was what my old neighbor called "the drinking gift".

I never accepted the ability to drink as a "gift" even though I might have inherited some of those genes. Hard times never tempt me to drink, although upon occasion I do like to drink socially. In the first year of college I socialized quite a bit. On weekends I would go with a group of friends to classical music concerts or to other shows. The classical music was very much on vogue in that time.

During the last years of the Communist Regime, everything had to have a political touch, so they came up with a festival which toured throughout Romania called "Romania's Song." Young people went to the show in the hopes that they would be selected to come up on the stage, live, on the big stage of the homeland, and be recognized as ardent patriots.

It was great schtick for the Communists and it succeeded, though, in pulling much of the younger generation out of the classical music scene.

After concerts, we would go somewhere else to listen to more music and maybe also to have a drink. My colleagues wondered why I would always stop after my first drink, but that was my rule: one drink. It still is.

It was interesting to watch my friends, though, and all the phases they went through from their first drink to their last drink. Some of them would drink for pure enjoyment and others to drown their amorous troubles in a glass of whiskey.

Blessed with Twice the Freedom

It was interesting to see what alcohol does to the brain. First, they would become more jovial, next they would enter the noisy stage (everyone talking but nobody listening), and finally they wouldn't even know what they were talking about. Their exit line would be: "Please call me a cab'" Luckily, they could usually remember their addresses.

After a few episodes like this I found excuses to not join that group anymore and to see those folks in the classroom only. Other girls did the same. Maybe it was the boys' attempt to impress us. We remained friends throughout our school years, and at the end, as young men, many of them found the right way to impress us. The college boys were really good people, and many went on to become doctors.

Both my parents left their village for Bucharest to study teaching. I didn't have as many connections with their village as Sonia had with her parents' villages. Going through her journals I thoroughly enjoy the description of her times with her grandparents. Sonia believed it was the most beautiful part of her life.

My parents were happy to hear that I wanted to become a physician. My mother thought that it was a great choice because she always saw that vocation in me. I was always ready to help those who were suffering. That was my great desire. That was also what connected Sonia and me so strongly. Her reflections on my desire not only made a lot of sense to me but also gave me a deeper understanding of myself.

She would say, "A gift from above is not to be kept for oneself, but rather it is to be shared with others, serving a purpose, and fulfilling a responsibility. Think about the feeling you got growing up when your parents entrusted you with an assignment that looked a little beyond your ability. Their trust in you was a fortifying pill for a still fragile will. Finally, your will, like a little stream, grew into a river."

I was lucky to meet Gil who shared beliefs with me, but Sonia was not so lucky, or maybe she was. Although she didn't find such a partner in Sabin, she found him in Adrian. She found him, lost him, and found him again. The events leading up to the revival of their love story still amaze me.

CHAPTER 37

Reborn from the Ashes

The most beautiful letters Sonia sent to Gil and to me were about Corina's ingenuity in trying to bring joy to her mother's life. Using her great abilities, Corina created a repertoire full of originality. Here's one of the episodes Sonia told us about:

"One Sunday morning I woke up to a Beethoven violin concerto in my ears. I was off that weekend and I could sleep in a little later than on a work day.

At first, I was confused. Was it a dream? Was I attending a concert?

I heard music, but did not know where it was coming from. I looked around and noticed a yellow light with red sparkles that suggested a burning flame on the floor next to my bed.

Gradually, I recognized that it was one of my scarves draped over a lamp that was creating the impression of flames. Down on the floor I could see Corina portraying a Phoenix bird, trying out its wings before triumphantly standing up. She had synchronized the bird's movement to the music like a good stage director. With joy in my heart, I hugged my little bird tightly.

Not too long before that Sunday, Lee and I had been talking about the symbiology of the Phoenix. Corina was fascinated to hear about the mythological bird that burned down to nothing and then rose from its own ashes. She listened carefully and then concluded, "Like us Mommy, right?" Corina was always sincere and very profound for her age by seeing out coming out of the difficult time, without being crushed.

"That's right, my little nestling, we are Phoenixes."

She continued to be mesmerized by the magical bird story with its great message of the new only emerging after the old has been burned to the ground. But no fire can put an end to the desire to continue, to rise again into life.

On Michael's weekends with us, he was happy to be part of these improvised shows. They not only made me happy, but they had a lot of fun themselves. Their impersonations of funny characters kept me in stitches. They were adorable. As I have said, when Michael turned 18 he decided to move back home and live with Corina and me. Sabin had just remarried and all of us were happy in our various ways. With Michael moving home, I had to think about finding a larger place. Corina and I started to go house hunting. It was fun and exciting and full of memories. Whenever I drive on the streets where once I walked in despair, I push those memories out, and paint them over with brightness. Being grateful – finding the silver lining – is the most powerful antidepressant.

CHAPTER 38

Not Lonely

"I am as equally pleased by an overcast day as I am by a sunny one. I think of the clouds as givers of rain rather than the hiders of sun. The rain's wet fingers, knocked on my window all night long. It was a soothing sound that gathered all my thoughts like a lullaby and put them to sleep. I listen to the rain for a while, thinking of how long the thirsty land has waited for water. The grass has been looking burnt as if by fire and its green face was almost gone. But what a miracle it is, when rain comes at the right time!

In the morning the sky is an azure blue, and so clear that you can see the light spreading about at will. The color of the flowers on my deck is refreshed as if everything has been given a fresh coat of paint. A flow of positive energy gushes out like a stream and charges everything around it. I am a part of everything. I feel great joy and gratitude.

From out of the blue, a breeze. It moves like a playful child stirring the branches back and forth. All the trees shudder, shaking the drops of water from their rustling leaves as if it is still raining. There has been plenty of rain.

The birds sound a cheerful operetta on their open stage. After the show ends you can hear them calling each other and answering back in their own language. I imagine that they must be words of love.

Let us not forget the little brook! The rain woke it up, and it is rushing past the house. Yesterday it was just a wisp of water and could hardly be heard, but now its strength has returned, along with its noisy but pleasant song. Soon it will be clear again and be so perfectly transparent that every stone from its bed could be exhibited in a gallery. Many stones and pebbles have lost their edges and have become rounded from being washed by so many waters. Their endurance is brought out in each of their smooth edges.

I notice a little white ball carried by the waters. Who knows where it is from? It let itself get caught in the water's whirl. It hesitates for a moment, before being whisked off by the stream.

You can see that being alone doesn't mean being lonely, and I have never had that depressing feeling…

CHAPTER 39

Tragedy Hovering in the Sky

In the beginning was the Word and the Word was with God; and the Word was God.

John 1:1-18.

"I remember this phrase of wisdom: my father would start many of his sermons with it.

Today I can't find the words to express the agony that will be written on the American calendar in bloody lettering, "September 11th" or simply "9/11."

That number, 911, is the number we use in America to call the police in an emergency. That S.O.S., number, sadly has more meaning now since that fateful day.

Behind this atrocity, there is certainly an earthly reason, rather than a heavenly one. God is Love. God cannot be divided. One way is not better than the other if we're truly looking to find Him. Neither can the word "love" be split – if it is divided, it is emptied of its essence.

God gave us free will and many ways to use it. Without choices, free will wouldn't make any sense. Yet, we pray for guidance and mercy that His "will be done on earth as it is in heaven."

We pray, yet God knows every moment of the future. It is hard to understand things that don't fit our limited mind. He is omnipresent and can be found only in the present, in His everlasting present. Such a concept is truly difficult for the human mind, as difficult as the infinite or the nonexistence of time.

September the 11th started brightly like many another day. I watched the sun rise from the Eastern horizon, as I like to do when the sky is cloudless. As always, we were busy with the first chores of the day, free from the slightest suspicion that a tragedy was hovering above us. The brightness ended at 8:46 A.M.

I try to imagine the panic and the fear that spilled the dread adrenaline from the hearts of those confined in their planes before they died. It is unimaginable, and more than my heart can handle. We will never know what those people felt. Their dread vanished into smoke and their bodies into ashes. The Twin Towers fell to the ground, burying both victims and predators. A legitimate question is here, though; how could one tell apart the ashes of commemoration from those of condemnation?

And after all, who benefits from this? we don't inherit the earth but rather, we return in ashes to it. Fighting and killing each other on earth most certainly won't get us to heaven. If two people of different beliefs try to kill each other in the name of God, they do not serve either God or the dust they are created from".

That is what Sonia wrote on that unforgettable day.

Until today I listened to Sonia's advice not to look for Gil in the cemetery. However, today felt special; it is the anniversary of both his entering into and departing from the world. My visit to the grave was in part motivated by the dream I had last night. In my dream, we were in Baia-Mare, his hometown, at the house where he was born.

In my dream it was a very colorful spring yet there was still some snow here and there. The flowers were different from those of this world. They were moving earnestly on their own to chase the snow out. I found it funny.

In the same moment a lark that had appeared out of nowhere ascended to the sky. I recognized it right away by the song it sang. I knew that it was too early for its trill, but it was so unusually beautiful, that I looked for Gil, so we could listen to it together. There was no way to find him. I woke up sad. I would have liked to have seen him, at least in my dream.

Anyway, I decided to go to his grave and made myself believe that it was a date he was aware of. I picked the most beautiful chrysanthemum to lie on his grave.

On my way home, I walked and wandered through all the dear places we used to visit together. I still had the lark's song and the image of Gil vividly in my mind. I stopped in front of the Art Gallery on 6 March street. It was a place very dear to us. Over the years, we followed the artists path from their start to consecration. It was closed at that time. I looked through the gallery's windows and a few works caught my attention. One reminded me of Auguste Rodin's sculpture, "The Thinker." It was a sculpture of a man seated and resting his hands on his knees. His head was bent forward but without any particular, target for his eyes. For a moment I tried transposing myself in the sculptor's mind.in the sculptor's mind. In fact, it could resemble any of us when the head is too heavy with thoughts.

Then suddenly, it was as if Gil was whispering to me, "Close your eyes and you will see that only a thought is between us." It seemed so real to me that I turned my head to see him. It was just my imagination. But now I walk with the most vivid image of him in my soul.

As a flash from my dream, I turned my eyes again to the sky, to saw some far-off lightening. That's strange, I thought, we do not usually have lightning in September. In a few seconds I heard thunder. I remember how Gil tried to explain it to Corina, the child who wanted to know everything. It was difficult to resist her insistence. She would say,

"Why, why Uncle Gil, why does the scribbling in the sky come first?"

"My little darling, it is because the lightning and the thunder cannot run at the same speed."

"What, are they running? Now you're kidding me, aren't you?"

Then Gil would pick her up and spin her around saying, "I am not kidding, I am not kidding, little ducky."

What great moments, how dearly I treasure them…

Walking home I could feel the pulse of the street. But this time something even more was going on. People seemed to be more agitated than at other times, so I hurried home, sensing that something must have happened.

I practically jumped over the few stairs of my front entrance and went into the house. I turned on the TV and saw the image of the Twin Towers falling, being played over and over again. The TV channels talked about nothing else: AMERICA WAS ATTACKED AT HOME!

Right away my thoughts went to my dear friends. I could see people on the streets of New York disoriented but running, some of them petrified with fear. You could even read fear on the faces of the news reporters.

Before waiting to see clearly what was happening, I called Sonia; I knew she was living close to New York City. She answered on the first ring. She was still home; it wasn't long before she'd leave for work. She feared for Corina, who was on a flight coming home from Europe.

Although there was no one she knew working in those towers she was crying from the bottom of her heart, as if all of the people, who would lose their lives that day, somehow were connected to her.

Hours later, I also learned that soon after taking off, Corina's flight got a message to return to London. The crew didn't know what was going on until it landed at Heathrow airport. The entire world joined America in its grief.

Corina was stranded in London for a week and all of us, no matter where we were, had a new fear. I heard from them again when Corina got home. We all watched the news closely but avoided talking about it. The events were too raw and painful in our hearts. Rather we talked about the coming fall. We let autumn fall over us and we humbly received it, grateful for the lives we still enjoyed.

I watched autumn stepping down from the Hoia Hills of Cluj

246

leaving a tint of yellow on every tree it passed. Sonia loved those hills in every season. Gil and I used to take Corina there on short trips. It wasn't just to help Sonia: we enjoyed spending time with Corina. She took pleasure in running around freely or playing hide and seek behind the trees. I am glad that where they settled in America, they also have four seasons. Sonia would say, "Here the time flows through the seasons just like it does there, and every season has his own beauty. Even Fall competes with the other seasons, displaying its beauty, whereas in Romania, Fall was a colorless season."

During good weather I prefer to walk home through the park. It helps me forget that there is so much evil in the world. Nature has a calming effect on me. Sonia doesn't have to look for a park because her backyard already looks like one. I spent a summer at her house and I know every corner of that beautiful place. There are towering trees housing all kinds of birds, some of them new to me. They would come very close to us while we had our breakfast and coffee on the deck. And before we knew it, the birds' chorus was keeping us company. We didn't say a word until they finished. It was like a well-trained symphony of sound.

The flowers on her deck were crimson. Sonia told me they are called impatiens and she picks a new color every summer. She loves impatiens, she said, "because they never disappoint, even though they are *impatient* flowers." That was her joke. There was a brook in the backyard that was the best part of all. Sonia loved the brook. It was as peaceful as it was beautiful. She would comment on it:

"Watching the tireless running water of the stream makes me think of its continuity and of its urge to pass over obstacles. I'm impressed by how quickly it becomes crystal clear after a torrential rain. Despite all the trouble in the riverbed it triumphantly comes out transparent as if nothing happened. How much I would like to do just that ".

CHAPTER 40

Thinking Back to Transylvania

"The heavy rain has intensified nature's colors and as soon as the sun frees itself from the thick veil of the clouds; it provides a shiny mirror to happily reflect their bounty. Everything looks refreshed. Some few clouds still wander slowly across the sky, drizzling a little more rain, as if they are having a hard time saying goodbye. It reminds me so much of my childhood in the countryside with my grandparents, nestled in the humble beauty of the Transylvanian Hills. Each one had its own name, just like the people in the community. I am wondering how they got the name and who was the first to give it to them.

I was happy when it rained, for I would have more attention from my grandparents. They would take a break from the fields to work in the house or barnyard instead.

It amazed me how in touch they were with nature, reading nature's hints about future weather. Grandpa would say, "Don't you smell the rain? It is coming." Of course, I couldn't.

Or I could hear Grandma saying, "Oh no, a red sunset! Tomorrow we will have to look for work at home."

She was very organized and would already have work put aside for the rainy day. Everything in her house was homemade from scratch.

She was a great cook and always formulated the next day's menu in advance. On rainy days I was her assistant in the kitchen. I paid close attention because I was eager to learn all her secrets.

During the winter, when the fields freed them from work outside, it was the turn of the work in, and around the house.

Women in the village were very busy in the winter with the preparing the yarns for the weaving of canvas. She would have rolls and roll of it at the beginning of spring.

On rainy days in the summer, she would cut out pieces from a roll of hemp cloth and sew shirts by hand for her and Grandpa.

She had an assortment of woven fabrics — the result of her hard work from the previous winter — stacked in one of the rooms. The finest ones were designed for shirts and the others for towels, bed sheets, and pants. Some of them had designs and would serve as tablecloths.

Sitting on a low little stool, she put her glasses on and in an instant, I was next to her. Her eyes were getting weaker and it was my job to pull the thread through the needle. I was so proud of my job! I liked to stick around in case she needed my help again.

While she sewed, Grandma hummed. It was always the same tune, crooned, as if it was coming from the depths of the earth and had forgotten its words on the way out. Listening to it, looking out the window, I recognized its harmony with the background sounds outside.

I could hardly wait for the rain to stop so I could go outside and search for the waxy-yellow and very tasty early summer apples, hidden in the soft grass. I heard them fall when the summer breeze blew. I would gratefully have picked them up in a brand-new basket my grandma would buy for me from the fair at the beginning of every summer. I loved it when they called me their precious helper. They always found a way to make me feel special.

I still remember looking for the poles of the string beans loaded with yellow pods. Grandma and I would pick them eagerly, knowing that after every harvest more would come. Then they would end up in the best yellow string bean soup anyone ever tasted. My mother was also a good cook, but grandma had no equal.

Every season — even autumn — has its beauty, but regrets plagued me at the end of every summer. Vacation was ending, and I would miss being with my grandparents in their magical village. I thought, that there was not another place where nature and life displayed their beauty better than in that village.

And there wasn't any harvest there as important as the wheat harvest at the end of summer. It gave them the daily bread that they prayed for – without fail – every day. At the end of the harvest, they would take home a bunch of wheatears braided into a crown as a sign of gratitude for the plentiful harvest. They would keep it in an honored place in the house, as an auspicious sign of that year's harvest until the next year.

During the summers of my high school years besides being a help to my grandparents, I read the great thinkers' books in my father's library. I must admit I had a difficult time understanding the conclusion to some of them that life is just an illusion. It seems unbelievable, and yet, I have learned that is true. All existence is a fascinating illusion built on mystery.

The celestial archway vault, is like a transparent tent, which rings the horizon. Can you reach the horizon? As soon as you think you can reach it, the skyline runs away, teasing you with another more elusive horizon.

My limited mind would ask, but what is beyond the infinite? I would imagine the Creator smiling indulgently at my question. He might answer the way He answered to Moses; instead of saying *I am who I am*, He might say, *the infinite is what it is*. Then I would add: as *we are who we are*, the question and the answer merge into the same words.

Then I would hear grandma calling me; dinner was ready. My philosophical interlude was over. Grandma would have prepared something delicious, maybe chicken paprika with polenta – a frequent summertime favorite in Transylvania. At the table we had our rituals; we didn't taste the food until we had expressed our gratitude for its being on the table. All three of us bowed our heads in front of a

Blessed with Twice the Freedom

table loaded up with food and uttered words of appreciation. Then, a moment of silence, while we watched the steam ascend, like our thanks to the Eternal. It was that simple.

CHAPTER 41

Grandpa's Last Journey

"I was still a college student in the fall of 1964 when I was told the dreadful news that Grandpa had passed on. Grandma called my folks to tell them that he was not feeling himself. My parents took it seriously because Grandpa was never sick and had never complained before. The doctor concluded it was a stroke. At least my parents could be there for his last days. And at his advanced age, it was not altogether surprising that he would pass.

This was the first time that death hovered over my family to take one of us away. In time, I would lose more people that I loved, but no other death was like that of my grandfather's.

My family knew how much I adored Grandpa. Before calling me to come, they asked Grandpa if he would like to see me. In his Transylvanian dialect, he said, "Of course I would like to see my dearest Sonia, but she is so busy at college with her studies. Please have her come later if it seems to be needed."

Then he told Grandma about his little secrets, "Look for a little purse in the other room's alcove; you will find some money I've been saving for a while. Please give it to Sonia." I never wanted to spend that money because to me it was priceless.

Knowing they were my favorites, he also told Grandma to look on the right side of the hay barn for some Bosc pears for me. That's where my grandparents stored the harvested apples and pears.

They also had a way to keep the table grapes fresh by hanging them on ropes stretched between the beams of a cold room. Grandpa

Blessed with Twice the Freedom

knew that Muscatel was my favorite of all the many varieties of grape, and again, he made sure that I received some. I always knew that Grandpa loved me because of all the little loving things he did just for me.

I got to the village by noontime. As soon as I approached, I could hear the church bells tolling. That was how they let the people know that a village family was about to lose one of its members. It was hard to believe that at that time it was my dearest grandfather. I guess it was just me, but I felt that the bells had a crying sound in them that I had never heard before. It might have been a homage to him. He had brought the bells with him when he came back to the village from America.

I entered the gate to the front yard and a lot of people were already there to give a hand as they did on such occasions. They came to set up the procession for his departure. The villagers did all the work so that the family could be left to mourn. I always admired the sense of family in the village community. They were there for each other in both, good times and bad.

As soon as they noticed me coming through the gate, they stopped whatever work they were doing and lined up on both sides of the pathway to let me pass. They bowed compassionately and through barely audible whispers said, "God rest him in peace." I couldn't answer, so I just nodded, barely able to hold back my tears.

Meanwhile my parents learned of my arrival and came out of the house to meet me there. Grandma followed them as well. The four of us clutched each another in a big hug and cried on each other's shoulders. The cadenced cavalcade of the bells pouring over us made us feel that heaven and earth were one single piece.

I stepped into the room where during the summers I would listen to Grandpa's many stories, the room from which he would soon leave. They understood that for a few moments I would like to be alone, just he and I and my sweet memories. There was a deep silence but strangely I could listen to it. That silence was already a

253

part of Grandpa's realm and now he chose to share with me. There is no other way to explain that feeling. I closed my eyes and I let my thoughts talk to him. I tried to restore our old conversations, so I could keep them fresh and treasure them. I let him know how grateful I was for having him as a part of my life. Then I let him go… Maybe he was heading far, far away to the stars we looked at in our summer research of the sky. In my heart I understood that he needed me to let him go. Those moments helped me to find dignity in death, the same dignity as in life.

Back in the village, an event like this was, unfortunately, commonplace. However, this was my family's first time to deal with the death of a loved one in this village. I watched and understood the way that the villagers deal with the afterglow of life. The village was so much a part of my life and at the time of my grandpa's death, I was reminded again of what a special place that village was.

As soon as the men approached what was still – for a little longer – Grandpa's house, they demurely took their hats off and bowed their heads humbly to present their condolences to the mourning family. One after another they said, "May God grant him forgiveness and peace."

Women, clad in black, approached with the same reverence, following the same ritual as the men. The closer female relatives untied their hair from the buns they were required to wear after marriage. Their disheveled hair, resembling the weeping willow trees, was a sign of their grief.

Nowadays when capital crimes regularly make the front page of the newspaper, death has lost its dignity. Life and death have become trivialized and are little more than two dates on a calendar…-

My father chose not to serve my Grandpa's funeral Mass, but stood instead between my grandmother and my mother on one side of the casket, wearing his priestly attire. I stood in the row next to the other close relatives on the other side. In his funeral speech, the priest didn't forget to mention Grandpa's generosity to the poor, who seemed to grow in numbers, especially after World War II and during the Communist Regime. "Nobody who knocked on his door left empty-handed. Many of them are here today to honor him and will be chanting in his memory forever. You see, we can only leave behind our good deeds and nothing else."

It was a sunny day in late October. Coincidentally, that day was also the day he was born, back in 1885. There was a gentle sun up in the sky and through my sad eyes I found it sad also. The front yard and its surroundings were all well-manicured. A few days before Grandpa fell sick, he had done all the yard work around the house. It was as if he knew that he would have a large crowd coming to pay their respects.

At the cemetery, I heard the phrase, "For dust you are and to dust you shall return" as the casket receded more and more deeply into the earth. There was no better place to understand that such a truth is so real. It is more real than the mind can comprehend. But in my beliefs, it was not only the dust but the spirit ascending to heaven.

My faith pushed all my fears and anguish away and I stood there still, until the wooden cross with his name and the two important dates on it, was stuck in the ground for Grandpa's return...

Many years have gone by since that mild autumn. The cross has since aged and the writing on it has faded too. A white climbing rose cheerfully runs over it every summer, as does one on my grandma's cross and two others on my parents' stones.

Grandpa never would have thought that my destiny would bring me to the New World, as he called America.

The trip across the Atlantic, which took him three months on a boat, had taken me only one day on a plane.

On summer evenings when the sky is clear I like to watch the little moving lights of the airliners overhead at their scheduled intervals. They are the flights heading to Europe, which I still think of fondly. Both America and Europe share my heart equally just as the sun impartially bathes them in light at different times. While America is deepening into night, Europe is taking in the dawn. We are unaware of it until we cross the ocean in flight. Every time I go back home to Europe I see it. My biological clock gets confused by the time change and is stubborn in adjusting to the jet lag. It doesn't like the shock of losing seven hours of American time. Losing and gaining time is just as much of an illusion as life itself. At the same time, I find it interesting to think that one side of the earth is always illuminated; it might be part of the Creator's plan to give us a sense of security and safety. It would be frightening to have both sides in the dark, without any guard, wouldn't it?

For a day or two after I cross the ocean, my brain is baffled as it tries to recover the hours of sleep the American clock owes it while it catches up with the European one. It makes me think to the plasticity of the brain and its most marvelous assignment: to think. As a rule, what is not used must atrophy. Such a weakening allows ignorance and indifference to set in. If we look up to the sky and ask, "Why is it blue?" our curiosity is triggered to find out the truth about blue. Interest, no matter how faint, is a resistance against a predatory void. Thinking fills up the void while it makes room for wisdom and then for the true happiness.

CHAPTER 42

From the Heart of a Transylvanian Village

"I loved my grandmother dearly. Over the years, she shared with me the many inspirational words and stories she had received from the generation that went before her, words and stories that I now share with my children. This "get and give" is a continuous flow, and every generation enriches a tributary in the *folkloric* river. This river is as sacred to us as the Ganges River is for the Hindus. Folklore is a community treasure that I was lucky to have access to. Even now that I am so far away, in difficult times, I return to my grandmother in my imagination and rummage through the stock of wisdom I have from her. Nothing keeps me grounded and on the right track better.

If I were to translate the word *Grandma* from Romanian to English, keeping its content unaltered, it would be *goody*. The Romanian word for grandma *bunica* comes from the adjective *bun* which is the equivalent of *good*. My grandma was a great *bunica*.

My father, who also sought a deeper understanding of the world around him, might have inherited his insightfulness from her. He would come up with the right words and always at the right time. He was not very talkative, but he was a great speaker. I was very lucky to have such loving people around.

In my grandparents' Transylvanian village, I encountered a spiritually pristine life. There were unwritten codes of conduct that were not created or imposed from outside. The most important link in the chain of community was family and the entire chain itself was considered a family. Every link of the chain was considered sacred. The older generation in the village were honored and revered. They were active and appreciated in every part of the community. They held the unforgettable secrets of many generations and were guided by them.

Nobody started a family without taking the first steps towards it in the church. Then it was a solemn promise, first to God then to each other, and to the entire community. The ceremony was always officiated during a Mass, so the community could witness their pledge. The bride and the groom were crowned during the sacrament of marriage, to underline the royal importance of the moment. The phrase, "What God has joined together, let no man put asunder" came unequivocally as a Memorandum of Understanding between the spouses and the community as they lay the foundation for a soon-to-be-new family.

As a child I wondered how people developed feelings for each other, and how the circle of life held the community together. Later on, I was amazed to learn that such ties had a deep and mysterious meaning. Married people became "one heart of one will." Family responsibilities were never thought of as burdens, but rather as joyful duties that were an honor to fulfill. I understand.... I truly understand why people from my "childhood wonderland" longed to get together for important events in their life, no matter whether they would celebrate or mourn.

Once Corina asked me innocently, "Mom, how come you never get discouraged?"

I smiled and right away my grandma came to mind. I remembered the endearing and simple words she would use in difficult times, "Never lose your hopes for the better. Believe that God has knowledge of you!" I explained to Corina that my courage was the result of my beliefs.

"Be humble, humble, all the time. Humbleness and love towards each other will wipe out the evil in the world," my Grandma used to say. And I shall always remember her saying it. My grandma taught me to always look for God's favors and she was right; His kindness would come down on me, just not always when I requested it. She also taught me how to address my wishes to Him; they should be humble and always wrapped up with, "your will be done."

Nothing can illustrate a villager's prayer for the beneficent intervention of heaven better than Rusalii Holiday. The English version of such a celebration is Whitsuntide or Pentecost. It comes fifty days after Easter and often marks the beginning of summer.

At this time, Christians celebrate the Descent of the Holy Spirit to humanity. It was considered as important as Easter or Christmas.

This was my favorite holiday as a child. Every year it was celebrated outside in the fields where the grain was growing. It was a most beautiful time of the year. It wasn't only the beauty of the field preparing for a new yield, but the anticipation of a good future crop that filled every heart with joy. Everyone's lives depended on the harvest to come and then, more than anything, on the generosity of heaven. Any devastating vagary of weather could leave people hungry and penniless. They would have nowhere to turn for help but to heaven.

The village came together, young and old, in the field; they thought it was the best day to ask for mercy and blessings, this day of the Holy Ghost's Descent from Heaven.

Every June of my childhood I joined the villagers in the fields. I remember how I could hardly wait to be dropped off at my grandparents' house on the day before Rusalii. I was keen to be there. It was such an experience for the child in me! No church could open the gates of heaven for me the way that field did. It was enchanting; no other word can describe it. People knelt in the middle of the field and prayed. They prayed that the crops be protected from the wrath of storms, from scorching drought, from predators, and from many other enemies. I was touched by the humility the villagers adopted towards heaven. I let myself be a part of it – even though I was just a child and there was still so much I did not understand. I was grateful to have a connection to both the city and the village. There was always something special about the faith of village people. This faith never wavered, even under Communism. In the countryside, celebrations like these in the fields could be hidden from the regime, but such celebrations could never take place in the cities, where the Securitate was everywhere.

On Rusalii Eve, the village's lads would prepare the place for the following day's procession. Branches from linden trees were stuck in the ground in a circle to create what was to be the assigned prayer place for the villagers. The linden symbolizes peace and fertility. The lads built a sanctuary with linden walls and an arch to the heavens above. It was truly uplifting. This is where my love for linden trees, perhaps, began. I had always admired the humble linden's yellow, pleasantly-scented flowers, but it was seeing how peaceful the village was, when the linden trees were used for this celebration, that opened my eyes. In the month of June, no other tree got more honor than the linden.

After the young men had set the place up in the field, they would bring linden branches to the village. Robust oxen adorned with red tassels on their horns were harnessed to carts, so they could parade the streets of the village and deposit two linden branches at every house, posting them at the entrance gate. It was the symbolic gift of June to the village, and the village accepted. For us children it was a pageant, a spectacle, that also spilled its joy over the entire village.

The aroma of sweet bread was everywhere as each home-made preparations for the holiday. There was ecstasy in the air. Everyone in the village was ready to celebrate life with Nature herself. On Rusalii Day, after the church service, the entire gathering would head to the open-space church in the field to share sacred moments. I vividly remember my feeling of melding with the beautiful field speckled with so many colors. It was an unparalleled, uplifting feeling. Each flower was more beautiful than the next. There were spools of red clover scattered into the grass with much taller yellow flowers of bedstraw and blue bells that bowed with every touch of breeze. Red, yellow and blue, our national banner's colors, were sprawled around us. With the mind of a child, then, I made an easy connection between the flowers' color and the colors of our national flag. I thought that they had come to the field by themselves, answering to a higher and mysterious call, just because we were Romanians. I smile remembering those thoughts. Children have their own special way when viewing the world.

A handsome lad, dressed in our national attire held our towering flag. I thought to myself: it makes it easier for us to be identified as Romanians from above. Even though I knew little of His omnipotence, I thought that on that day He had an eye on us, on that field. During my childhood, Romania was truly the center of my universe.

On the field for Rusalii celebration, I imagined every wisp of grass coming back to life, proving its survival by defying and leaving behind a harsh winter. And every year the grass would do it again. Not far from the place of the sermon, there was a wheat field stretching around us as green as the sea. With every breath of wind, the wheatears would bow and ripple continuously after each other. When I was in high school, with my knowledge of physics, I saw Huygens ripples in them.

When it came to religious beliefs, the Communists didn't put the same pressure on villagers as they did on urban people. The Communists tried to push their doctrines on new generations by trying to push out all incumbent beliefs. They relied more on the fruit of the generations than on the roots. They never knew how wrong they were. However, fruit doesn't fall far from the tree. People of true faith, no matter where they are, receive nourishment from the same sap — both the root and the fruit.

Because of my connection to rural life, I could live out the authenticity of the three major Christian holidays every year. Each of them express people's deepest gratitude for the intersection of heaven and earth. In their belief, every is taken in account, because in each there is a sparkle of God Itself. They had no questions on this, because the answer was already there; it was through their Faith.

D Before Easter, during Holy Week the entire village was in a state of grief. For that reason, wearing colorful clothing was taboo. In remembrance of all the suffering Jesus went through, a heavy silence would fall over the entire village. It would have been sacrilegious to party or to have any other joyful gatherings. Women wore only black clothing, a symbol of mourning.

Holy Week left a deep impression on me, even though not everything from it fit into the mind of a child.

Like many others, I was not exempt from bearing a cross that was sometimes even too heavy for me to carry alone. Nor was I exempt from drinking from the cup of the bitterness of life. I freely accepted it without looking for revenge. I had a strong belief that one day the reason behind the difficulty would be revealed. Looking back, I can clearly see how I learned patience and found real strength.

Other times, I let my memory wander, so it can recreate the entire colorful meadow and the sprawling fields on Rusalii Day.

Then I want to feel the jubilee of Nature again, under the early summer sun. Once it starts, nothing could stop it from its course. It's hard to believe how tenuous the generosity of harvest really is.

From the joy in a community of faith, I have learned commitment to sacrifice, when it was called for, and I have learned tenacity to endure.

The lessons I learned in my early life are my "a secret tool box" for use in emergencies. I call them my *Transylvanian field teachings*.

Another tool in my kit is my belief that I am a favorite of heaven, even when to worldly eyes I do not seem be anyone's favorite.

The beliefs I acquired in the village protect me and dissipate the fear around me. They say that it takes a village to raise a child. We're

Blessed with Twice the Freedom

not talking about daily food but rather whole, spiritual growth.

In the village there were beautiful traditions that taught the new generation moral discipline and a sacred belief that the Hand of God is always stretched out and ready to rescue us from the fire of despair.

In the village, people didn't know anything about anxiety, depression, or any other derivatives of fear.

However, times have changed and so did life in the village. I have kept all the memories unaltered in my mind though. They were not there just to keep, but to use to recover from almost insurmountable hardship.

One day, Corina remembered my grandma's words and asked if the Almighty also had knowledge of her. And without hesitation I told her, "Of course He does. It was meant for you to be in Ms. O'Neal's class. She was not only an excellent teacher, but she had a golden heart. She and her husband Gary took us under their wings, so we could belong to a family, which we will always treasure.

And, what about our lawyer, Julia O'Day? She was one of the best lawyers in the state and she offered to protect us with no expectation of payment. She chose to do it pro bono, out of genuine goodness.

And, what about Lacey? Remember how she appeared in front of our door with a brand new, typewriter. I couldn't afford to buy one for you, and very often you had to borrow one from your friends to do your homework. It was not out of pity but from her great generosity that she did that for us. That's why we rightly call Lacey, "Mother Teresa."

And don't forget our other friends Rick and Sandy; they picked you up from school when I was working late, and they took us every Sunday to church. And the list goes on and on. You better believe that all of them were a part of a rescue plan."

My little listener was quiet again but nodding affirmatively. Then she said, "What about my brother, do you think that Somebody has knowledge of him too?"

"Certainly, without doubt. Think about how lucky he was to be spared in that car accident, so we could have and enjoy him."

"But he left us to go with his father," she complained, and I amended her sentence, "You mean your father, don't you?"

Her response was angry, "It is better not to have one than to have one like him".

"I hope that in time you will change your mind on this; we have to look in a bright side, we are free now. And this is a big thing.

Your brother hasn't left us, he was taken from us. And I know, it is your right to look at him like that, but I promise you that a time would come that you will make peace with him. You cannot dwell in anger forever. No matter how hard it sounds now, we must move on.

Regarding your brother, you cannot judge him too harshly. Michael is still a child and not able to make the right decision on his own. Don't be upset that he got a computer and you didn't. That computer came with too big a price. Michael, unfortunately, will have to pay, maybe for the rest of his life. But I promise again, my precious listener, a computer, for you. And I always keep my promises. Remember that your father said I would kidnap you both and take you back to Romania? Michael believed him when your father said so. But I assure you, your father knew that he couldn't convince you of that. You are a kid with an old soul."

There might have been a reason she didn't like to talk about all of this, but instead preferred me to tell stories about my childhood. So I went on...

More than anything, I liked spending the holidays with my grandparents in the countryside. My parents would come, as well, after they were done with their duties in the city. There was so much to learn in the village, no city could compete with it. The many traditions of the village enhanced its beauty and cemented connections between people; people loved and respected each other. And that it is what life is about.

All the holidays were great out there, and difficult for me to make one, my especial favorite.

On Easter Sunday, very early in the morning, as soon as they heard the little bell call, the people gathered, in a hurry, at the church. It was a privilege for them to participate in that great moment called the Resurrection.

My grandma knew how excited I was to take part in it. She came to my bed and whispered a tender song in my ear, "Up, up and let's go, so we can be in the first row." Everyone wanted to be there first for the event. I jumped right up out of the bed, got to my feet, and in no time, I was ready to go.

One could see from all directions flocks of people heading to the church. It was still dark outside; the spring air was crisp but refreshing. As I inhaled it deeply, I felt the Resurrection penetrate not only into my lungs but into everything around us; it was so real; all of Nature came back to life as did Jesus. We would arrive by sun up. It was magnificent!

I would meditate on how physical suffering was rewarded with everlasting life. We all, one by one, lit our candles from one main candle posted at the front of the altar, which gloriously spread its light throughout the entire church. It was the light of life's triumph over death. Then we walked around the church holding the lit candles and singing, "Christ has risen." Our song was loud with joy and could be heard over the entire villag".

Like Corina, I listened to Sonia's stories with rapture. I grew up in the city of Bucharest and had little contact with village life. No wonder Sonia loved those customs so much. They were beautiful, and that beauty has shaped her life.

How true it is, as Schopenhauer says, "the contemplation of beauty, or *aesthetics* as the philosopher calls it, heals the soul's wounds".

265

CHAPTER 43

Reflections on the Present and the Past

The scenery at that end of the day is absolutely, magnificent. The sky is crimson. The sun stumbles in a few silky clouds, and finally lets itself be escorted out past the horizon.

I wish I had a canvas and many shades of red at hand to capture the beauty of sunset. The transition from one color to another is subtle, quick, and too elusive to be pinned down. It beggars paint. Such a transition can only be captured on the memory's *canvas*, and then played back, in great details, with words.

Colorful bliss used to linger in my mind long after night swallowed what my eyes saw. But even night has its charm...

I recall the nights of my distant childhood.

Once, Grandpa and I were watching from the grapevine-covered porch of his house, the sun passing from twilight to darkness.

I must have been in primary school, yet very much captivated by the mysteries of the sky or the "heavenly vault" as Grandpa called it.

We pretended that the little porch was our observatory. In a corner, the dense vine opened to the sky. That gap helped us to concentrate our imaginary telescopes on a little patch of the sky. I was amazed by my grandpa; he was all-knowing. I remember how I would blink my eyes first at him and then at the sky, as he went on and on...

"Around the middle of June, here in Romania, he would say, we celebrate Sânzianes' Day, which for the believers coincides with St.

John the Baptist Day.

As you might know, Sanziana is not only a female name, but also the name of a wild flower. Their yellow, humble flowers, with a subtle scent, bloom around this holiday. We all here, are looking for that yellow tint to the fields. It heralds for us, the summer. Their blooming is bound to a celestial event, the summer solstice, marking the longest day of the year. After that, the days become shorter and shorter until the autumnal equinox, when a day's length equals the night's. The descending length of the days continues until it reaches the shortest day and the longest night of the year at the Winter's Solstice."

Ever since, and without mistake, I could tell the solstices and equinoxes apart.

My grandpa used a teacher's tone of voice, making sure that his pupil understood every bit of information.

Oh, how I cherish these memories!

The sky looked like a page from a book with its many constellations, for each of which, my grandpa had a name. He would say, "This is the time for the shining stars called the Pleiades, or Găinușa (meaning hen with chicken) as it is known around here. We missed the Big Dipper or Ursa Major; it has already left the Northern Hemisphere. I promise though, that next year around the beginning of May, when we're back on the prowl, we'll catch it in the sky."

I knew that Grandpa always kept his promises. I went to sleep with my mind full of the beauty and the mystery of heaven. Even as a child, I had many questions about that silent, fascinating world above.

It was so long ago…but I still ponder some of those questions. I know that for some I will never have an answer. Other generations will come, though, one by one, and unravel the mystery until the entire cortege of questions would finally, be answered.

Now, faraway in time and space from that Transylvanian village, with my grandpa long gone to the realm from which nobody returns,

I still look to the sky with the curiosity and fascination of a child.

The trees in my backyard display an arrangement, like a living altar for me. They make me think of a sacred landscape.

In the morning I see the sky between those trees, and ask heaven for its blessings and at night, with gratitude, I count them.

On clear summer evenings the sun sets behind those trees, but not before flickering between the branches and playing hide and seek with me.

As soon as the sun is gone, the sky becomes studded with stars. I can tell the seasons apart by looking at the stars, as Grandpa had taught me. It is June again and I look to the heavens to find the Pleiades. They are the same as those that my grandpa and I had watched so long ago. I wonder if my grandpa is above, somewhere between the stars, watching me, and is glad that these sweet memories are still so vivid in my mind.

CHAPTER 44

True Love Never Dies

"It was 1967, in the middle of June...

The sky suddenly became overcast, without any warning. A little later, some distant thunder thrummed in the background, but the sound was easily covered by the noise of the streets; the only proof, it had happened was the lightning.

It was unusual to have clouds before thunder; normally it would be the other way around. I guess, the wind oversaw the changing of the usual order, and it brought us a heavy rain faster than expected. I was glad that Adrian arrived before the rain started.

I recognized his steps, but I was surprised not to hear his whistling, which always announced his arrival. I knew it by heart. He always whistled cheery tunes that we both knew. I ran to open the door. The first heavy drops rolled over our hug as a blessing after an unusually hot day.

We planned to visit the City Park that afternoon. The park was known for its many linden trees, hence its nickname Linden Tree Park. The linden's blossoming was the park's main attraction. People flocked to it to enjoy the first scents of summer.

When Adrian and I were in college, we always visited this park after our exams. Nothing was more relaxing and in tune with our love than sitting in this lime-scented bower. On this stormy day, though, we were no longer students, even though the park reminded us of that carefree time.

With my head on his arm, we quietly watched the rain shuddering

269

down, like a curtain pulled over the window.

Adrian was much taller than me. I couldn't reach his shoulder unless I wore very high heels. He didn't mind me being petite. In contrast his remarks made me feel special. "In my eyes you will always be the first and the tallest. The height through your heels is not real, it is fake. I love you the way you are. You are perfect."

Adrian had a way when talking of love that reminded me of how special our love was. This time, though, Adrian was unusually quiet. It seemed like something was bothering him, but I didn't ask any questions because he was usually so open with his thoughts. He moved the arm I was leaning on and put it around me and hugged me tightly. I felt in that hug something more than love; it was like a hidden hurt. I looked in his eyes and instead of explanation I got a kiss on the top of my head. Even in that long kiss there was something more than love.

It was still stormy outside, the gusty winds turned into gusty rain, tempestuously knocking on the window. It was like an intruder which kept us from being ourselves. Adrian bent down to my ear and whispered,

"I don't like this storm."

And I whispered back, "I don't like it either." I had a feeling that we were not only stranded inside, but something deep in Adrian's heart was also stranded. I was patient with Adrian as he always was with me. If there was something important for Adrian to tell me, he would tell me eventually. I tried to chase away any anxiety and felt grateful being in the safety of his arms.

The storm passed as fast as it came. A few last clouds shed their remaining drops. It gave us time to look around my mother's flower garden. I couldn't tell whether we were waiting for the rain to stop or if we were just postponing an imminent talk and moving our attention to something else.

We felt sorry for the flowers that didn't make it through the storm. The multicolored cups of petunias haughtily posed before the storm and humbly fell face-down on the ground.

My mind strayed to how my mom loved flowers and had many varieties with many colors. There was also a linden in our backyard, which filled the garden with a fragrance that was the attraction of all the bees in the area.

On sunny days, when all the bees were out, we watched how diligently they went about their chores without bumping into one another. Curious! They came in a hurry, checked out every flower for nectar, picked it, and then brought their harvest to the hive. It was also their job to turn it into honey which Adrian often compared me with, saying that I was much sweeter.

I loved Adrian with all my heart and I had no doubts about his love either. We were truly soul mates. Adrian was a deep thinker, which was exactly what I enjoyed the most in our friendship. We shared the same values and had the same questions about the world. We admired its beauty, but detested the ugliness so often caused by our fellow humans.

We liked to watch every small thing around us and looked forward to learning about its purpose. We were amazed by the bees' accuracy in finding their own hive after wandering long distances in search of pollen. There is a wisdom in nature that challenges us. Think, for example, how the colors and the scent of the flowers first attract the bees and offer them sweet nectar in exchange for pollination and the perpetuation of the species. My father would mention the

Ecclesiastics saying: "to everything there is a season and a time for every purpose under heaven. "How true!

We wondered what would make a bee work with such devotion, and be willing to sacrifice its life, for its queen. It was like there was a device implanted in its tiny body responsible for its behavior. If that device could be decoded, and set in other beings, that would be the greatest achievement of science.

We watched the ritual as the bees bowed in front of the flower, perhaps as a sign of gratitude and joy at the glimpse of its nectary riches. Then they made their pre-harvest hopping dance.

One-day Adrian, amused me by humming the tune of Brahms' "Hungarian Dances" to the thrum of the bees in the background. It was funny, but not far from the truth. The bees' buzz had the same cadence as the Brahms 'piece of music.

Other times we were in awe that such a large variety of colors and fragrances could come from the same handful of dust. How you might not be amazed?

Adrian was an architect and I was a chemist. We let our two professions blend with our fascination for the things around us; our love was much more than a simple attraction. Sometimes we joked about it; he was the architecture and I was the unseen chemistry.

This fascination helped us to keep the fire of love ablaze. We spent our time together to the fullest. We were Cupid's kids. We didn't let our inner kids die and therefore we were never bored. We found joy in learning new things. For some, such a joy might have been insignificant. Many are too busy to notice or too numb to feel such joy.

Beyond this we had fun. We loved music and dancing. It was enough for us to hear just a few notes for our steps to catch the rhythm right away, and we would be dancing in each other's arms. It was pure love coming from Heaven.

We also found nature's music everywhere: in the soft sound of a stream, in the birds' chirp, or in that of the bees' humming. Even the wind made a song that we sometimes enjoyed.

Nature showed us its hospitality in the garden in my parent's back yard. My mom, out of her love for wild flowers, always had a patch of them. Lying down on the colorful carpet, we watched the clouds floating like feathers on the quiet sea of the blue sky. There were bees swarming around us. They belonged to my parents' hives and they were thought of as being part of our family. No matter how far away they traveled in search of nectar, they would return home without mistake. We liked to think that bees were left behind by a

Blessed with Twice the Freedom

vanished world. They might have been left here to teach us duty, generosity, and appreciation.

Before we knew it, the sky had regained its blue color and the air its freshness. All of nature, unfettered in the storm's tension, became calm again. We headed out to the park as planned.

The walls of the buildings around the park were still wet, giving the impression of fresh paint. The lindens were heavy with their yellow flowers as was the air with their fragrance.

But now Adrian was not only quiet but looking sad. I anxiously waited to learn what was bothering him. The way he was holding me tenderly with his arm made me believe that it was not at all about me. On the way to the park we didn't exchange many words. But sometimes that was the way we were, contemplating and thinking. Though this time, it seemed different.

There were many leaves and twigs with bunches of lime-yellow flowers along the alley. One of the more robust jutted into Adrian's way. He kicked it aside with rancor, which surprised me; it was uncharacteristic of him. I looked at him and couldn't help myself from saying,

"Why are you doing that? It was struck already once today; don't you think that a second hit is too much?"

"I am sorry, Sonia. Today was terrible for me."

"Yes, I can see that, but I was waiting for you to talk. Is it about your work, your parents, or me? What is it?"

He didn't answer right away, he stretched instead his arm , and grabbed a bunch of linden flowers from a short tree, and hung them on one of my ears. He bent down and whispered in that same ear,

"It is about us. We have to flee this country, so we can stay together forever."

He emphasized "forever" …

I am still stunned. I have no words for this.

Apparently, love is a thing, which politically, can be snatched from us and then made it disappeared. In this respect, Adrian and I must

273

be considered dead for each other, unless we could manage to escape such a verdict. I cannot see right now how.

I did not realize until now, how much control the Communist Regime has over us all. Here I am, confronted with a new Chapter in my life. My mind refuses to process such an intrusive decision in our own lives. The peace of mind I had before the storm, it was taken away from me ,leaving behind a turmoil I was not prepared for.

I didn't pass through my mom's room as I usually did when coming home at night. We were used to chatting a little before going to sleep. But this time it would have been more than just a little chat. I didn't want to disturb my father, who because of his poor health, always went to bed early. I couldn't face them tonight. My tears didn't listen to my strong will and began to roll down my face. I kept thinking that this could not be happening, and yet it was. I could not control the tears. As a child who cannot take any more hurt, I pushed my head deep into my pillow, and started to whimper. My mother must have heard something and quietly opened the door of my room. I didn't hear her come in. Sitting on the edge of my bed, she touched my shoulder. "Sweetheart, what happened? Why are you so upset?"

I answered through gritted teeth, which was not my way at all, "The Party…"

"What party are you talking about?"

"Mom, what kind of question is that? There is only one Party, the Communist Party."

"That's true, sweetheart, there is only one, the Communist…"

I think my mom suspected what was behind my distress, but she was waiting to learn the details from me. It wouldn't be a surprise to her. She knew that the Communist Regime controlled every single aspect of our lives.

For sure my family was not at all in its favor. Adrian and I were not politically compatible. I am sure we were under Party scrutiny for a while without us knowing. Once under scrutiny of the Communist Party, it is hard to emerge. Adrian's parents were both teachers, well-

Blessed with Twice the Freedom

respected people in the community but members of the Communist Party. My parents were not.

It was a rule. All the educators, in order, to prepare students in the Communist spirit, had to be a part of the Communist Party. It was hard to know who was merely affiliated with the party just to keep their job, and who in fact, believed in it. I am sure Adrian's parents like many others, had to save their careers. There was no way to advance in such a career without a Communist Party affiliation.

"Well, Adrian was called in early this morning by the Communist Party Committee, and he was asked bluntly to revise his personal conduct. As you know he is a highly regarded as future member of the Communist Party Committee of the Architecture Institute. They are looking to offer him a great political future, but a relationship with me puts his future in jeopardy. In their eyes my family and I are nothing more than societal rejects, which in time should disappear."

That was a tough but true statement.

Even though my social provenance was not the same as Sonia's I was very familiar with the communists practice.

Beginning with high school, everyone was minutely surveilled by the Communist Party, as a part of its process for recruiting new members from the younger generation. The folders in the Security Service drawers became fatter and fatter. Unfortunately, informants would sometimes destroy careers and even lives by twisting the truth. Students, without any warning or explanation, were expelled from college. Recovering from such an event was not easy. It was like being bankrupt and expecting to have soon a good credit report, again.

Some people were pushed to disguise themselves and flee the country, hoping that their spoor would be lost.

The hidden information in the filing cabinets' drawers controlled our personal lives the same way that a chromosome inserted in in our DNA, would do its vital work, inside of us without us knowing.

Surveillance was used to hunt for, and announce any political indiscretions from the past. The only cure, for those with any inherited political *error* in their past, was to be destroyed. The Communist regime had zero tolerance for such *errors*.

But how can one's past or identity be changed? One person's past includes preceding generations. One carried not only the own political *errors* but those of parents' and grandparents'.

There was only one way, empirically, to make the past obsolete — and that was a fantasy: obtain a new identity.

We couldn't even mention the word "transcendence" because it was an irritating word to the Communist ear. Not long ago, highly regarded people from different institutions in Bucharest were accused of practicing transcendental meditation and as a result were thrown out of their jobs. Transcendence, was thought to be part of the metaphysical realm and, like God, had to be out of Romanian minds and vocabularies.

Spirit was also a forbidden word. Materialism was the only philosophy allowed and we were pushed to believe in it.I was an inescapable obligation.

Power was in the hands of the Communists and everyone feared that power. Being a suspect was often a straight line to be a convict, because no proof was needed in the courts. People were found dead on the streets and others were lost without a trace. The victims' families couldn't even ask any questions about their loss, for fear of becoming victims themselves.

After the fall of Communism, the gruesome truth was revealed. Many of those who had disappeared were found buried in the basement walls of the town's Security Service building. Little nameplates that endured with time helped to identify them. It is believed that after being tortured, the detainees were buried alive in their cells. I wonder how someone could sleep after committing such an atrocity.

But to give *love* a hideous political face, and kill it for that only reason, it was atrocious, also.

Love was not a part of the Communism Doctrines, and the

Blessed with Twice the Freedom

heart was nothing more than a physiologic pump without hosting any feelings. Love coming from heart was considered superfluous. There was only the rational love coming from the superior organized substance, how they called the brain.

And, of course, a real Communist should have more patriotic things in mind than love.

I am sure, these terrible things were not only in my mind, but also in Sonia's, and not less in her mother's, while delivering to her the news she just learned about. It would be an absurdity, to think about a person, as you think about a robot without feelings. Yet such absurdity has become for Sonia and Adrian a reality.

Here is how the two of them, in dismay, are going over it, weighing the possible and the impossible.

" I read my mother's face, while we kept quiet for a few minutes, yes, she was also still troubled. My anguish rose up again,

"Adrian is ready to flee the country and have me follow him."

"Something like that is impossible," my mother said outright and then explained,

"They will know and do much more…you know what I mean. They will certainly seek revenge for your actions, they will blame you for Adrian's defection. You will be held responsible for that."

My mom pleaded again, revealing her own anguish,

"My dearest Sonia, I am sorry that our faith has led to such a strain on your relationship. It is a shame that somebody or something so hostile can impact two people who love each other so much… It is hard to say, but for now it may be better for you to be away from us, pretending that you don't have anything to do with us. We understand the world we are living in and we accept it because we have no other options".

I totally disagreed, and answered her vehemently,

"I have learned from you both, from an early age, about the importance of righteousness in life. I could never go against my conscience and not be true to myself. Living a double life would be tougher for me than the Communist oppression. At this point, no matter where we move they will easily track us down. From our files they know more than we know about ourselves. The file is like a fingerprint. You know that hiding from Security's eye is almost impossible. All of this is not because Adrian is a fierce Communist; it is because he has the potential to be a loose thread, unravelling further from the fabric of the Party. By the same token, if Adrian were to be expelled from the Communist Party he would have no future."

I left my mother speechless. I begged her though, to use discretion and spare my father's health by not telling him anything that night. Above all, he would feel guilty for the social background I was born into. It would have been too much for him at once. In time he would have to learn about it, little by little.

The next day I was on call for a twenty-four-hour shift, so I had an excuse to leave the house earlier and come back only the next day. I was glad I didn't have to face my father; he surely would have noticed signs of the turmoil I was going through.

"Let's go to sleep now, and let all these thoughts go numb, as in a short hibernation. The light of the day will bring them out, and maybe they'll be less dreary," my mom said in a weary voice, looking towards the door. We needed to protect our secret.

I felt a little better sharing my distress with my mother. She always passed her calm onto me, like a bandage over a child's wound. Nevertheless, at that point, I would have liked to be alone. My mother, with her sixth sense, seemed to understand.

"May God keep us under His protection," she whispered, hugging me tightly and kissing the top of my head, then stepping slowly out of the room.

I wish I could have fallen into kind of hibernation, but it was simply not possible. I tried and tried to chase away my troubling thoughts, but they returned to me just as the tides return to the shore, continuously. With my mind's eye I could see Adrian caught by the same tide. I still felt his arms holding my head tight against his chest, so tightly that I couldn't talk, only listen. He said clearly,

"I could work as an architect without being as ideal a Communist as they would like me to be. Nobody should have the right to rip us apart." He said it without realizing that desertion from the Party would come only at a high price.

Deep inside I had a comforting feeling that destiny would bring us together again but when and how, I didn't know.

I was sure that my mom had the same hidden thought. I also believed that Adrian clung to that hope. Nobody and nothing should have the right to destroy us. We had to be wise to not make things worse.

The following morning, I tiptoed out of the house before my parents were up. I stopped for a moment at the front gate. I wasn't yet sure what direction to take or where to go. I walked to a little church not far from my house. The college students called it their "secret church." I knew that place well and hoped that only the old nun who was always there would see me. She did. I was glad that there was nobody in the church but her. We greeted each other without any other words.

I lit two candles, one for Adrian and one for me. I watched them burning in a flickering dance. I didn't know what to pray for. I imagined all my questions and answers burning in the humble candle's flame. I felt, weirdly, that I was floating when I got up from the wooden bench. I felt ethereal, my body and my mind were two separate entities. The lack of the sleep made me weak and the stress almost made me forget to breathe.

Going to work I walked the back streets like a sleepwalker, for fear of seeing anybody I knew. I didn't want anybody to step into my painful world. I was hoping to have an easy time at work without many emergencies. I was lucky to have only two prescriptions to fill for the entire night.

In my locker I had one volume of Proust's *In Search of Lost Time*.

279

During slack times on night duty, I read the entire series, one by one. I liked his writing style very much. Small and insignificant things were graciously turned into jewels by his mind and pen. Tonight, his words were a tonic for my wounded heart.

We all encounter hardship in life and Marcel Proust encountered his. He was born before the world of medicine knew anything about the causes and treatment of asthma. There was no explanation for why the lungs would constrict and cut off every cell of the body from vital oxygen. Without oxygen, life was not possible. For that reason, Proust was forced to live in total isolation.

Something just as dramatic as asthma would isolate Adrian and me from each other. For more than five years, Adrian had been the oxygen that I couldn't live without; as I was for him. We didn't have any other choice then, but to try to survive the Communists' suffocation. It was unbearable not seeing see each other. It was like we were in boiling water under the lid of the Security Service.

I looked for an escape and found one. The Pharmacy Headquarters approved me to work on the Black Sea shore in the summer. Heavy tourism during the summer months required more workers, pharmacists were no exceptions. Within a week I moved to Olimp, a very nice recreational resort. I got to work in a new and modern pharmacy with new people, who knew nothing of my sad story. My heart was still heavy though. I left my love behind without saying a word. We knew what we had to do to ensure our safety. It was like treating an open wound with alcohol for the sake of healing. That short pain would spare us from one that would be even harder to survive.

Adrian knew nothing about my temporary move out of our town. He was confronted with same answers as he frantically looked for me everywhere,

"At this time, it is better for both of you to continue on your separate ways," my mom told him. He would also hear it from the Head Pharmacist where I worked, to whom I had confessed, so I could get his clandestine support.

After Adrian learned that the Communists' "eagle eye" was still hovering over us, he decided to move out of Cluj to Bucharest. We hoped that those in charge of our case, would consider themselves winners; "mission accomplished." We wanted them to move their binoculars away from us, granting us a bitter freedom.

They would never know what was still in our hearts. Our love for each other was not quenched, but still alive, hoping and waiting for better times to come. I made myself believe that Adrian was far away for a while, and that distance was the only hindrance between us. And then it became real.

CHAPTER 45

Turning Back Pages

I learned more about the original Sonia-Adrian love story from Sonia's journal than from her personally. When I met her that story was buried deep in her past. She talked to me about him only once and in a very casual way, never mentioning his name.

But I know a lot about the second part of their story though, as I was the one who brought them together again. Even to this day, it is hard for me to believe how these coincidences came to pass.

I don't think the past buried their love, but oddly it covered their love over, to protect it from dying. It seems that there was always a trickle of love flowing within them, waiting for the right time to stream out. And then their love was rekindled, and the embers ignited into flames.

I could see that Adrian and Sonia were true soul mates, each completely intense. Sonia's intensity was, in part, the natural consequence of her perspicacious memory.

She admitted that her good memory did not always work to her advantage as it was also hard for her to forget events that caused her pain. This made forgiveness a longer process for her. She would often say, "Forgiveness must come from depths of the heart, while forgetting comes from the brain. They should not be and must not be confused; forgiving and forgetting are not the same." I totally agree with her, they are not the same.

Throughout her life though, it was a real struggle to balance the forgiving and the forgetting, no matter what she said to the contrary.

Tirelessly, I combed through the fragments she left behind, trying to follow her life's path exactly. No matter how much I would have liked to keep chronological track, it was not possible. Her past and present were intricately entangled, like an elaborate design on a canvas which would have been distorted just by pulling out some threads.

Sonia was complex in nature yet pleased by simple things.

I would say that Adrian waited a lifetime to get her back, while Sabin stumbled into her complex nature and pushed her away. Sabin was too shallow to understand her.

He must have made a gargantuan effort to impress Sonia, for her to have ever thought of him as special. There was a glossy surface to him, just enough to catch the eye. That was his way; to impress, to catch, to discard and start the game again.

He never learned from his mistakes or even admitted to making them. He expected others to tolerate them. I know Sonia put up with him for so long for the sake of their children and to keep her family together. She respected their marriage vows as sacred commitments. For her, marriage was not a simple play.

For a long while she refused to see the plain truth, in order to nourish hopes of change. But surely if there had been no children involved, she would not have stayed in that marriage for seventeen years.

In Sonia's journal once, I came to a page entitled "Corina's Birthday." I read it many times as it gave me great joy. For a moment I tried to transport myself back to the first days that we welcomed Corina into our lives also. Gil and I adored her.

We were given a gift just to enjoy, without the diapers or sleepless nights. We got the best time of her childhood too. She was at the age when children willingly accept love from anyone who gives it. Corina received plenty from all of us. Let Sonia tell it.

"It is the 14th of June again. My dearest daughter, your page has turned over 20 times. I still vividly remember your first cry, your face perfectly round and your incredible hair, which seemed too long for a newborn. But I guess you asked heaven to allow you to be perfect to make me the happiest mother of all timer. I will never forget that moment. It is one of my greatest blessings.

Then as you grew up, that same beautiful face, adorned by braided hair and eyes like two playful beads, would greet me every morning, always smiling. No matter how many years have passed and how famous you might be I think of you as my baby girl. I guess that is a mother's privilege…

Even though I am trying not to mingle moments of joy with moments of sadness, I do always get a little sad when I think of my children's birthdays. As a new mom, I never got a basket of roses in my hospital room, but instead I got the cheapest possible bouquet of whatever seasonal flowers could be found on the market. I tried not to pay much attention to it then, but somehow the gift of cheap flowers – which I consciously tried to suppress – hunted me down when I least expected it. I must have forgotten that he was stingy and that the time for impressing me was over. But I will never forget that with the birth of my daughter on a beautiful June day, I got an entire line-up of June's flowers.

In fact, that very morning I did received a real and very beautiful bouquet of wild flowers. It was huge; I could hardly see the person behind it. There were yellow bedstraw's, red poppies, and blue cornflowers all blended with light yellow wheat-ears. I stared at it and let my mind place every detail into my memory. Later, I retrieved this memory and made many paintings for my friends. It was my way of sharing the happiness I took in June's gifts (one of which is Corina) with them. The bouquet was not from Sabin, as he had forgotten how much I loved wild flowers.

There was a time, though, now lost in the past, when he knew how to remember. It was our first spring together. Who would not have been be impressed to hear a confession of love like his? I remember it word by word;" for you, and only for you my love, I would like to bring an entire field of wildflowers and cover you then watch you shine out of them."

Very often, he would tiptoe behind me and stretched a handful of flowers to me, while whispering in my ear, "They are for you, and only for you."

That day, I did feel that I was the only one in the world. If I had asked Sabin for the moon, he would have tried to get it for me. Now, such a thought is risible. I guess there was not enough room in his heart for both children and a wife to coexist.

However, Sabin did bring Michael to see his sister. Michael came to sit next to me in the maternity ward. He was only three and it was hard for him to understand how I could belong to him and his sister at the same time.

In fact, one day when they both were still little, I heard them arguing over who I belonged to. Corina always vehemently, claimed me as totally hers and Michael, who would never hurt her feelings, begged Corina for a compromise. I wish I could have recorded it.

At that time though, Sabin wouldn't get into the dispute; he let them have me entirely.

I look back and cannot believe how long it took me to understand that I could not change Sabin. I had learned a bitter lesson; you cannot change people, so you can love, they have to change themselves, to be worthy of love.

CHAPTER 46

An Old Scar of a Distant Spring

I guess, Sonia wrote this poem-draft after learning about the obstacles the Communist Regime was putting between her and Adrian. But revolt and despair were not a good trade for love. The price was too high. The price would have been their own lives.

"I run to you, still having in my hair,
The scent of June's linden blossoms
That will spell to you my love's fair.
Then held tightly in your arms,
I could listen to your heart's whispers
Coming in tumultuous waves,
Which then turned into love's river
And as it rushed tenderly over me,
turned me into spring.
That you may love each spring
Without any hindrance.

Then it let me slip slowly, into summer,
Flowing at time's will.
Love me even when I am disguised
In golden autumn
So, we both can slide into the whitest winter

Then vanish into colorless eternity.
Nobody should know
That it was you and me."

More than anything, I could feel in these lyrics the unbearable distress of a human being to whom it has been taken away an elementary right. For the sake of a sublime love, metaphorically she would have like to be anything just to escape from the Communists' eye.

Sonia knew that she could have disappeared without a trace just to save Adrian from a relationship that they found not only inappropriate for of a Communist Party member, but dangerous for his future. At least that's what was in their minds; Sonia and her family were enemies of the regime. People like them were oppressed in many ways, until — so the plan went — they would become extinct as a social group.

Once in the Communist Party, an unwritten right of ownership hung over its members' heads. It was like an invisible net that stretched over them so nobody could escape without their knowledge and of course without penalty.

I suspected that this was not a subject Sonia would have liked to talk about freely, and I never dared to ask her more than I had been told. I thought that it was still painful for her. It might be one of those things that are very deeply and secretly buried in one's mind.

I knew though that their love story turned into a drama and that took place in the City's Linden Park. I noticed that she would often avoid taking walks through that park. We spent a lot of time together and also walked a lot, even though Corina's steps were still short. She didn't mind at all, she would always be jumping in front of us, with her inexhaustible child energy. Corina, one day, wished to go to the park. The other three of us thought it was a good idea and agreed at once. I guess Sonia was either very discreet with her hidden scars or she decided to plunge herself into a thing she was still vulnerable to. On that walk, though, she brought up something from her past. She said, "Love is not something we can buy, sell or steal, but surely it can be killed." After reading in her journals about how they were forced apart, I remembered that it was in this park, at the same time of year, and that, that was the last time they saw each other. Sonia could not help but remember Adrian on that day. And she was ready now to talk about things, which were until then, had been locked up.

We walked slowly and talked at the same pace, enjoying the fresh air. If Gil were with us he would explain the benefits of negatively charged air to Corina. I am sure she would have said, "but I know that negative is bad, isn't it?" Gil would have told her that sometimes there were exceptions to the rules, as in this instance; the negative (negatively charged ions) would bring a positive effect. We didn't want to even go close to such a subject with Corina. It would have been an endless list of questions that only Gil was never too tired to answer.

The alley was still wet from the heavy rain that had just ended a few hours before. Now everything was calm, and an amazing afterglow adorned the sky. Only the fallen flowers of linden could remind us of the past storm. Corina left us alone for a while, but she suddenly came running up to us holding linden flowers in both hands. "This is for Mommy and this one for you, Auntie Neli." She said it with a smile stretching across her entire face.

"Oh, Corina you are very nice to offer me flowers," I said.

"Yes, and I would like to be as nice as my Mommy."

Sonia couldn't help herself from saying it with a lovingly smile, "Sweetheart, you are perfectly nice on your own and I shouldn't take any credit for your niceness."

Very often Corina, would aim for the last word. At this time, she came out with a compliment to her mom, "But you have noticed it, haven't you?"

Then Sonia ended such a conversation, because with Corina it might have gone on and on.

Blessed with Twice the Freedom

Corina liked the color of the flowers. She was always looking around to find them and saw beauty even in the weeds. And I adored those two little hands holding flowers. Of course, our talking about the love story stopped right there.

On another occasion, I had a talk, not with Sonia but with Mrs. Sava, a.k.a. "Mama Elena," on the subject. The three of us paid her a visit at her new house in the countryside. While the girls went to Corina's neighborhood favorite "Ruffled Hair Salon" for a haircut, I preferred to keep Mrs. Sava company.

Then we were planning to take Corina to a puppet show. We grown-ups joined the little ones and shared their enthusiasm. It was like a steam bath for the soul.

Taking advantage of the fact that we were alone, I dared to reopen the already closed Sonia-Adrian subject.

"It's true; their forced break-up not only broke their hearts but scarred them. You know what I mean. It was totally unfair," Mrs. Sava whispered sadly and kept her eye on the door. She knew that Sonia avoided talking about that bit of unfairness. Then she added, "Sonia has her own way of accepting the twist of her destiny. Now that she has her children, she wouldn't exchange them for anything in the world. As for her husband, I have my doubts. I think Sonia has them too, but she tries to make the best of it. That's what I hear."

"Mrs. Sava, I know the word "unfair" is too little to express what they had to go through, but what is fair when it comes to this regime?"

I made this affirmation and glanced apprehensively at the door. It was not so much that Sonia might catch us talking about her, but the fear that spies could be listening to us too. Then Mrs. Sava added, "Sonia is not one to accept a double-life; for her truth is a virtue. Adrian's parents and Sonia's father and myself tried to find a middle ground for them, but even as a child, Sonia never accepted a "halfway." I guess it's part of their destiny, what else can I say?" she concluded with a sigh.

From our talk, I also got Mrs. Sava's impressions of the two men in Sonia's life. About Adrian she said, "I know that Adrian admired Sonia's character, even though he knew that somehow it was to his disadvantage. He knew that he had to give up on her so her safety was assured. He was also aware of his own safety. At the high level he was at, he must have known a lot about the behind-the-scenes Communist activity, which was hidden from the common people It was not that Adrian would have been involved; he was a great man, but as many young people, he became a part of the Communist Party without knowing what it would entail. Remember some of the highest-ranking officials had problems of this kind and wouldn't approve the marriages their children wanted. They didn't kill their adversaries, but people were sent into exile."

"We live in hard times that's for sure," I said.

"Of course, the Adrian-Sonia story is not a story of that magnitude. Nevertheless, the Communist Party had high hopes that one-day Adrian would be one their consecrated even though Adrian was not at all what the Party wanted him to be… If he had been able to follow his heart, he would have chosen Sonia over anything.

For Sonia, being the cause of wrecking Adrian's party affiliation would have been not just unpatriotic but a true crime. So, as you can see, there was no other way," Ms. Sava said, nodding and closing her eyes as in deep reflection.

"Their story is more than a sad story, Mrs. Sava. I hope with all my heart that Sonia doesn't have to go through more sorrow due to this other man in her life."'

Mrs. Sava replied quickly, "This other man? Oh, it is better not to mention him now. I have never had great feelings about him. And what he did lately confirms my suspicions. I think he is selfish and that he tries to control Sonia. He treats her like she is a thing he owns. A loving husband would never do that." Mrs. Sava appeared ready to cry but controlled herself, knowing that Sonia could enter the door momentarily.

"I know Mrs. Sava, it is difficult to admit that a person whom

Blessed with Twice the Freedom

Sonia trusted, could do such a thing. But let's look at this as positive for Sonia. It's good that she didn't have knowledge of his plans. First, no matter how much the Communists hurt her before, she wouldn't have agreed to let her husband leave the country illegally. Sabin knew that. Secondly, no matter how heavy her file was in the Security's Service drawers, they spared her. Sonia can make a strong case for her innocence." I didn't say it, but as much as I knew of Sabin so far, Sonia and Corina could both have been disappeared and Sabin still wouldn't have returned. He seemed to not care about his wife and daughter. I did not say so.

Mrs. Sava listened to all of this and at the end said, "What can I say other than God knows best." No sooner did Mrs. Sava end her sentence then we heard Corina's playful footsteps coming up the stairs. She was first to open the door, then she stopped purposefully onto the threshold for a moment. We understood she was waiting for compliments on her haircut. Sonia left her to do her show. And she knew her poses very well. We looked at her like a picture framed by the door's panels. Her haircut suited her very well. It was an adorable variation, in miniature, of the French singer, Mireille Mathieu, whose haircut was then in vogue.

There was only time left for goodbyes and hugging, so Sonia said while hugging her mom, "Hug, hug, and let's go."

Mrs. Sava had goodies for her girls and also some for me already packed and ready to go. She made sure we wouldn't forget them on the counter. She would always prepare something special ahead of our visit; it was a sweet treat. Corina would ask, "Granny, what is the most important ingredient in it?"

Mrs. Sava would smile and say, "It is love, my dear."

We took our packages loaded with love and left in a hurry. We had to be on time for the puppet show.

CHAPTER 47

Escape into Colors

"Hey, Gil where are you? You have to see this. I want to show you what I found in one of our photo-albums."

"I am right here behind you. What is it?" Gil answered full of curiosity.

"You remember that write-up in the newspaper about Sonia's exhibition, don't you?"

"Of course, I do," Gil answered with a gleam in his eyes.

"Here is a clipping about it. Look it is dated February 20, 1980."

We had read that article in the City's newspaper, praising an exhibition of "good quality amateur art," as the critic called it. Other people who saw it left with the same comments. It was a must see. We did go. We didn't make it for the opening, but we got there a few days later. It was Sonia's first solo painting exhibition.

Even though it was years ago I still vividly remember the poster on the gallery window; **Sonia Sava-Cătuşan** in bold and multi-colored letters on a blue-sky background. We had no clue that Sonia would become our precious friend. We also remember that nobody could believe that the artist was only a beginner in the art of painting. The critic would reveal that Sonia's talent happened spontaneously or as they say, "overnight."

"The first time Sonia Sava-Cătuşan got a brush in her hand, she made use of some oil paints she found lying around."

(In fact, we learned from Sonia after we met her," that she bought those paints for Sabin as a gift, knowing that he enjoyed painting.)

292

The article continued:

Without any previous training she painted a beautiful bouquet of flowers in a little carafe. Astoundingly, the painting expresses the beauty of simplicity, a chromatic freshness, and a convincing existence in space. Flowers are one of the most defining subjects in a creative person's poetic universe. They are tender receptacles of light, noble in their humble appearance. They are fragile yet beautiful. We are tempted to believe that we have in front of us someone who has burnished her craft for many years, but she is an ingenue. Such knowledge of the craft, such a subtle degree of refinement, and such near-melodious combinations of colors, can only be credited to a professional. This artist exudes confidence, and the exhibit captures a wide range of warm, human emotions, transcribed with specifically feminine discretion."

We read this review many times. We refreshed our memories from the time when Sonia's artwork emerged as a theme or even when we were just admiring her as a person and a dear friend. She made our lives more colorful.

Over the years so many flowers have marched, like a parade, in front of Sonia's eyes. Her eye, like a camera, would take pictures and pictures of their ephemeral exuberance and store them in her memory. Then triggered by an impulse known only to Sonia, they would be scrolled and unfolded. The parade would come back to life in the long-lasting liveliness of her paintings.

I remember our first visit with Sonia at her home. Her many paintings vividly colored the house's walls. Then I learned that her paintings were also on many friends' walls. So many people loved her artwork. Jokingly she would call herself a florist. She would paint excitedly when she received a request for one of her paintings, then she would give it away. I have never known someone else who took such profound pleasure in sharing.

After her boys left for America she rarely painted. I am not sure whether she was physically too busy or if she was just creatively drained. She tried to hide her feelings, but she was visibly affected by the way her husband had trapped her. Nevertheless, she was hopeful that once in America the painting muse would find her again and then she would spoil her new friends with colorful work.

In America she started painting again, but out of despair. She could hardly speak English and understood the language even less. She had to find a way to express herself and deal with the stress that she was under. Just thinking of what Sonia and Corina had to go through traumatized Gil and me. We felt helpless and wondered if she should come back to Romania.

It was during the divorce that Corina's teacher, Lee, visited them and saw some of the paintings she had brought with her from Romania. The next day, Lee delivered all the supplies that Sonia needed to begin to paint again. We considered Lee their guardian angel. I prayed constantly for Sonia and her family, since there was no other way to help them. Lee was the answer to my prayers. Sonia even called Lee the American version of me! We were glad that even though we couldn't be with them, Lee and Gary filled our place. In one of her letters she wrote,

"I listen to music while I paint. I let myself sink into a virtual world, fortifying my resistance to the real one that I have to struggle through."

Very often I look at Sonia's paintings in my living room. The shift in colors from one to the next gives the paintings a vibrancy that reflects hers. Every painting reminds me of her joy of painting and giving. Every color precisely displayed reminds me of Sonia. I know that she very often worked without a model, using her imagination, freeing her creative spirit.

"When I paint I feel the longing of one color for another and then I let them complement each other like in a perfect marriage."

She always dreamy about the perfect marriage.

Maybe that's why Gil and I loved her paintings. They were not copies of things but rather expressions of the feelings that stuck in her memory and passed through her heart. Sonia's memory was so powerful! It was difficult for her to simply draw lines between past, present, and future because the events that happened were glued together in her mind. Years later she would chuckle about the "parallel" that Sabin had thrown her in. She would call it her "launching pad to freedom."

One day she said, "I cannot believe that the Security Service isn't following my steps anymore. I also cannot believe that Sabin is not around to rummage through my shopping bags and admonish me for the things I bought for our house or for our children. To avoid this scolding, I used to secretly leave my purchases with a friend. She would give them back to me as presents, and always in his presence, of course. What was wrong with me? Why did I let him push me there? I wanted to protect our children from his reprimands. It took me a while to realize that the stingy man was not around anymore. Imagine that deep breath of freedom!!!"

Again, it was her belief that in life nothing comes without a purpose. She would learn patience from encountering limitations and learn serenity from uncertainty. She learned tolerance when sometimes her too-high-standard demands were not achieved. More than anything she would peer through things to turn them around. As they fell in her favor she would appreciate how lucky she was. She truly found a bright side in everything because there always was such a side.

CHAPTER 48

Just a Thought Between Us

Both Sonia and I believed that we are not finished at the grave. Otherwise the concept of life – creation – which is so meticulously designed, has no meaning. There is continuity in the universe and in life, there are no exceptions. Even though there is mystery beyond the grave, mystery keeps us going. One might ask, "Going where?" And I would say, "To beyond the grave." Life is just a link in the great continuum between the seen and the unseen worlds, it is another dimension, a dimension we don't have palpable access to in the same way we do with the physical world.

When I was in medical school, I got in-depth knowledge about every piece of the human body, about its complexity and its magnificent design. Would you throw away a great piece of art after you have created it? Likewise, the Creator wouldn't discard his works of art as debris or waste in the universe. That must be the reason mankind was given the gift of thinking, to seek a truth that can only be seen with the eyes of the mind.

In the beginning it was difficult, but with all of this in mind, I could deal with my dearest Gil's death almost a year ago. He passed suddenly and at first it broke my world apart. Then I put all of my beliefs to work. For me, there is a Truth that doesn't need to be verified. I keep Gil alive in my heart and that is an extraordinary feeling. Sometimes he comes to me in my dreams and vividly shares a connection with me as if we were in the same world. I found it curious and I smile at how he comes into my dreams precisely when

Blessed with Twice the Freedom

my days are not so easy. He must know that those are the days I miss him most! He left me so quickly and I was so unprepared!

I wish Corina and Sonia were still here. Having them with me in this difficult time might have made the loss of Gil easier for me to manage. In such situations, a friendship that is via phone or mail doesn't seem to be enough. There was too much to be missed. Fortunately, after the Revolution, Romania became free country, at least it was not a problem to travel abroad freely. Unfortunately, I did not love to fly, and I actually had a fear of flying, which made travelling to see Sonia more difficult for me.

With that freedom also came my retirement and I could spend time with Sonia and my little friend Corina. Whenever I use the word "little" in association with Corina, she hugs me tightly and says, "Hey, Auntie! I am an old teenager now, but I still like how you call me that. It reminds me of the great times I had with you and Uncle Gil when I really was little."

She remains the same genuine kid that I can't get enough of. She is very busy with school and her many extra-curricular activities. I enjoyed seeing her play sports and of course, also loved to see her play the piano and proudly she would tell me that she had been the newspaper editor all along, starting with the primary school years and into high school as well. Jokingly I would say, "Get out of here, have you mastered English so well that you were given such a job?"

"Oh, yes, Neli, I love my new language, but I'll never forget Romanian."

I noticed that she finally called me by my name, after I insisted on it many times. Of course, she was an editor.

I was filled with joy to resume our always-interesting chats with her mother. Sonia's house had a beautiful deck surrounded by flowers and a stream in the backyard. Sonia wrote and talked about it so many times that I was eager to see it. No wonder she loved that stream so much. It burbled just one song, yet you would be able to listen to it forever without getting bored. I let its clarity run through my mind to wash out all the silt of the thoughts I wanted to get rid of. We would have coffee in the morning or tea in the afternoon in the stream's company. It gave us so many reasons to reflect as it seized our attention. Jestingly we would say, "Let's gossip about nature again, it won't mind."

Sonia took the lead. With her eyes half closed, as was her manner, she said, "Would you believe that the water we are looking at is nothing other than two gases in a tight embrace? There is an interesting paradigm in nature: the hydrogen that "burns" in the sun, and the oxygen, which is desired in the fire, are both running in that water which is on call to quench the fire."

When she paused I knew that it was my turn to take over the conversation. We never let ourselves get caught in an argument about our beliefs, even if sometimes our beliefs were not the same. "And then what a twist – water itself becomes the most feared enemy of the fire."

"That's very true," she said, and then elaborated. "Imagine, the same water that we are watching moving in a hurry, the same water will turn into a cloud, scouring spaces, before returning back to earth. Think about a cloud as water's bliss. We know how short-lived bliss can be. In the winter the clouds sift snow instead of rain. So, you see how the same two gases can manifest themselves in three ways."

Everything that she said to me came out like a stream of words revealing a truth as clean as the river's stones. I couldn't help from saying, "Oh, Sonia I just got the answer to a question I've been struggling with for some time. I had difficulty understanding the Christian Doctrine defining God as a Trinity. Now I feel like I have the answer to the mystery of the Holy Trinity. More than that, I think that other answers will unmoor themselves from places that might look un-researchable at first sight. There are things that surpass our understanding but that doesn't mean they do not exist. Why then shouldn't I believe that Gil is still around? If I feel it, I do not need any other scientific evidence to justify such truth. We don't see the

Blessed with Twice the Freedom

hydrogen and the oxygen in the water we are looking at, or in the clouds above. And yet the two exist tightly bound together."

Sonia looked up smiling at me, glad to have a new accomplice in a theory that might seem too complicated and that some might never bother with it. Thinking deeply can always help us discover a new piece of the infinite world. Such thinking not only makes life more interesting, but it also adds substance that anchors it to reality, so no wind can blow it away. We were quiet for a moment but then learned that we were thinking the same thing: how lucky we were.

We thought that in life people don't meet by chance, however they often meet without seeking each other. After that, they spin their lives together like two colored threads on a spool. If one thread gets interrupted the ball still keeps its color wound in. There is no other way to take that color out other than to unravel the spool back to the point where the colors started their journey together.

Even though Gil's thread of life was interrupted I still keep his color blended into mine. Now, I have added it Sonia's and Corina's bright colors to the spool.

I visited the states many times and was finally able to meet Michael. I was so eager to meet him for such a long time. What an amazing young man. Indeed, he did have blue eyes like a "patch of clear sky" as Sonia would often say. He was tall and well-built and was a carbon copy of Sonia's father. He was quiet but at the same time witty with a special humor. So, I was happy to wind his colorful thread onto my spool as well.

Sonia and I approached the Sabin subject in our conversations randomly. Sonia as always, would look on the bright side.

"Probably my destiny had to teach me something new. Forgiveness was not something I could handle easily. I couldn't see my dignity obviously riddled by malicious words and deeds. As you know I am a Libra." She said it smiling, knowing that I was one too. "My nature is to be always in search of peace. But when I am deeply hurt, I don't want my wounds to be seen, so I cover them with unflinching

299

determination and keep my chin up. It is actually no more than the wrap of a timid nature that doesn't accept humility. I never thought that I could become so merciful that I would ask Heaven to have mercy on the one who hurt me so deeply. It was a tough lesson; I had to learn it step by step. And maybe I couldn't have learned it if it hadn't been so tough."

She was absolutely right. Revenge was not her way of dealing with enemies. That would have stolen her sleep at night or her joy in the successes she won against all vicissitudes. Approaching her fifties, she managed to learn a new language, so she could use it in her pharmacy practice. The American pharmacist licensure that she regained thirty years after her Romanian Pharmacy School graduation, brought her so much happiness. She would say, "Neli, it is so heavy a joy I can hardly carry it. Can you imagine that?"

"Yes, I can. I remember how heavy your work was also. Maybe only Corina and Michael are as happy as I am for you."

Corina, like her mother, was very talented and attended some of the most famous schools in the world. It was just Michael. He attended good schools eventually but there was still his seizures and its consequences. Post-traumatic stress is like a storm's aftermath; pick up, sort out and build again. The most important part is stirring up the will to do it. Psychological trauma heals slower than physical ones. Sabin had it all wrong. But he would never realize it, because he was stubborn and always needed to be right.

That day, listening to the lovely stream, Sonia unexpectedly brought up Adrian's name. Suddenly her eyes lit up and nothing divulges the mind as the eyes do. I had a feeling that she needed to unleash some thoughts that may have been locked up for too long. I looked at her hinting that I was ready to listen, and she picked up on it right away,

"Maybe I was too tough and not fair enough with Adrian. It was not him but the imperfections of the world we were living in that didn't tolerate a relationship like ours. Adrian claimed that love could overcome anything, no matter the obstacle in front of it. I knew it should have, but it was more than my will, involved. I was painfully honest; I couldn't play games or tricks. I couldn't pretend to be a Communist proselyte under any circumstances. I couldn't give up my beliefs or the rules that guided me. Or as Adrian used to say; it was my architecture…

When I look back I see those two men in my life. One I had to give up on because our love was forbidden; from the beginning, there wasn't any freedom or right for it to even exist. The other one, snatched me out from the Communist regime to freedom, but confronted me with a marriage that had already died. Isn't it strange? What one lost, the other found, but didn't appreciate. It was love. In other words, I let myself be crushed between two destructive forces: The Communist Regime and Sabin. Here we are, Adrian and I, free people in a free world."

At this point without trying to cut her off, I said, "Do you know that he never got married, but climbed up the professional ladder as high as he could?"

"Yes, I do know. I like to keep in touch with Romania, as you know, not only by visiting or talking to you but also by reading Romanian newspapers. I learned that many of the important buildings across Romania bear the imprint of his ideas."

"That's quite right. I read about him too. And I have to confess though, that my Gil, after the revolution in Romania, wondered if the future still had something in store for you and Adrian."

She was all smiles as she asked, "Really? It would be interesting to see if we still recognized each other. A good number of years have passed since we saw each other last. I remember that it was a colorful June, which I always thought would never repeat itself like that again."

We left our talk about that past right there. We had resumed the same talk a few times on the phone though, and I can see now that she was doing it in her journal too:

"I learned from an old friend that Adrian has been keeping track of me for years. After my friend told me this, I was alone, and I cried. I cried like a child who doesn't know whether to be sad or happy. I was both. A deeply buried feeling bubbled up. Maybe our love is still alive. I hadn't thought about loving a man after everything I went through with Sabin. But Adrian is my old love. Could it be true? Yes, it is true, very true, a voice of a hidden thought whispered it to me.

Then Gil's words to Neli came to my mind,

"Look back and see that there is just a thought between us."

I think about that phrase a lot. Like Neli, I realize how true it is. No matter how far the distance between us, there is only a thought that can devour both time and distance. There is just a thought; only a single thought that can cut through even what once seemed impossible.

To my dismay, suddenly, all the smoldering emotions from the distant past became real again.

I searched for Adrian's address at work and found it; Professor Doctor Docent Adrian Muntean, Architecture Institute of Bucharest.

I wrote the entire address down. Then I carefully wrote it on a little package with a disk of one of Shawn Colvin's songs on it, "I Don't Know Why," then a short message borrowed from Gil: "There is just a thought between us."

I signed it and put it aside.

CHAPTER 49

Lines Other Than Parallels

Remember how Sonia always believed that she was a favorite of heaven? This story is proof of that. I, too, located an address for Adrian, but did not tell Sonia about it. I was saving that information for when I thought she would be opening to re-connecting with him. Shortly after finding Adrian's address, an amazing thing happened.

Late in the year of 2000, I was invited to an awards ceremony for those who in their daily work had brought important contributions to the field of science. Gil was among them. He was honored with the Horia Hulubei Prize, given in the name of a Romanian physicist whom Gil greatly admired.

Unfortunately, he couldn't be there in person for such an honorable moment. My beloved husband was no longer among us. His death was caused by a fatal aneurysm, which up until then, had been hidden and silent.

I was left feeling helpless and unprepared for such a loss, who couldn't have been? As a physician I felt guilty. All of my medical knowledges were not prepared for such a stealthily enemy.

His life was a part of mine and it was so painful to see it broken apart. I had no sign that Gil was ill. It came at lightning speed and Gil was taken away from me.

I now understand Sonia's pain about being left behind more than once, numb, bereft.

It took me time to realize that Gil was not physically around anymore. But I hoped for his presence in another way. I knew that

303

reaching him would require the peace of diligent acceptance. No guilt, no resentment, and then he would return to me in my dreams. Slowly his memory began to flow and fill the empty part of me, and make me whole again. Even though he was an expert of the physical world, he had a sharp eye for the world one could see with only the mind. I imagine him smiling at my thinking. For him, it was a physical truth that both matter and light are nothing more than two manifestations of the same entity of energy. Maybe others would also smile at the thought of Gil and me, still so much in love, discussing the laws of physics.

I was proud to represent Gil at the award ceremony.

For my part I was ready to award Gil with the most distinguished prize a husband could get: the prize of integrity and the gift of self.

I looked around and realized that I knew no one. There was a printed program that contained a list of all those being honored with awards. One name from list of nominees caught my eye though, it was a Professor of Architecture, Adrian Muntean. I muttered to myself, "Oh my Lord, could it be possible or is this just a wild coincidence?" I looked around again to find somebody who resembled the picture Sonia had given me to keep before she left for America. Sonia never let that photo come to light, as she did with some of the other deep feelings buried in her heart. She couldn't find a reason to take it with her to America either. That past had to stay back in Romania.

Scanning the auditorium, I noticed a tall, handsome man, entering the door. His hair had a touch of grey to it; he wore stylish framed glasses and was overall in perfect attire. There were just a few minutes until the ceremony would begin.

It seemed like he knew some of the people around because as soon as he entered the auditorium he shook hands with them and then settled in with that group.

During the reception I approached him, and I introduced myself simply, "Excuse me, sir, I don't want to bother you, but if the name Sonia rings a bell, you should know that I am her best friend."

He was puzzled at first, but then his face lit up with a warm smile of pleasant surprise. I noticed it in his words as well. "Sonia? Sonia Sava? Yes, that name means a great deal to me. I was also her best friend in the past."

"Do you know that she left years ago for the States?" I asked and waited curiously for his response.

"Of course, I know that she lives in the U.S. For a while I lost track of Sonia but recently I was talking with some of our mutual friends."

I had a feeling that he would have liked to ask more but at the same time he was trying to avoid asking too many questions. The light on his face betrayed him though. I didn't want to hold him up and maybe he was unsure too if he was holding me up. So, I thought that exchanging phone numbers would be safest for us. I had a feeling that Adrian wanted to talk to me as much as I wanted to talk to him. This would not be the last time that we would speak. I couldn't wait to call Sonia. When I reached Sonia on the phone, I did not even say "Hello!"

"Sonia, you won't believe it! I met Adrian, your Adrian."

"Really, are you kidding? I don't believe you. Where? When?"

Our conversation flowed rapidly. I tried to tell her every detail as quickly as possible and she anxiously wanted to hear it.

A week hadn't even gone by when I received a call from Adrian. He had an ongoing project with the Cluj Architecture Institute and would be in Cluj and thought it was a good opportunity for us to meet.

"No trouble at all, on the contrary I would be glad to see you. Please give me the date and place." I said without hiding my excitement. I knew from Sonia that he was a genuine man and wouldn't play with words just to make a good impression. He let me decide.

"What do you think about Belvedere, the highest point of the city? We could see far across the city that you and Sonia at one point called home."

He then said, most politely, "Perfect; may I see you at noontime? We can have lunch together, please be my guest."

I got the impression that I had known him forever. Sonia had only recently begun to talk about that part of her life. I could immediately see why she loved him. Adrian, and the stories that Sonia told of him, reminded me of Gil. Both men had that trustworthiness that every woman looks for and admires in a man. Rather than with words, it can be read in the eyes.

He was punctual. I remember that Sonia always appreciated punctuality from people, but she didn't get a lot of it from Sabin.

Adrian was first to speak, "Here we are, two of Sonia's best friends."

"Agreed, we are those two indeed."

A festively arranged table was waiting for us. I thought of Sonia and how much I would have liked for her to be with us. I was sure though that'd she be in almost all of our conversations.

We had the best view of the city from our table.

It was still cold but a sunny day. The sky was blue; the kind of blue that Sonia would elaborate on for a few pages of writing.

Adrian did almost all the talking, which brought a certain serenity to his heart. It must have been a long time since he had the chance to talk about Sonia.

Nobody could understand him better than someone who knew Sonia the way I did.

I got to learn both sides of the story and I also got some answers to questions that had not been totally clear in my mind until then. It was always hard for me to understand why Sonia sacrificed the pure love that they had together. Sonia couldn't live a double life, though. In her heart there was only room for one. On the other hand, Adrian couldn't escape unharmed. There was a social gap between them that even the purest love couldn't fill. I heard it from Mrs. Sava and now the same from Adrian. That love had to be hidden and live underground forever.

There was only the hope that a radical change would occur and all obstacles to freedom would disappear.

Romanians needed to get back their most basic rights: to be, to believe, and to love freely. It took a very long time for that to happen though, but finally it did.

"You know I did receive a sign from her yesterday. It was just a disc with a song on it that answered a question I've had in my mind all along."

"Sonia has been blessed with twice the freedom for a long time now. You know what I mean. She talks to me about the extraordinary things freedom brings to one's life. You must hear her. She will enthusiastically tell you how freedom can heal scars and turn them into stars; a phrase I 've often heard from her.

You remember how the Communist regime kept us subdued and suppressed without the right to speak up, even in situations where revolt boiled inside us. The words could only get up to our throats and sometimes they almost choked us. That definitely applied to Sonia; she was born with fewer rights than others, as you know.

In the land of the free, she has become a totally different person. She can freely display who she is. There is not a regime or a husband to try to mutilate her personality. She became a successful transplant in the new land.

Her children and her profession are her biggest priorities. I cannot say too much about her divorce. Her luck was disguised in that divorce. As she learned who her husband really was, she was burdened with so many changes and difficulties. But you must remember her attitude; behind every obstacle you might find a treasure so don't give up. Don't you like that?" At that he nodded his head and smiled.

"She didn't talk about you often or much, but I did get the truth about your sad love story after she moved to America. She regretted that you were both born in Romania during the Communist Era. Yet, she would say, 'You know Neli, the Communist Regime threw Adrian and me on two different paths, but not parallels. You know

307

what I mean.' America was part of her destiny. That part of her life built out a road towards America. In her mind she believes that in life people meet each other for a reason and once the mission is fulfilled, they leave."

Up until then Adrian had been listening to me carefully, answering from time to time with just a smile, yet he remained genuinely connected to the conversation, nothing could distract him. He never took his eyes from the direction where I was sitting, assuring me that he was not interested in anything but my talking.

Without hesitation Adrian would sensibly take his turn to keep our conversation flowing. It was only interrupted from time to time by delicious bites of food and sips from the flavorful Romanian Muscatel. I was ready to pay the same attention to his part of the conversation. With a grimace, that allowed a discomfort from deep inside to surface he started,

"The hardest part for us was not only having a tall wall between us, but we were not even allowed to get close to it; we could only look at it.

At the same time, we could sense the malicious eyes glued to us and happy for our distress.

As you can remember, there was no respect for feelings at all. They pertained to the soul, and their godless mind couldn't see beyond the matter. In their view a real revolutionary communist should never stumble over feelings. Love had to be nothing more than nothingness.

I thought of it as a holocaust of the spirit. Nobody could mention the word spirit without being laughed at or being accused of political heresy.

You can remember that time. We, as college students, were joining the Communist Party in a crowd without thinking of the consequences if we ever tried to break away from such an organization. I don't have to tell you why we rushed to belong to the Party. After graduation the best jobs were reserved for Party members. That was not a secret.

Blessed with Twice the Freedom

In any competition between two people, the Party member would win. However, such benefits were not without a price. Remember? As for myself, I learned it firsthand. Stealthily, and inch by inch the Party took over my personal life. I was no longer a free man but constrained to do whatever was imposed upon me. Either way – leaving the Party voluntarily or being kicked out – would have left us without a future. It was like stepping out into a void.

However, some were ostracized. They were those labeled anti-Communists, mostly due to their family's past. Sonia was one of them. But love doesn't follow such laws. I would have given up any Party just to be with Sonia. It was too late though; I was sold out. Plus, I was always more afraid for her than for myself. Yet, they could never destroy how much I loved her. I was never an adventurer, chasing women for their beauty or wealth, but for what they were deeply inside. It is hard to explain.

I let myself stay in love with my profession though. It has filled the emptiness…"

He was a special man, I could see it. I understood why he and Sonia would have been a perfect couple. Now, after having heard both sides, I've come to own conclusions. These two should try again, even though their story had been interrupted a long time ago. It still feels hard to believe. What a twist of fate! I was so lucky to spot Adrian at the awards ceremony. I think it was the hand of Providence.

They say that sometimes during dreams we are given feelings that are impossible to have or experience otherwise. Here is a reality, which seems to belong to a dream.

I believe that Gil played a role in all of this. His award came with the best gift he could possibly offer to Sonia and Adrian, from the other side.

Given the enormous coincidence, it does appear that someone from the other side was guiding each moment.

Gil knew just a little bit about Adrian but he knew a lot about

Sonia's life. As I did, he felt sorry for the ordeal she had to go through with Sabin. Gil was reluctant to call Sabin a man. He would say, "You could call him anything but a man."

Without that ordeal, though, Sonia and Adrian couldn't prove the durability of true love. I was to learn that their friendship started like ours—at a concert. Adrian gave me all the details about it. Both, he and Sonia had a way of telling a story, making the listener feel as if they were part of it.

"It was one of those concerts called "The Autumns of Cluj," he said. "Every fall for one-month, great selections of the world's best music were performed for city concertgoers. It was challenging for even members of the City's Philharmonic to get tickets for the each one of these concerts. However, there was always a chance at the door. Every time there was someone who couldn't make it, they would resell the ticket. That night I was lucky. I didn't even have to look for a ticket because the lady in front of me stopped in a hurry and we made a fast trade. Now I consider her an angel. I had no clue that something other than the concert itself would make that night very, very special.

I took a glimpse around and saw some friends of mine. There was a girl with them. I had seen her a few months earlier at a dance in the City's University Hall. She had left before I could ask her to dance. I had looked for her since the first time we had met, but I had no luck finding her until that night at the concert.

She was fully clad in black. It was a sign that she had a death in her family. I kept my eyes on her. Her black attire helped me spot her every move. I missed my first opportunity to meet her and now I was ready to do everything not to miss my opportunity again.

During the intermission, her group didn't walk outside but instead stayed glued to their seats. I didn't blame them, as it was difficult to move through the crowd. I had never seen such a big crowd at a concert and I had been to many. I still remember that the second part opened with a piece of music by Antonin Dvorak, "Song to the

Moon" from his opera "Rusalka."

Everyone in the audience was touched by the way the singer expressed Rusalka's grief at being unable to connect with her loved one.

I have to admit that Rusalka's misfortune has come to my mind often. Rusalka, a water fairy invisible to humans, fell in love with a human prince.

They came from two different worlds, but no sacrifice could keep them together. Sonia and I were also thought of as coming from two different worlds. Impassable obstacles were put between us.

After the concert our all groups of friends decided to go to a fine restaurant. She was in one of the groups.

I learned that her name was Sonia. Later on, I also learned that she wore black because she was mourning her grandfather.

We saw each other a few more times but always in a group. I anxiously tried to get closer to her and ask her out. But there was something particular about getting closer to her. It was not only her state of mourning, but it was a reservation that put first a distance between us. It was not arrogance but rather discretion.

One day I built up the courage and invited her to join me for a walk. I will never forget how she said simply and with a smile, 'All right.'

On the day of our date, I found a gypsy girl selling little bouquets of flowers on the street. They were the first sign of spring and the first flowers I gave to Sonia.

She received the flowers gazing at both the flowers and at me. She whispered a thank you, which I could have read more easily in her eyes. Then like a child she began reciting a little poem, which you might very well remember. It was from our generation's second grade reading book.

'You little snowdrop and frail flower,
How dare you come out?
Don't you see, I wonder,

How winter's still around?'

"I answered her questions as if I were that snowdrop: 'I am not afraid of snow, and I came out just for you.' She looked again at the bouquet and moved it against her cheek as sign of appreciation.

Without any shyness she displayed her gentleness.

It was her smile which struck me from the very sight of her. I called it, later on, the *masterpiece* of her beauty. It wasn't enigmatic or seductive, but rather a sincere communicator with her inner world, which I would love so much and never let it go.

For a long time after that I called her Snowdrop; she had something of its gentleness and its bravery at the same time.

I also noticed that she came out the door at exactly the right time. I didn't have to wait even a minute. Some girls like to be waited on. She was always genuine and never played games. I said to myself, 'This is the girl' and she was indeed.

She came out of the house cheerfully, and I remember that I couldn't help myself from saying that she was very pretty. She glanced at me and said, 'Don't you know that all happy people are always beautiful?'

"'Yes, they really are, and so are you' I said, without taking my eyes from her.

There was a shine in her eyes. They say that the eyes are the windows of the soul and I could see her tender soul through her shining eyes.

All of this made me feel like I had known her forever. It was as if we were apart for some time and now we were again together. Or, we were created for each other and just had to wait for the moment to meet. Certainly, this was the moment. It never happened to me before or after.

Even though it was late March it suddenly started to snow heavily and we had to make our way out, it was like going through white curtains. Before we knew it, the trees were loaded with fluffy snow, which didn't come to stay but to offer us a day from a fairytale. It

Blessed with Twice the Freedom

was a playful whim of both winter and spring before one season was ready to leave to make room for another.

The sidewalk became slippery and from time to time she was forced to find support by holding onto my arm. At that point I wished for a sheet of ice to lie before us. We stopped for a treat at a famous pastry place in town called Spring. She turned to me and looking in my eyes spelled softly but meaningfully, "S-P-R-I-N-G." I responded without words while our gazes merged.

Many seasons had come and gone, and we found a way to identify with each of them. So, our story began, and it went on for five years. The rest is history…"

Until then he had refrained from calling me by my first name. I made the first step.

"Please call me Neli. Our ages and circumstances entitle us to do so."

"Alright, then you should call me Adrian."

I said only to myself and only in my mind; I wish Gil were still here. In my belief he was. He had connected the dots and a lost love was retrieved.

CHAPTER 50

Reviving the Past, Again

"I have passed by that place many times. On one evening in that place a long time ago, I remember waiting for the six o'clock bus. In less than twenty minutes it brought me home. In good weather both Corina and Michael would be waiting for me in the front yard. They were anxious to see me home after a long day.

To my surprise, those places have finally stopped triggering any emotional feelings. And yet, yesterday something unusual happened when I was on my way to a business meeting. A piece of music on the radio reminded me that I still had scars that have not totally healed. The radio was playing Beethoven's Waldstein Sonata. In the very moment that I was passing by the bus stop where I used to wait many years ago, I burst into tears. The music touched a string of my soul and it resonated with me.

Then I remembered Toschi, the Japanese girl who sold roses on the street. She was there on certain days of the week and I knew that she worked for charity. One day she approached me and offered me a bouquet of roses. She said nothing but let her smile connect with mine. Although we both were in the process of learning English, kindness speaks the same language.

Later on, I had learned that she was working for an organization that helps children in need. I never envisioned that mine might be among them. We came to America for a better life, but I had to fight for it on my own.

I would never disappoint my children. That was the last of the memories that needed to be freed.

The Waldstein Sonata opened the door for it to come out and then to let it vanish. On that evening heavy rains and strong winds came unexpectedly. I called Sabin and asked if he could give me a ride home. His answer was unequivocal, "Absolutely not."

I had no choice but to wait for the bus. The strong wind made my umbrella useless. Streams of rain not only whipped me mercilessly but also washed away all my tears. When I got on the bus nobody would know that I was crying. I was soaking wet when I got home.

Corina, my sweet Corina, was waiting for me at the door. She was always scared when I wasn't home on time. The possibility of being left behind alone really frightened her. She jumped up to hug me but she was too little, so she couldn't reach higher than my waist.

"Mommy, Mommy, I am so sorry that you got so wet. What can I do for you?"

"Nothing right now, my sweet heart, other than to let me change. Then we can talk."

Michael came out from the bedroom he shared with father also showing concern for my deplorable situation.

"Mommy, why didn't you wait until the rain stopped? You always say that cold rain could make one sick."

"You are right honey, but the last bus is at 6:00 in evening. I couldn't risk missing it and being left on the street at night."

"But why didn't Dad give you a ride?"

"Ask him," I uttered in the moment but then found it wrong of me, and changed my mind, "No, no Michael please say nothing to Dad, I am okay."

"But you are not, he should have given you a ride, where is he?"

There was no answer. For the longest time I thought that crying was associated with only weak people. But if crying served no purpose for our beings then it wouldn't have been included in our behavior's marvelous design. Crying must have a purpose behind it. That purpose might be to cool down an overwhelmed brain. Or it might explain what pain is for the physical body, an expression of getting close to the limit.

Well, the Waldstein Sonata was a key that opened the box of my repressed feelings about that rainy bus stop. That box should have been filled with the gratitude. After my friend Lee heard the story, she would wait in front of the pharmacy and take me home on a daily basis. I didn't know that Lee was also worried because that bus stop was not a safe place to be at night.

The Waldstein Sonata reminded me of the time that I kept my cries tightly inside. And now the radio is playing that very piece as I pass that very bus stop. I could finally let go of the painful memory of the time Sabin would not give me a ride home. It was the time to move on…"

CHAPTER 51

A Resumed Path

Sonia made the first step. She flew from New York to meet Adrian in Bucharest. It had been almost 40 years since they had seen each other. I could hardly imagine how anxiously they were waiting to see each other. I was also anxiously waiting to hear the whole story, directly, from Sonia.

She called me the next day and I got more than words alone could have told. Even from a distance, I could feel the intensity of her emotion. It was pure happiness...

"My dear Neli, how do I tell you? That feeling I had many years ago when Adrian asked me out for the first time came back to me. It was overwhelming....Adrian was waiting for me at the same airport where, more than twenty years ago, I had gone into the unknown, following another man. I had a strange feeling. My heart marked one place with two different men; for one I left the country and for the other I returned."

Sonia's joy was like a beautiful song, lovely to listen to...

"It was a mix of winter and spring. I could see through the airplane's window the green of the landing site. I smiled to myself. Our long hibernation was being awakened by the coming of spring sweetness! Before my trip, like a teenager in love, I paraded in front of the mirror deciding which outfit to wear, so Adrian could spot me in the crowd instantly. I remembered in detail the colors Adrian most admired on me. I wanted to remind him that I hadn't forgotten even the smallest details of the things that were ours. I was also glad that

I put my high heels on, as I noticed even from a distance that he was still tall. All those years together I always had the desire to at least reach his shoulders. The sweet memories came one after the other, I guess deliberately, to rebuild the bridge that had been broken such a long time ago.

"Suddenly, there he was. My heart was beating so hard that I thought the people next to me could hear it. We approached each other wordlessly, with a mesmerized look in our eyes. Our exhilaration burst and we melted into each other's arms. We stepped back from each other, just to confirm that what was happening was real, and Adrian whispered in perfect English, the first lines from the song I had sent to him, 'I don't know why the sky is blue, I don't know why I am still in love with you." I answered, 'Same here.' Both the mind and time can be so tricky. It seems that just yesterday we broke up. Like in a fairytale, time stopped and took us back to our youth. On the drive to Adrian's, I noticed the first signs of spring moving in. The same spring flowers that we admired walking down my street during our first spring together, seemed to have been grown also here. Adrian and I would start anew with this spring and enjoy each season together.

"Suddenly a playful cloud shook off maybe the last flakes of the season. At once we found ourselves saying, 'And all the snowflakes are melting by our gaze.' It was a phrase we remembered from our distant past. We started to laugh like two children who remembered magic words from a magic time.

Spring felt entirely new and revolutionary to me. The secret of youth infiltrated my entire being, like a living and miraculous water, bringing dormant feelings to life. Inside I felt as young as I was when we saw each other last. We would just have to resume our journey from where we left off. I was not yet done thinking about all of this when Adrian said, 'We are home.'

"He said it looking at me with that gaze I was once so used to and later missed so greatly. That gaze made me feel like I was the

Blessed with Twice the Freedom

only one in the world that he saw, and now he brought me home. If only he knew how many times Sabin had cast me out of the house he brought me in. I should not be thinking of Sabin and those bad times at such a wonderful moment. We were in a nice place on the outskirts of Bucharest. He stopped in front of his beautiful house, which I knew right away had to be of his own design. The house reminded me of one that Adrian had once said he had in mind for us. It was not meant to be then, but it could be a home for us now.

He didn't have to open the door because somebody else did as soon as we reached the top of the front stairs. It was his housekeeper; he introduced her to me as Mrs. Maria. From the first I felt that she was a special lady. Before we settled down, I learned that she and her family were originally from Transylvania and that she had spent time abroad working for a wealthy family. Upon her return to Romania she started to work for Adrian. She treated him like a prince and at the same time a son. I could see it. Everything in that house looked impeccable.

"Adrian had remembered all the things I liked —favorite flowers, foods, colors… A huge azalea welcomed me in the entrance of the hallway. In the living room on a short oval table there was a cobalt vase with freesias of all different colors. He hadn't forgotten the crocuses that herald the spring either. I couldn't help myself from asking, 'How in the world have you remembered all my favorite things?'

"'I remember everything about you, my sweet Wise. How could I forget?' He used to call me *Wise* because the meaning of my name is wisdom. We were still amazed. We still couldn't believe that we were together again in the flesh. I couldn't take my eyes off of him. I had an unexplained fear that if he were out of my sight I would lose him again. But I said firmly to myself: do not be afraid anymore. This is not a dream, but the most real moment of your life. Pinch yourself and feel it.

"Mrs. Maria asked me to call her by her name. It was not hard, as

319

I am accustomed to calling people by their first names in America. Her gentleness reminded me of my mother's. It was such a great feeling to get the sense of being home and being loved. That was the way I truly felt. It was just a few hours past noon but by that time Romanians are ready to have their main meal of the day, something similar to the American dinner. And the dinner was served. I couldn't believe my eyes.

"'Oh, Maria what is this, do you think I am royalty or something?'

"'Yes, you are more than a princess, and I am sure you will always be part of this house in time to come.'

"Involuntarily, I went back to my first day, that first New Year's Eve in America, where our arrival occasioned no celebration at all. It took me a long time to forget Corina's whimpering and her desire to return home to Romania the same day. I had to wipe the tears from my eyes. Some of the tears were from my past and my glasses could hide them as they had often done for me. Others were tears of disbelief. I was not used to joy any more. It was as if my joy was stopped by a dam, which had now erupted because of excessive pressure of my hidden feelings. I had no reason to be afraid anymore, I was in Adrian's protective arms. He had always been an exquisite man. He had me in his mind and heart for who I am. He didn't care about my possessions. It seemed that Adrian intercepted something of what was crossing my mind so he tightened his hug. My ear was next to his chest and I could hear his heart beat. It was the same heart that I used to listen to when we sat lounging under the trees in my parents' backyard.

"'A smile came to lighten your face, what is behind it?' Adrian asked, looking into my eyes.

"'It is a piece of our sweet memories. Remember the bees bouncing around the flowers? You were whistling that playful melody from Brahms' Hungarian Dances and they seemed to be bouncing on its rhythm. We pretended that their show was just for us to watch. The entire spring was a show. How intrigued we were by them, and how they sacrificed their lives for their queen, remember?'

He responded by looking directly into my eyes again. Nothing connected our souls more, as they merged into one, than the gaze from his eyes. I was fascinated by how bits of memories rearranged themselves in a perfect mosaic of the past. It was like a piece of valuable art stolen from us had been returned. The strong and reciprocated feelings that we had for each other had deep roots in our youth; they just needed to be reconnected. Those feelings let us to reunite.

"The next day we were ready for a trip. Because of my dual citizenship it was easy for Adrian to plan all of the details ahead of time. I didn't understand why there was such a rush. I still felt like this was a dream. It was not only the jet lag, that made me feel like a feather flying, but there were the emotions that had thrown me into a state of pure bliss. It was like a wonderland. To all of this Adrian offered this explanation, 'Hon, I know you would like to sleep some more but today is the first day of our new beginning and we have to catch up on so many things.' He said it as he tenderly lifted the pillow that my head was resting on, so I could wake up in his arms. I could hardly believe it.

"While rubbing my eyes I asked, 'Is this a dream?' Through one of the doors I could hear music that sounded like the Telemann's Don Quixote suite.

"As if Adrian read my mind he lifted me out of the bed and then let me down on my feet and said while bowing in front of me, 'Dulcinea, do you want to dance?'

"Returning the bow, I answered gladly, 'Of course, my Don Quixote.' Our steps moved to the rhythm of the music as they did many years ago at one of the New Year's Eve carnivals. One year, we chose to dress up as those two characters from Cervantes' novel. I wished we could have been disguised forever so that we could have been together under the Communist regime. But the music and memory of that night returned to us again. We didn't choose to live in the past but took the essentials from it, which were the basis of our lasting relationship. They quickly filled the chasm that kept us physically apart.

"At the end of the dance I was in his arms again. He looked at me and said, 'This trip is not a dream. It is something we've dreamed about for a long time.' I let him have the last word. I didn't know anything about the trip; Adrian strung together as a series of surprises. He couldn't have planned it better. Nothing keeps one awake better than the anticipation of many surprises.

I was told only the starting point and we traipsed along until we got to Rimini, Italy. He let me know that we'd be spending a few days there, then we'd be taking a cruise on the Adriatic Sea towards the Mediterranean. Only heaven knew how much I needed this piece of my life to become whole. I am sure it was no different for Adrian.

"Without saying anything to him I pondered for a moment; why Rimini? Had he been thinking of Francesca da Rimini? To test this hypothesis I said, 'Nobody carved love into marble as well as Auguste Rodin.'

"To which he replied, 'And ours is carved in time.'

"Then without taking our eyes from one other, we again unfolded some of our greatest and unforgettable memories. One by one, the events of our past were resurrected. Some of them brought us tenderness and others made us laugh joyfully. He reminded me of a funny thing. 'Remember how we fell in the water off the footbridge over the Someş River? We were soaking wet and our thin summer clothes stuck to our skin and made us look like a sculpture of lovers placed by the riverbank.' That's the Francesca da Rimini tie-in. We had a lot of fun waiting for our clothes to dry out. We didn't care one bit about the inconveniences or the strange looks from passers-by; we owned that time and the world.

"'Remember our playing in the snow in the winter? You used to bury me in the snow leaving only my face out so our eyes could talk love.'

"We continued to reminisce - it came so naturally to us. That might be the answer to why our love was so easily revived and resumed. He didn't interrupt me but looked adoringly in my eyes and said, 'I remember it all.'

"We woke up very early on our first morning in Rimini. It was Adrian's wish to walk on the beach and watch the sunrise. It can be more than spectacular to watch a blast of light come out from the sea and stretch across the sky. The light leaves behind a landscape that challenges painters to propagate amazement. But a sunset splash on the sea is also a majestic beauty.

The beginning and the end share the same magnificence. I remember my father's thoughts on this theme, 'Under the shield of God, death is a victory'. It was difficult to understand it when I first heard it. Now I do.

There were only a few people on the beach at that early hour. I guess they were there for the same reason; to see the sun coming out of the sea. I had a feeling that for us there might have been an extra reason. Adrian had asked me to wear one of my most beautiful white dresses.

"It was unusually warm for a regular spring morning. At one point I took my sandals off so I could drag my feet playfully through the sand. I could feel not only the warmth of the sand but the water was also warm as I walked through it. I made a few splashes with my feet towards Adrian. Instead of walking away from the splashes he came towards me and hugged me dearly whispering in my ear, 'You are so attractive in that dress, you're like a Sea Fairy.'

"Holding my hands, he knelt down in front of me. At first, I was astounded but then I had the desire to do the same. A high wave came and covered us as a blessing from the sea at exactly the same precious moment that he asked me to be his wife. I didn't wait for him to finish his question as I leaned my head on his chest saying more than once, 'Yes.' He took a little box out of his pocket. When he opened it, a diamond caught the sunlight and became a drop of sun itself.

One wave after another rolled to the shore continuously throwing ephemeral but blissful garlands of what looked like white roses. I had never experienced such happiness as I did at that moment.

The ascending sun on the sky brought us a new day. We would have liked to connect that day to the past, from before we had been separated. We wanted to forget the hard times in between. Even though it was too early for swimming, we plunged into the water and swam out a way. It was the day of our epiphany; such happiness signaled many good days to come."

I knew Sonia almost as well as I had known myself, and I know her story by heart as well. I heard this story, first-hand, and then I read it again in her journals. I like to reread her journal entries. My Gil teased her by giving her the nickname Alpha. It comes from an herb Medica sativa that she told us about. It amazed us to learn that this herb, or alfalfa as it is more commonly known, sucks up nutrients from soil as far below the surface as fifty feet. Gil would say, "It is like your words Sonia and how they extract the deepest feelings from the soul." She would giggle at that. She always enjoyed Gil's wit.

Then jokingly, I added, "Why, not the Alpha and the Omega? Sonia doesn't go only deeply but also comprehensively."

"Come on guys, I don't do it alone but with you also, so such compliments belong to you as well. That's why we get along in such a way, isn't it?"

But all of this is only sweet memory, now… I wish Gil were here. I wish I could hear him say again that true love is like good wine; over time it turns into something better.

While the reflections that mirrored their special day in the water were short-lived, their story is carved in time, and for them it was unforgettable. I thought about that day tenderly myself. Both Sonia and I were blessed to have men like Adrian and Gil in our lives.

Last night I was alone. I stayed quiet in my room, in the dim light of my *candela*, a little oil lamp on the wall above the nightstand.

Unfortunately, there is no equivalent in English for such a lamp. A *candela* is more than a candle. It has something sacred to it. There is light intertwined with prayer. I stood in front of it trying to find the right prayer to say. "Alone doesn't mean lonely." I had heard that often from Sonia. There is a page in her journal that proves just that.

"As soon as the weather got warmer I pulled out the colorful paints and the canvases from the cabinet where they were stored. It is enough to see the colors lying freely on my work table for me to immerse myself in their world. They give me an instant motivation to look for changes within the reach of my hands and my heart. This is the bliss of creative moments. To create means to be free.

Longingly, I was looking for one of the green colors: China green. I liked that color; it couldn't be missed in any of my paintings. I could get all the shades of spring from a mixture of white and that green. I rarely used brushes but rather fine spatulas. This technique flattens and mixes the colors, letting them come out differently every time but in beautiful and unique shades.

Because of my thirst for colors I mainly enjoyed painting during dull-colored seasons.

I had my secrets. I easily found both solace and joy in the nature that was around me. Things hastily overlooked by others were pillars of balance for me and I used them to brush off uncomfortable states of mind.

I would feel uneasy disclosing to others that I liked storms (excepting the very dangerous ones). I like to see the clouds build up on the horizon and then send the first "scribbles" of light on the sky, as little Corina used to call them. Then thunder in the background would give another signal for the main event: the rain. I enjoyed the sound of the first drops striking the ground, leaving behind a scent that only the rain can bring. Nature was ready to share that joy with me like colors and music did.

As the built-up tension in the sky was finally released, I used to compare the phenomena to our own lives; tension, lightening, thunder, and then silence…

As summer ended I thought longingly for all of it to come again. The cold drizzling of the fall was not my favorite kind of rain at all. I remember knowing as a child that the first frost was imminent, which made me feel sad for all the flowers. I had no choice but to let them to die. It was a remorseful goodbye.

Later on, I had an undeniable resentment towards any type of "good bye".

Thinking back, I can see there were many of those instances in my life. Maybe they were given to me to learn how to handle them without any hard feelings. Life is about learning. They say that there is no downhill without climbing the hill first, and there wouldn't be a *goodbye* if there was not a *hello*.

Whenever I think of climbing the hill, I think of Sisyphus. I was always more than amazed at how in the face of futility he patiently carried his burden repeatedly without any objections."

That's right. For her boulders were path breakers. I can say that with certainty, I witnessed it. Sometimes when following these life events step by step they can seem aberrant. But when the same events are examined on a larger scale they have a different look. How little I understood the part of Sonia's life when she was forced into a divorce. But her destiny still had Adrian in it. She had to be free, so they could prove that true love never dies.

She adored her children and if she was asked to go through the whole ordeal again, she would still do it for them. They were embedded in her life and she in theirs. I smile thinking back to Corina asking me one day,

"Tanti Neli, you are a doctor and know everything. Do you think it would be possible that I inherited 75% of my mother and only 25% the other's? You know what I mean."

"Hey, my little friend let's not go that far, I don't know everything. But in this case, I don't want to disappoint you. As far as heredity goes, partiality is not permitted. Instead there are very strict rules to

Blessed with Twice the Freedom

it. But you know sometimes good things can be retrieved even from the other part that you call the 25%."

Much later when the subject was brought up again and Corina was older, I dropped a science-bombshell on her I was sure she would like, "The mitochondrial DNA, without mistake, is inherited only from the mother."

I still remember her exuberance. "Hurray, Neli I love you for this golden piece of science. See, my question and presumption altogether were right. I think this is a recovery for all women who have been told that God cloned them from a man's rib."

She had finally accepted my proposal for her to call me by my name. It was appropriate for her to use Auntie when she was younger, but now she was older, and we were close enough to drop the formality.

Corina and Michael had a special place in my heart and in my world.

Corina was especially drawn to Romania, I think, because her old country was a place where she found much love. In her new country she was confronted with tougher times than a child should have to understand. I could hardly wait to have her back on her vacations. Those summers I was in heaven and as for her, I spoiled her rotten, more than Sonia would have liked to see.

Corina was a great storyteller. I don't have to wonder why or how. Sonia had told me about her visits to the United Nations, but I would also get all the details later from Corina. She won several prizes for her paintings in a World Painting Contest. The award ceremony was held at the UN. It is so appropriate, that even on American land there is building that belongs to the world.

"See? I have pictures from those events. There is you and your mother. She couldn't have been prouder of you for all your great achievements."

I dared to interrupt her from time to time because Corina was too modest to admit all of this proudly. She would say, "You know, my mom sometimes thinks that I am the center of the world."

327

And I replied, "Yes, Corina you are the center of her world, you know that."

"I know, I know." She said it with her eyes half closed, exactly how her mother used to do as if she was in a reflection with herself. I realized how much they were alike.

"Your mom was glad that you never forgot your Romanian roots. Even before getting on the podium to get your painting award at the United Nations, she told me that you asked if you could mention that you were Romanian also."

"That's right. I remember that. I would have liked to represent the Romanians also, so they could have a winner as well."

"You were a magnanimous little Romanian, weren't you? Even your name discloses that. 'Core' in Latin means heart, and there you go. Corina is the right name for you."

"So, does yours. Your real name is Cornelia, isn't it?"

"Yes, I guess every name carries a message within that sometimes fits a person perfectly as if it was predestined. But let's move from this subject back to the UN. I remember your mom's excitement for that trip. I could feel it in her voice. It was an uplifting moment for the both of you. All of the painful events disappeared that day.

"You are right, Neli. Who would keep them in mind when you're sitting at the same table as the Romanian ambassador to the UN?"

Every attending nation had its own table and people could order their traditional food. It was no surprise that my mom and I chose chicken noodle soup and of course that much-appreciated Romanian dish, stuffed cabbage. It was as tasty as Grandma's. When I saw the doboş cake, it reminded me of the delicious layer cake from my childhood. It was a little piece of heaven. My mother and the ambassador also enjoyed a glass of Romanian wine."

"Oh yes, I remember your mom told me about that wine from Romania's Jidvei's vineyards. With her romanticist flair she would tell me how in every sip she also felt the sweetness of the grapes from her homeland. In the same spirit she depicted the Romanian flag

Blessed with Twice the Freedom

waving through the window among all the others."

"I remember my mom telling me about a feeling that I actually had also. Seeing the Romanian flag reminded us of all of our friends and family that we left behind in Romania. We could see the face of each of our loved ones."

CHAPTER 52

End of the Summer

"It is the end of October. Even though it has no place in the official calendar, summer still lingers, trying to make a comeback before next year.

It is Saturday. All the parking lots are full. It seems that everybody is outside preparing for the weekend and enjoying what is left of the summer. As they say, "Before fall is ready to fly in, summer has to give its wings a last flap."

It might be the last weekend for picnics. In the fall, the parties move inside, into the Americans' spacious houses, which were built with such gatherings in mind. In my first year in America I was struck by how many opportunities Americans find to celebrate. On summer weekends, friends and families gather around picnic tables in their well-manicured backyards or decks to celebrate various aspects of life. In the cold seasons, joyous indoor gatherings gather friends and families in warmth, culminating in the sumptuous Yuletide holidays.

But what moved me the most during their celebrations was their concern for and generosity to those less fortunate than them. They would make sure that such people would have a meal and wouldn't be forgotten or left to be alone.

I was one who received a bounty of their kindness as well.

The profound gratefulness that characterizes Thanksgiving permeated the entire year. People would travel long distances and long hours just to have dinner together with loved ones. I had never seen such a strong bond before.

Blessed with Twice the Freedom

There is a great spirit of community in America. There are special kitchens that function on donations and compassion. It reminds me a lot of the Transylvanians' generosity and my grandfather's good heart.

I never felt like an outsider in America. Everybody comes from somewhere, creating the proverbial melting pot. All of us, who have been transplanted here are fond of it and shall always be grateful.

But above all today is an incomparably beautiful day. I am out in the grocery store parking lot with a trunk full of goodies. I am ready to head home and prepare an American picnic for tomorrow bringing in my Romania cuisine. I very much enjoy doing it.

However, a colorful landscape in front of me has captivated my attention. Even though I know that such beauty is common in nature, this landscape looked magnificently unreal. The summer's green had been totally erased from the panorama and colors of fire came to replace it. A crimson red engulfed the leaves scattering around a diffused light, while thin clouds like giant feathers headed towards the horizon. The sun behind the clouds let itself filter and then blend into the same pink and reddish shades with a golden edge around it.

I often stopped for a moment to admire the fall colors; but I had never seen something like this before.

The background looked like a magnificent gate inviting the imagination past the physical horizon. The music on the radio was equally enchanting. They were playing one of the movements from Morten Lauridsen's *Lux Aeterna*. Such music came just in time to add itself to that picture for which I had no other word but sublime. I could easily reflect on that music and imagine that it came from beyond that gate.

It was like a heavenly chorale coming from "the other side" on the waves of a sacred light, specifically to comfort us in our much-troubled world. I kept my eyes on that scene and my ears to the radio. Through both senses I reached the same revelation: in the universe there is neither a prelude nor a finale, but a constant change. For a moment I was so captivated, that it was difficult to discern on which side I was.

I glanced at my watch and caught myself saying, "Oh, it is late. The parking lot is almost empty."

Nowadays most people are too busy with their daily life and their duties to revel in such beauty. Often people think that what is free has no value in it, but money and wealth have no value in a life either, if not well lived.

A sense of gratefulness for the small things might eliminate the pills people rely on for happiness, or a dream, always kept alive, might eliminate feelings of boredom or bouts of depression.

As soon as I got home, I reviewed my Romanian recipes, and chose what to have at my picnic. I remembered that Lee had once mentioned a favorite Romanian dish that she didn't know the name for. From her description I guessed it was cabbage noodles. Back in Romania cabbage noodles are a favorite fall dish. So, I made that recipe a favorite here too, until another dish came to replace it. I challenged myself, trying one recipe after another; I liked to spoil my American friends with the best of Romanian cuisine. I not only brought the recipes from my old country but the love of cooking too, inherited from my beloved Grandma.

I still keep that weekend in mind. I made cabbage noodles, plum dumplings and eggplant salad - all Romanian favorites.

People still talked about the abundance on my table and the joy surrounding it; for me, it was the joy of preparing special recipes for them and reading the joy on their faces. But the biggest joy of all was that they embraced us as a part of their family. That was indeed the greatest joy.

Autumn was not my favorite season until I came to America.

For a while it was difficult to forget the cold, dark, and rainy month of November which a month before the fearsome winter was; anyone would have shivered just thinking about it.

The American holiday, Thanksgiving, helped me to erase the

Blessed with Twice the Freedom

stubborn, bitter memories of a Romanian November.

Every day, I gave thanks for all I was given.

Christmas then came to help me forget my painful divorce with its papers being served just before my first American Christmas, and also the distress of having to hide Christmas for 46 years from the Communists.

My children wondered why Santa would not bring presents for their mother, whom they considered the best in the world. But I didn't want them to ask themselves why I was the only one in the house not getting presents on Christmas. I didn't like seeing Santa blamed unfairly and I stood up for him.

"Don't worry too much about that. It is not Santa's fault that there are so many children who keep him so busy."

They jumped in with another question,

"But why does he find time for Daddy?"

"Now come on, don't be so critical, Santa is very old and can be forgetful. Maybe he still has your Daddy on the children's list. He forgot to cross him out."

They had nothing to say about Daddy being on the children's list.

CHAPTER 53

An Unbroken Connection

"Corina, returned to Romania often, not only as a young girl, but also as an accomplished pianist.

Her old hometown proudly announced Corina's return on imposing posters. Sometimes I would eavesdrop on conversations around those posters. I was almost compelled to say, 'I've know her since her first steps into music. I was part of the audience when she had played her first piece of music, the "Fur Elise."'"

I was that excited! Not only was she born in the beautiful land of Transylvania, but she also took her first musical steps in that place.

She studied music with the illustrious piano teacher Gina Voicu or "Tanti Gina" as Corina called her.

Corina's shows always sold out. Romanians appreciate their own and like to share their fame with them.

For some time, she purposely chose to play pieces of music that she and her mother used to listen to from their first beginnings in America.

Before she played, the announcer would mention in his introduction that the recital itself is a tribute to that beginning.

Corina also would say a few words at the beginning of every piece she chose.

For example; "I remember as if it were yesterday how my mother and I listened to Beethoven's Appassionata. I used to blink my eyes with the fall of each heavy note on the piano's keys. I felt those strikes in my heart. I asked my mother if Beethoven had a reason to

334

be upset. But my mother told me that it was not about distress but passion. That was how he expressed the intensity of his feeling.

I promised my mother that one day I would play for her and for others as passionately as the Appassionata. Here I am, keeping that promise."

She continued that recital with a few movements from various Mozart piano sonatas, and she dedicated that segment to a good friend from childhood.

"We often chose Mozart's cadenced music for our dance recitals. Unfortunately, my good friend's dream of becoming a ballerina was cut short and she is now in a wheelchair. In this world we never know why a dream is taken away before it can be realized. But, my friend has since become a famous designer. She is still using her many talents, but in different ways."

I thought to myself that Sonia would have said the same thing in a situation like that. I was glad to see Corina keeping the same keen optimism.

Leaning her right elbow on the piano and standing tall, she looked like a carved topaz sculpture in her blue dress. Her gaze swept the entire concert hall before she said with melancholy,

"Now, in memory of my unforgettable piano teacher, I will play Frederic Chopin's Piano Concerto No. 1. I remember that she liked it very much and I would like to believe that she is listening now with the same pleasure from above. "Do you hear me Tanti Gina? I thank you again from depths of my heart."

When addressing her, Corina looked up to heaven with her eyes fixed in one place, as if she truly had found Gina. Gina Voicu was a very well-known personality in the city. All who became great performance pianists from our town studied with her. Even though Corina didn't have many years of study with her, they connected strongly during Gina's life. The entire hall gave a standing ovation for both Corina's performance and Gina's Voicu memory.

As I watched Corina throughout the program, sweet memories

flooded my mind. I still have the keyboard I bought for her, so she could keep busy when she would visit. It is a relic that I treasure.

At that time, Corina was too little to make sense of our talking.

I smile, thinking back to our whispering when she would come around. For a long time afterwards, she associated whispering with love. In some ways it is true, the two are associated, but then, our whispers came from fear.

Then I heard Corina say, "The last piece of music I will play tonight goes out to a dear person, and let me say again, to a person very dear to me, to my Neli." She looked in the direction where I was seated and spotted me. Other people did the same. I tried to get smaller in my chair. It was not the time or place to be the center of attention and yet Corina made me feel that way.

"For her I have saved a piece of music whose title my mother thought was associated with the way we chose to assess our past. It means a great deal to my mother and me. It is the Consolation in E Major by Franz Liszt."

She played it impeccably. It truly was the music of their life. Soon after she finished playing, a beautiful young lady in a wheelchair, appeared on stage from behind the curtains. It was Victoria. She could hardly be seen behind the huge and beautiful bouquet, that practically covered her. One could read the surprise and emotion on Corina's face. She approached the wheelchair and tightly hugged her old friend and they both let their emotions out and began to cry. Then Corina gently took one Victoria's hands, and introduced her to the entire audience,

"This is Victoria, my dearest friend from when we were little. When we were young girls we lived close to each other and spent a lot of time together after school. Most of all we enjoyed dancing and making our dolls the audience. The music was always the same: Mozart's Turkish March."

Then turning to Victoria, she asked, "Do you have any clue why we always danced to that music?"

Victoria said smiling, "Remember, it was my mother's Oriental carpet in the living room."

She giggled as Corina added, "Yes! Yes! the Oriental rug and the music made the dance more authentic. We were pretty educated at that age, huh? And we danced and danced until we fell from exhaustion and our mothers had to pick us up off the floor." She said giggling too.

Then there was another surprise. Somebody came on stage to play the finale on the piano: It was the "Rondo alla Turca" from a Mozart sonata.

Corina and Victoria were both baffled by it and then suddenly, holding hands, they started to dance, moving the wheelchair gently and gracefully. Again, there was a standing ovation. I think many of us had tears in our eyes also. Surely, I did. Both of them bowed in gratitude saying humbly at once, "Thank you."

Then Corina acknowledged that those were the most beautiful days of her childhood. I couldn't speak for the others, but I knew why she said that.

The concert was an emotional one and it was talked about in the town for a long time after. Unfortunately, Sonia was not able to be at this concert, so I called her and told her about the event and everything that happened. She loved hearing everything in detail, or, as she used to say, "drop by drop."

CHAPTER 54

2011
Moments of Grace and Remembrance

"It is a beautiful morning.

I'm having my coffee on the deck surrounded by an unusual tranquility for this time of the day. The old trees around the house still look asleep. There is no breeze to bother them. Even the birds aren't giving their chirping signals of being around. Occasionally, I notice them moving quietly from one tree to another. Otherwise, all of nature looks still. It is the calm before the storm. A much-needed rain will come soon, I hope.

Suddenly I had a feeling, otherwise, familiar to me, but at this time more intense: my appreciation for the simple fact that I exist, that I am a living speck in the universe. The chance of being who I am is as unique as it is arbitrary. For some reason, the word "dust" came to my mind, and I said silently, "God please heal this earth."

Looking at the sky I saw a plane crossing it. Shortly, another one followed and then another. Then I could hear bells tolling. It seemed that their sound didn't come from a single church but from all around. I rushed inside to turn on the TV. I heard the names of those killed tragically ten years ago.

John William's "Hymn to the Fallen" played in the background, adding to the solemnity of the moment. It was September the 11th, a day of mourning for America and a day of deep grief for those who lost their loved ones.

There were the bells, the "Hymn to the Fallen," and then all the names of the fallen; they all came together as an outcry to heaven, begging that such a tragedy would never be repeated.

I was alone and yet in the midst of all of it. I broke into tears, joining their outcry. The heartbreaking emotions in the air would have moved even a heart of stone. The Twin Towers falling to the ground were still vivid in my mind. The World Trade Center disappeared, leaving behind what we would call from now on, "Ground Zero," a Land of Painful Remembrance.

With bowed heads, heavy with the memories from that day, Americans would visit that place or keep a moment of silence at the same time on every 9/11 after 2001.

Yet in between the two commemorations evil and hatred is still present. But what or who is the evil? I like Albert Einstein's thoughts on it,

"God didn't create evil. Just as darkness is the absence of light, evil is the absence of God."

It is well known that evil's strategy is to lure us into the dark. In darkness nobody can tell a friend from an enemy, thus creating chaos and fear. The destructive forces of darkness push the earth out of resonance with the uplifting forces of the universe; and self-destructive tendencies spread like the plague.

If brought into the light, people can see and find no reason to fight.

We are proud to consider our nation a melting pot, but at the same time we let it degenerate into a conflicting pot. There is an old strategy throughout history: divide and conquer. It looks like our once-beautiful nation is not far from going through that. But what seems to be even more alarming is an ostrich-like ignorance, not thinking that it is easier and smarter to keep it whole, than to fix it after it breaks. It is easier and smarter not to let the darkness set in than it is to chase it out.

In the human mind greed and selfishness are the greatest generators of darkness. As Einstein explained, "Where there is no light there is no God," or as my father would have said, "no consciousness."

Now, I realize the intensity Sonia lived with every moment. Just as embers in the hearth, with a little loosening, can rekindle into a crackling blaze, Sonia's intensity nourished her memories. Nevertheless, she would confess that her strong memory was not always in her favor. Her mind stubbornly stored even the events she would have liked very much to push out and forget. Sonia would plead that forgiving and forgetting weren't part of the same mold. She was right, they didn't. Neither did they reside in the same place. Forgiving comes from the heart, while forgetting is from the brain. She struggled with the conflict of those two feelings, most of her life; I know it from our talks and I confirm it in her journals. She was happy when she could smooth a conflict and so was I.

I compare her life to a fabric with a complicated design; it is enough to take just a few strands out to distort the whole thing. I have been as genuine as she was in telling her story. Without getting tired, I sometimes chose to run on what seem to be fragmented paths just to keep the complicated design unaltered. No matter how much I would have liked to keep a chronological order, it would have been impossible. The past and the present are part of the same fabric. And Sonia's fabric had all of her characteristic colors on it.

From my first talk with Adrian, I understood why he was spiritually captivated by her and why he remained loyal to his deep feelings. He kept a platonic love for Sonia after they were condemned to live apart.

Years later, still longing for a politically, free version of Adrian, she mistakenly believed she had found one. However, later on, Sonia painfully learned that Adrian was the only one; his shoes were too big for Sabin to fill, and frankly, Sabin never actually tried. Sabin was comfortable in his own zone. Sonia was more than happy to learn, though, that she was never replaced in Adrian's heart.

Now I understand why they both preferred to stay captive to that undeniable love, which had waited so long to be redeemed. Nowadays, finding an old love seems impossible, yet Sonia and Adrian proved that it can still happen. It was their refusal, at the end, to surrender their love for one another. That is the real secret, indeed. In everyone lies a potential of passion, just waiting to be revealed.

CHAPTER 55

The Priceless Years, Adolescence

"I approached the school where I had spent my most beautiful and precious years in excitement and timidity. A wave of emotions from those innocent years suddenly washed over me. As often happened, I was blushing. I have always wished I had control over my red face, especially in matters amorous. Anyway, I was on my way to a class reunion.

The stately buildings of that time were not the same and neither were we. Time left a mark on all of us. We frequently had to whisper our names discretely to each other, to escape the awkwardness.

Sorina, the one who always claimed to have a ray of the sun in her name (in Romanian "insorit" means "sunny") made herself heard from a distance.

"Hey pals don't be sad, only time has passed but that hasn't changed us."

"Really, Sorina? You know that time is built into us, and it just doesn't stand still and neither do we," I said.

"See, I recognized you as soon as you spoke. You are Sonia Sava, the class 'truth seeker.' It looks like, in that regard, you haven't changed a bit." She hurried to embrace me.

Sorina was right. I always followed the rules, seeing many angles and probing the depth in things. I would split things into pieces, analyze them, and put them back together again for a better understanding.

342

Blessed with Twice the Freedom

By nature, I had all the excuses in the world to do that; I was a Libra.

I didn't want to say anything about the tour I had already had of the school. Because I wanted to see it alone, I had arrived a little earlier.

Back when I was in school, I often enjoyed having a chat with friends before class. There was one friend in particular, Dan. He was a very handsome guy and he was in one of my classes. He was a tall boy with blue eyes and wavy hair. We really liked each other. Each morning I would check to see if his hunter green jacket was hanging on the corridor peg, signaling that he was already in. A pleasant emotion would flood my heart. I knew that soon he would crack open the door to my classroom and his blue eyes would look for me. We would then walk together down the long corridor minutes before classes started. Those joyous minutes started our days. What an innocent love.

Here I was many years later, quietly, walking down the same corridor trying to retrieve my memories, put them together, and recreate a picture of my youth.

At that point, I would have ignored any mirror in the world, to revel in the belief that I was as young as I felt inside.

I was glad that our graduation anniversary fell on a Saturday. There weren't any classes, so I could have the old school to myself. I opened the door to a classroom from my freshman year. Even though it was very different from how I remembered it, I closed my eyes and created a snapshot of the entire class which I still had in memory. I was amazed at how accurately I had stored it. I saw the faces of my fellow students and the desks that they would sit in. Unfortunately, if the students' names from our class had been called, many of them couldn't have answered; they were no longer among us. Consoling myself, I said, "And life goes on."

My school was among the largest and was one of the best among all the high schools of Romania. Not only were there students from primary grades throughout high school but also there were

343

also three ethnic groups. Together with Romanians were Germans and Hungarians. Even though our mother languages were not the same, there was no difference between us, no discrimination, and we obeyed the same rules.

The uniforms were mandatory. Navy blue was the compulsory color and they came in all sizes. They were made from high quality fabric and were the same for all the schools in the country; pleated dresses and white, starchy, embroidered collars for the girls and a light blue shirt with a dark blue tie that matched the color of the suit for the boys. Along with the uniforms there was a mandatory neat haircut for all. Yet that uniformity didn't chip one bit from our personalities, which were better expressed in our academics rather than in our apparel.

I remember how the streets around the school looked like a moving blue tide, fast in the morning and slow in the afternoon, but never loud or undisciplined. Looking back, I find that such discipline was very important; it was the most critical stage in our life, the transition from the innocence of childhood, through adolescence, and into adult life.

Theory of Materialism was a required class and it made its way into all of our lives. As soon as we entered college, our political affiliations became important. That was the time when students were sorted out; some were selected with the goal of creating a future generation of passionate Communists, while others were targeted and kept under observation, hoping to convert their beliefs. I wasn't in either group and preferred that. Nobody and nothing could force that switch upon me. However, our political beliefs were not a subject we would fervently debate at that age.

I smile thinking about the innocent talks we had, walking down the school's long corridors during recess. One day my friend Paul was looking for me after my first class. He could hardly wait to tell me about an Austrian poet he had read. Without much introduction, Paul enthusiastically said,

344

"Sonia, I am sure you would like this poet." He was right; I fell in love with Rainer Maria Rilke's excellent poems. I was in awe. The poetry was beautiful, just beautiful.

Paul promised to bring me one of Rilke's collections the next day. It was called, The Book of Hours, which he took out from the library for me. It was exquisite. Both my father and I very much enjoyed the book and wondered at the same time, how such a book got to go through a Romanian translation. God was mentioned in it. We noticed though that it was an old version, a translation done before the Communist regime installed its rules on our lives. Somehow that book escaped the ruthless censorship and was not thrown out.

Later on, my main interests would expand beyond literature. My other friend, Dan, would catch me in his fascination with Max Planck's quantum theory, which had just been introduced to us in our last year of physics; it was great to learn about the nature and behavior of matter and energy at this level. There was no word in the classroom that such a level coincided with the realm of God. A mind infatuated with materialism couldn't be poisoned with such ideas. Yet, many of us were ready to conclude the other way around; that God came first. Unfortunately, neither Dan nor Paul are with us at this reunion. They have both passed into the other world, along with Rilke and Planck.

I recalled talking about poets and philosophers with these boys and realized that nowadays, poetry and philosophy have been replaced as topics of conversation with computer games and other modern topics.

Then I quickly reviewed the teachers who had inspired me over the years, my chemistry teacher, for example, with her keen eyes and haughty looks. She instilled a curiosity in me for the unseen world of atoms and molecules, and then a love for that world. I am still as interested in chemistry now as I was then. She was known as a stern but also an excellent teacher. I can say that I owe my choice of pharmacy to her, even though my parents thought that I had a natural calling for it. It might have been true; no matter how many times I was asked or how many choices I had in front of me, I choose that career.

Next, I remembered the history teacher who was our great chaperone on the long walk through history. Personally, I was very fond of ancient history and the study of a nation's roots; how countries ultimately change into the way we know them today. I reached deep into the first beginning of Romania's roots and then to our kinship with the surrounding nations. It made me feel proud to be a descendent of such great ancestors even though I had no role in it.

I didn't have the same interest in modern history though. It was all presented so as to fit into the Communist agenda. What could have been more disgraceful than distorting the truth and then forcing others to believe in made-up history? We didn't make a big deal of it at that age. Anyway, we couldn't change it back to its truth. It was just about getting a good grade. The same was with other political subjects.

We were young and full of life. There were strict rules for us every step of the way, which we obeyed without bargaining, so our school policy became second nature to us. But that didn't stop us from slipping in some fun moments.

We liked jokes and playing funny pranks on our peers and even on our teachers. Sometimes we'd take a word that had either been used too often or was very specific to a particular person's vocabulary, and that word would become their nickname.

Our history teacher's nickname was Tzetze. During his lecture on the Persian Empire dynasty, this history teacher mentioned the Emperor Darius, and his son, Xerxes. We found it funny how he pronounced the name Xerxes. Without fail, I remember "Tzetze" every time I listen to the aria "Ombra mai fu" from Handel's Xerxes. That piece of music became very dear to me. Later, Adrian blended those tunes into our wedding vows.

I found myself stepping along the hallway to the cadence of that music, it was so vivid in my mind. I immediately looked around because only I knew that I had just swapped a moment of the present for one from the past, and I wasn't sure if others had seen and misunderstood".

I admired Sonia for her ability to condense events in time without cluttering or overcrowding them. I guess all the feelings that touched her heart were easily encoded, stored, and retrieved and easily recalled from her memory. She was interested in listening to and grasping the meaning of any conversation. When she remarked, "that makes sense," it signaled that whatever the information was, it could be recalled from storage after a long period of time.

Here I am too, perfectly remembering "Ombra mai fu"; the distinct notes of the piano are softened somehow by the murmur of the cello. Adrian picked the music for their wedding, which was a surprise for Sonia. I could read it in her eyes as soon as she heard the first notes. The music tenderly filled the tiny room of the remote chapel nested in the mountains. The scattered yellow beeswax candles gave the room a sweet scent as they flickered. Then Sonia in a simple, elegant, white linen dress, gracefully stepped to the rhythm of that music towards the altar.

Adrian, her destined "prince" was patiently waiting next to the priest. All together, they created a page from a fairytale, a happy ending. It took me a moment to move my mind from that "fairytale" back to reality.

The entire ceremony was private; it was only the children and me. The old priest looked no different from the saints who were painted on the walls. In that tiny room, I felt that the life-size mural of the saints took part in the ceremony and touched the moment with their holiness.

In the middle of the ceremony, when the old priest invoked blessings from above on the two to be wed, an eerie glow from the sky came through the little window and rested on them. It was as if the sun, on his way up in the sky, took a peek through that window and then sent his blessing too. It might have been the wish of Sonia's father. It was really magnificent! Surely, that moment was a divine witness to their proclaimed love for each other… But I should let the journal resume the narrative…

"The funniest of the teachers was our Russian teacher. His name was Gregory Karpovich, but he preferred to be called simply Grisha. It was odd; nobody else asked us that. Every other teacher was respectfully addressed by "the single word "Comrade" followed by their last name. He was short of stature with a large forehead that seemed wider because of his baldness. His big glasses and few strands of surviving hair were what struck you first when meeting him. We all agreed with one of our prankish classmates that Grisha looked like a little mouse; therefore, his nickname was Mouse.

He would allow us to skip classes if we managed to properly formulate our excuses in Russian. We took great advantage of his leniency but got a rich, practical vocabulary because of it.

For the most part, we'd try to escape his classes, because he always wanted us to sing Russian songs like "Volga, Volga, Dear Volga" or "The lilac is shuddering next to the window."

The entire school knew that Grisha wanted us to learn Russian through songs. They would say,

"There they go, our comrades are singing again." For a while we sang them passionately because nothing made Grisha happier than singing those songs with us. He might have had some sentimental attachment to them that we did not know about. After a while we grew tired of the same songs and it was also kind of embarrassing when the other classes started to make fun of us. In response we began to skip his class.

One day the prankster who named Grisha Mouse brought a little toy mouse to class and put it under Grisha's desk. The class hadn't started yet when Grisha noticed it. Startled, he jumped from his chair shouting again and over again "Mouse! Mouse!" The prankster's

Blessed with Twice the Freedom

mission was accomplished and now Grisha was calling himself by his own nickname.

This was the fun of our young minds.

However, we didn't do things like that to the French teacher. We called him simply Aujourd'hui ("Today"). He would always start class with that word.

He was a tall, skinny man, who seemed to be suffering from something, but nobody knew what it was. I remember that as soon as the cold weather arrived he always had his coat hanging off his shoulders. He looked like a walking mannequin.

Soon some other colleagues appeared who were reconnecting with their past before the official reunion began. All together we went down the school's large staircase, joking about its steps, which knew where we were headed better than the teachers did.

We stopped in the front of the school and our group grew larger by the minute. It was difficult for me to recognize some of them because I had missed all the reunions since I left Romania.

Our happiness to see each other was overwhelming and deep emotions brought us to tears. We had a little time before the ringing bell would call us inside. But it was not the same bell; a hoarse electronic ring replaced its crystalline tones. We hardly recognized it at first and almost ignored it.

Only three of our teachers came to the reunion. We were supposed to go to classes as we did when we were young. But it had been 50 years, and year by year we were fewer and fewer in number. So, we flocked to one corner of the hall, a corner not far from being empty, to meet with the teachers.

The festivity hall brought back so many memories. I imagined festivity halls of the past, where monthly dances were held. I let my mind recall those sweet moments and let the room fill with the joyful music of that time. Two of those songs came right away to my mind; there were, "Non-ho l'eta" ("I am not old enough"), and "Que sera, sera" ("Whatever will be, will be"), so specific to youth. Now we

349

sang two parodies: "Now we are old enough" and "Whatever it was, it was."

I had to "return" to the present quickly, our reunion ceremony was about to start. After a short presentation that informed us of the important events our old school had gone through over the years, the actual principal handed the microphone to one of our former teachers. It was interesting. All three of the teachers still with us were former physics teachers.

"Everyone in?" One of the teachers stood up and asked the usual question from the start of class. He didn't wait for our answers, but rather concluded instead,

"I guess not." At the same time one of us, a physicist himself, responded, "Evidently." We all chuckled. We used to call this teacher, Mr. Evident. During his classes we heard that word constantly. It was understandable; the truth in physics is more evident than in other classes.

He used to leave the podium and walk in front of us; thus, his classes were never boring. By walking through the aisles while he taught, he engaged all of us in his discussions. It was a great way of teaching; by the end of the class, we were halfway there. It just took a little bit of studying to consolidate things. His reunion speech started like this,

"As we know very well, in nature nothing is created or destroyed but only transformed. This is the Law of Conservation of Mass…

" We didn't let him finish, but rather jumped at once to complete the sentence. Some said "Lavoisier" and others "Lomonosov". We all were right;

Mr. Evident was talking about the Lavoisier-Lomonosov Law of the Conservation of Mass.

"So, we see that the transformation spares no one," he said, smiling and then continued

"We were lucky to have been born in an era where the qualitative leaps of quantitative science happened more rapidly than ever before.

Blessed with Twice the Freedom

We have gone to the moon and we continually send messages into the universe about our existence, from our speck at the edge of a galaxy.

We entered the heart of an atom, opened it, and found mysteries within to unravel. Now we are allowed to say, without jeopardizing our jobs or going to jail, that the subatomic world behaves like the realm of God. We are convinced now of the wave-particle duality of light. In this respect I call Max Planck a physics-prophet.

The gates of science have never been more widely opened. We went to where God let Himself be touched; the intangible photon converted into tangible matter. We are talking here about the Higgs' boson, where matter can be born from nothing - the otherworldly ethereal that fills the void of the universe. Isn't it just incredible? It is indeed.

And all of this is possible because there is a continual transformation, nothing is created or destroyed. Nevertheless, I would like to add that we do continually gain knowledge about the universe and ourselves."

I don't know if all this time I took more than a few breaths. I didn't want to miss a single word. I realized the impact of not only this speech on me but of all of the hours I spent in his classes. He was a great teacher. A discussion on the subject followed. We plunged into the more recent theories, where only the eyes of the mind can see clearly. I saw in us the same ardent students that we were a long time ago. Unfortunately, our time was limited. The hoarse electronic bell let us know that class was over".

CHAPTER 56

A World of Our Own

I imagine how much Gil and Sonia would have enjoyed going over all of this. She was more into physics than I was. It reminds me of our Club, during which Gil served us baked apples one cold winter evening. He shared with us the latest news in physics, which applied to medicine also.

"A big part of any medical devices' function is based on the laws of physics. MRI (Magnetic Resonance Imaging) is the latest breakthrough." Gil pronounced. At that time an MRI was Sonia's most important piece of physics. It held the promise of revealing the cause of her son's seizures. Later on, she would call it "the bridge over the Atlantic."

Looking back there was so little from the outside to be happy about. People had to find something that might bring a bit of joy. For us, it was spending time with close friends and talking about things other than politics. It was safer to pick totally different topics. Sonia, especially, didn't need any more trouble. But ultimately, no one was safe from the eyes and ears of the Communist regime.

We also had to make sure that our *Mariana* wouldn't get sick and have to miss work. Without her, food was scarce, but it was unpatriotic to complain. Lack of patriotism could have equaled jail time. It was easy to be arrested for complaining. But there was not only the stomach to satisfy; we also had to find nourishment for the soul and we found that in each other.

Even Corina found her own patterns for happiness. By listening,

I guess, to our worries about the haunting flu in town, she created an ER service for her dolls in the corner of the living room. It was delightful to listen to her talking to her dolls. She used the exact words she heard from us but coming from a child they sounded so funny.

It was the toughest time of the entire Communist Era. There was not enough of many things including heat, electricity, warm water, and food. We had to believe in something, so we created a world of our own. We survived by believing in that world; otherwise we would have been doomed to live our common, depressing lives.

That was back when Sonia taught me how to knit. On freezing cold days knitting gave us a warm feeling. I enjoyed knitting and agreed with her that it was relaxing. We had to let our mind escape from the sometimes-overwhelming stress of our lives. Hands and minds worked freely without interfering and allowed the worries to go away. The knitting needles were not for Gil though; he would rather find work in his office or entertaining Corina.-

Years passed by, and now here I am alone, with only my thoughts. My thoughts are often of Gil and Sonia. I miss them both so much. I like to believe that Gil and Sonia found each other on the other side and that they have also had Adrian join them in the relocated Club. These thoughts make me smile. One day I will leave everything behind, as have those who have already gone.

I guess we are sent here to keep the gift of the world beautiful, the way it was given to us and to enjoy it. And that's all.

However, humanity often misunderstands the offer. We often stubbornly believe that the world is ours to keep and to mercilessly exploit during our short passage through it. I like to imagine that someone from a nameless planet is watching all that is happening here on earth and is appalled. There is so much hatred and so much greed. From the beginning of time, greed has been considered the root of all evil, yet instead of uprooting it, greed has been cultivated. Unhappy people try to fill the emptiness in their lives with something, and unfortunately that something is often a thing from the outside and not a thing from within. Surely, greed can't fill an emptiness, it amplifies emptiness. Maybe that's why selfish people don't find as much happiness as the altruists do.

When I reached the age of retirement I chose to keep working. For some reason I enjoy my work more and more. I am sure it is because I have the freedom to practice medicine correctly, without an illiterate comrade interfering.

And more than anything I like to be generous to my patients with my time and my knowledge. I like to walk to work or downtown, so I can feel the pulse of the street and make myself a part of the crowd. I see faces I know everywhere. I get the feeling that I am not alone. Even more, people greet me with gratitude. Right away, I know that they must be people who, at one point or another, have passed through my office and have not forgotten the help I gave them. There is no greater feeling than that.

I remember one of my neurology professors from college who used to say that a well-maintained brain is never too old to learn. He had a good reason to say so. He knew every turn of every fiber in the nervous system.

I was now free to practice medicine under auspices, I found virtuous: "First do no harm" and "Treat the individual not the sickness."

In the Communist years, the first thing they asked you in a doctor's office was the name of your street, because the regime decided who your doctor would be based on your address.

Communist Party bigwigs, though, never had to accept these assignments. They had their own, special medical offices equipped with best imported technology. It was as if a special world had been created just for them. It was a privilege to work in such offices and such people were selected from only among the Communists.

To be challenged in any field is a good thing but in medicine it is an excellent thing. More than ever, I looked to perfect my work every day so I can accomplish my profession the way it was meant to be.

The saying is that "one swallow does not make a spring season but still heralds the spring." I would also add "a flock of swallows travelling together makes a difference." I like to consider myself part of that flock.

I listen to my patients not only with my ears, but also with my heart. The Hippocratic Oath, which was spoken loudly and clearly at my graduation, is a true covenant. I remember it as if it were just yesterday...

There was a deep silence in the crowd, as we all repeated the words of the Oath. In that stillness, the words sounded sacred. I closed my eyes and let myself make believe that it was Hippocrates himself reading that oath in perfect Romanian.

Just a few days before the tragic accident that ended Sonia's life, we had a very long talk, unaware that it would be our last. I remember fondly all the different topics that we covered. Among them was the principles of Chinese Medicine.

"For your information, you must know, that my liver is free of anger and my heart of burning fire," she said jokingly.

I didn't understand and, interested, I asked her,

"What do you mean by that, why are you talking in parable, my dear? I don't understand."

"Yesterday I sent you a great book on Traditional Chinese Medicine. You will love it. It is in French, which you speak as well as you do Romanian. There is also a letter written in Romanian. I couldn't send only the book without saying anything. You know we never get to an end with our talking.

But let's return to the old Chinese view on health: interestingly, it is thought that imbalances in the body are caused by seven basic emotions.

Anger is not the voice of the heart, as we are used to believing, but it is of the liver. Odd, isn't it? And even more interesting, suppressed anger induces depression, inflammation, and the feeling of being blown out with rage. Can you imagine that? With my Adrian next to me, I have the most peaceful liver. While it sounds unromantic, it just might be true.

Expected feelings of joy belong to the heart, but when joy comes as a shock, it overwhelms the heart, which doesn't provide a restful place for the spirit. I was surprised by that, but it explains why my sleep vanished for almost a week after I reconnected with Adrian. My spirit had more joy than it could handle. In other words, this book speaks about moderation in everything, even in good things. Even more oddly, a devastating shock that might leave behind post-traumatic stress is known to reside in the kidneys."

"Wow, totally different from Western medicine, isn't it?" I managed to say, in my awe.

"Yes, it is very different. I am sure after you go through the book we might share the same thoughts on it. I'll wait to hear what you think."

Then it was the usual promises and wishes,

"Talk to you soon and stay well my dear." It looked like she was ready to end the conversation.

I answered as usual saying,

"It was great talking to you. Be good, and say hello to Adrian for me," and then our two "Goodbyes" came out at the same time, blending into one.

Hanging up the phone always reminded us that we were on two continents. Now we are more than that, we are now in two different worlds. It showed me again how little or nothing we know about what tomorrow brings…

I got the book and her letter only after my return home from her and Adrian's funeral.

We didn't have a chance to talk through all of the seven basic emotions. It was strange; I was left to reflect on my own emotions of sadness, worry and pensiveness.

The sadness, at this time, was more than just sadness but extended into profound grief. There was not enough room in me for my sadness. It flooded my entire being like a turbulent river. The feeling that I had lost all my loved ones stunned me at first, then little by little, one by one, the numbness abated and let my senses return to me.

One day I suddenly found myself with a smile of solace on my face, and after that a thought flashed through my mind. It was Gil and Sonia saying, "Come on, Neli we haven't abandoned you, remember the duality in everything?" Then I said to myself, "Yes, I remember, you have just turned into light."

I shook my head; it was not a dream. There were two voices in my mind, both so dear to me. Lament was on neither Gil nor Sonia's lips. I promised myself that it would never be on mine either. I was entrusted with the most precious career, I think, in the world: helping people protect and maintain their most valuable treasure, their health. It doesn't matter what it is called; Western, Eastern, Ayurvedic, Chinese or any other name, as long as they hold the truth of healing, I shall use them all. I didn't put that book on Traditional Chinese Medicine down until I had finished reading it. I also reread her letter many times. It was not because I didn't understand the message but because I felt as if Sonia was talking to me. And it was the last letter that she wrote to me. I know every inflection of her voice.

At first, some of the statements from the book seemed kind of weird to me; like that of sadness being associated with the health of one's lungs. I had to go through the pages over and over again until it made sense to me. I was finally able to grasp one of the tenets. Nothing else can release stress like breathing clean air properly Isn't the breath what life starts and ends with?

The other two, worrying and pensiveness, were associated with the spleen. Again, it seemed odd to me to find such an association. The spleen is viewed in Western medicine as an organ that one can do without. But it is said to be the first helping hand to an angry liver. No matter which part of the body you look at and analyze, it has a great purpose.

In ancient times they knew little about the chemistry behind physiology and health. But, any hypothesis of healing is nothing more than a natural self-tuning within the body. It is mind blowing. I miss having someone like Sonia to talk about this with. We could go on and on. But I still have her letter on my desk, which came to me after she left this world; it sounds like one of the dissertations we liked to compose on the phone.

I don't think Sonia would be unhappy if I made her final letter to me an open letter for others to read. This letter is more than a letter for me. It turns out to be a tribute to her, to my own beliefs as well. It was written on a piece of paper from the notebook that she used at work. It displayed her name and the other data she might have used as a pharmacist. I am sure she must have written it in a spare moment at work. I notice some interruptions here and there. She had smooth handwriting; you could see where her thought was interrupted and where it started again.

A graphologist could easily read her character in her handwriting. They would have said: Libra, the sign of Balance. Libra makes its first steps in the calendar in September marking the autumnal equinox. The day and night share the hours equally, suggesting a balance between light and dark. It seems that such tendencies to balance slip into everything and consequently in those born under this sign.

Looking at the sky, my eyes try to locate the constellation Libra. I wonder what is the empirical connection between date of one's birth and a constellation? I imagine her smiling at my odd questions without divulging the secret. There must be a spot in the sky for everyone.

For a while every phone call startled me. I was expecting to hear her. I was glad that Corina would call me often, but we both avoided words that could hurt more than heal. Then in time we began reminding each other of things Sonia would like to hear or do, so we brought her in in that way. The other day we talked about a sunflower plant, which somehow grew where no seed had been planted. At first, I didn't recognize the little thing. I was not a country girl. Yet, I spared it and now I am so glad to have it. I told Corina: I think this is a gift from your mom. I had never asked myself why that plant is called "sunflower," but I got the answer from watching it. As soon as the little yellow bud started opening it turned its head seeking the sun and kept an eye on it. Corina came up with a beautiful comparison,

"You see Neli, that flower fell deeply in love with the sun and became a sunflower to be always faithful to it. What a perfect marriage!!!"

"I would say, yes, yes indeed."

Gradually, we accepted our loss. There was no other way to have them back but to reignite the memory of them. It became very normal for us to bring them into the present.

Corina and Michael started to visit me more often. They became my children. A strange thought crossed my mind. With her generous heart Sonia allowed me to have a feeling that I never had before: the feeling of being a mother. Both of them became close to me. I knew that I would never replace Sonia but I thought of being more than a surrogate mother.

On one of their visits home to Romania, Corina confessed that the bond between her and her mother was so strong that nothing could destroy it.

"Even as an adult in my moments of indecision I ask myself; what would my mother say? Then my decision becomes easier.

My mother's admiration for me challenged me to deserve it more. She built my confidence. She advised me that the noblest challenge is the one you set yourself. I learned from her and from life that everybody's standard of what is the best is different. She gave me the good advice that I should be myself, that I should never try to match up to someone else's standards. Trying to copy others brings more stress than achievement. Everyone has to respect the unique standard of their own personal best.

Watching my mother, I learned how important it is to show appreciation and to never forget the good things the Americans did for us.

I have never seen my mother bend even when there were many burdens, heavier than she could possibly carry. It was like she had a rod of steel going all the way through her backbone. I have never seen her cry either, only when my father took my brother and moved out. Yes, that one was a heartbreaking cry. If she did cry other times she made sure to do it in hiding. It was not out of fear of showing weakness but because she knew that whatever it was, it was just a bump in the road, and she didn't want to make others worried about it."

While Corina and I had that discussion of the present blended with the past, Michael was quiet, but I am sure he was listening. Ever sparse with words he was quite sensible. He stood up and walked over to check out my disc collection. He picked the disc "Prayer" by Max Bruch. It was a piece of music their mother liked very much. I guess she often prayed listening to this music. This prayer is from Judaism and is called "Kol Nidrei." In the notes to the music, it is explained that they ask for forgiveness and mercy.

I was touched by Michael's gesture; forgiveness and mercy; two things to think about. Michael said nothing but listened quietly with us to that beautiful music. We all sat and listened and enjoyed the song. I was grateful Michael had chosen it. There was a lot to be forgiven, yet so much to be grateful for.

Then I remembered Sonia confessing to me about "Kol Nidrei" and how long ago she first listened to it. She must have been in her high school years. One evening she was walking on the street with her then boyfriend, Paul. Passing by the synagogue, which was on the same street, they noticed dim lights inside and heard music coming out through a cracked window. There was something sacred about this music. She noticed that the music could always be heard towards the middle of September, around the equinox. She learned from her

Blessed with Twice the Freedom

Jewish classmate, Claudia Wollock, that the song is played once a year on the most important Jewish holiday, Yom Kippur.

Suddenly Corina and Michael, as if on signal, stood up and hugged each other, then invited me to join them in song. This was not only a song that asked for forgiveness and mercy but also one that brought Sonia back to us.

If Gil were still here he would have said, "Here is her soul, crossing the universe on a beam of light." He might have been right; we felt her presence while listening to that song so dear to her…

In time I became for her children more than a proxy-mother. Sonia left me with the privilege of being called Grandma. Her grandchildren didn't call me Neli, but Granny Neli, and then they turned that into Graneli! Oh, how I love it!

I heard the stories about Michael's son and how much he loved Sonia. When Michael Junior, or MJ, was about three years old, he asked Sonia if he could marry her. He didn't accept Sonia's reasoning of being too old for him and said, "Granny, you are just a little old, but you are beautiful."

"That's true MJ, beauty is in the eyes of the holder." We used to tease him about that. It was even more hilarious when MJ would try to emphasize his commitment; "Granny, I am serious, I am very serious." Imagine that coming from the mouth of a three-year-old.

Over the years MJ continued to compliment his Grandma. He always wanted to tell her how beautiful she was. Year after year, whenever he visited her, MJ would come up with new confessions of love. He was about ten when he said,

"Hey Grandma, do you know how beautiful you are?"

Sonia would reply: "You say this very often. How do you find me so beautiful?"

"Oh, Granny you are beautiful inside."

"Really, how do you see inside of me?"

The answer came quick as a shot. "With the eye of truth." We couldn't say anything but "Wow" to that.

As he became a teenager, MJ grappled with the same issues that most teens have. He told Sonia one day, "Grandma, I have heard that, no teenager loves his parents and grandparents much." Sonia assured him that real love would never change with age.

Corina's twins, Bianca and Iris, were born after Sonia had passed. They knew their Grandma only from MJ.

"Mommy could you call Grandma back from heaven, so we can meet her?"

MJ would jump up and a smile and before anybody else would say, "You little geese, how could you ask Aunty Cora such a favor? Grandma will come only in your dreams."

When visiting Romania Sonia's grandchildren enjoyed going to the countryside. They were fascinated to see true animals and true birds so different from those on TV or even in the zoo. They fell in love with the chicks and the ducklings. The girls held them tenderly in their hands and whispered into their mother's ear,

"May we take them home?" And to their disappointment their mother said, "Would you like me to give you away when somebody comes to visit us?"

"Oh no, no" they both said at once.

"So, it is the same with their mother".

"I know she would cry," said Iris, always the speedy talkative one. As soon as we got home the usual question would come along,

"Granneli, what's for dinner?"

The children unanimously voted for paprikash. We all agreed. There is no better meal on a Transylvanian menu than paprikash with dumplings or polenta. Corina's husband and Michael's wife enjoyed Romanian food also, but they preferred to be out of our conversation and be spectators.

We enjoyed speaking Romanian when we were altogether. Every year they have promised to add something new to their vocabulary, but it is a difficult language to learn. After dinner they would let us have our Romanian time together. The understood how important

Blessed with Twice the Freedom

all this was to us.

It was my job to take care of the little ones, which was a little piece of heaven for me.

I was thinking of Sonia again and how as she left this world. I was able to taste the joy of being a mother and grandmother to her children and grandchildren.

It was their last night before returning to America. The luggage was ready, and we hung around in the kitchen a little longer for a Romanian chat.

"You know Corina, you were just a little older than your own little girls when I first met you."

"You are right, and I asked silly questions just like my little girls do."

Then Michael added, "Every age has its own silliness, doesn't it?"

"That's right brother. Do you remember how silly we were? Even though I was younger than you, I always pretended to be your boss."

"Oh yeah I remember that. But by the same token you helped me lace my shoes, at a time when that seemed a little too complicated for me."

I was glad that Michael was beginning to open up during his visits home. He had a nice sense of humor and was always making us laugh. I loved them both, as Sonia did. She saw in each of them the real potential and always encouraged them to stay close to it. Then Corina started to talk about "Mama." Sonia liked when Corina called her Mama. I also noticed that Michael always referred to Sonia as "my mom." It was as if he felt that he didn't get the chance to use that word enough.

Corina mentioned her mother's spirit of sacrifice, which Sonia only thought of as unconditional love.

"Sorry Cora, I have to say that we shared as much sacrifice as we did love," said Michael.

Her encouragement was always in our heads, "Don't be afraid to try. Sometimes it works and sometimes it doesn't, but never consider it a failure; it might be just a chance to look for a new opportunity."

Then both of them remembered another phrase their mother used to encourage them with, "Strike a flint harshly, and you will see how at once, both fire and light will gush out."

It was a line from a poem by a Romanian physician. Corina added, "Neli, hear me. You are as much the incurable romantic that Mama was, and one day the lyric muse might visit you too. You never know."

"What about a mathematician poet?" Michael asked.

"Everything is possible with a great imagination," Corina said and all three of us agreed to that.

It was my turn to add something that I brought up every time Corina visited with me. "It seems like only yesterday that we met on the train and had fun wondering about the snowflakes that fell on the windows and how they ended up as drops of water." This was the signal that we were at the end of our evening chat.

But Corina came up with another question. "Talking about those snowflakes I am sure that if my mother were here, she would have asked, 'I wonder where those snowflakes are right now?'"

I didn't answer. But I imagined Sonia with her half eyes closed, filtering the light through her eyelashes, and saying with a smile, "Oh yes, they are somewhere else, either dew drops or tears of happiness, or who knows what else."

We smiled to each other, as we did in the train years ago. It was late; yet it was hard for us to give up the chat and go to bed. I looked at both of them with love and said, "Tomorrow you have a long trip ahead. Now let's go to sleep and 'dream of things that could have been but never were.' That is what your mom used to say whenever we were visiting with each other and stayed up late chatting."

"Yes, she would say it to us also, remember brother?" Corina added.

"I think there's something more to it, Cora, wasn't there? Michael insisted.

"Yes, there was, but let's leave it for another time," I said, before

Blessed with Twice the Freedom

Cora could.

We hugged each other tightly, feeling Sonia's presence in that hug. We looked at each other smiling. We knew she was with us.

About the Author

Domnitsa Uilean, was born in Transylvania the northern region of Romania, in 1941. She is a graduate of The Institute of Medicine and Pharmacy, Cluj. She had practiced pharmacy in a few places of Transylvania, before settling legally in US. She has also become a licensed pharmacist in her new country. Being a graduate of both, Eastern and Western, Schools of Pharmacy, her work, naturally, is a blend of such schools' principles. As a result, she founded a new trend of pharmacy "Nature's Pharmacy, Inc" in Watertown Connecticut were she currently works as a pharmacist. As much as she is passionate of science, she is passionate of arts mainly, writing. She lives in Waterbury, Connecticut.

Made in the USA
San Bernardino, CA
28 October 2018